Nurses and Disasters

Arlene W. Keeling, PhD, RN, FAAN, is the centennial distinguished professor of nursing at the University of Virginia School of Nursing. She is also chair, Department of Acute and Specialty Care, and director of the Eleanor Crowder Bjoring Center for Nursing Historical Inquiry. Dr. Keeling is the author of numerous articles on nursing history and an award-winning book, *Nursing and the Privilege of Prescription, 1893–2000* (2006). She has coauthored or edited several other books: *Rooted in the Mountains; Reaching to the World: A History of the Frontier School of Nursing, 1939–1989* (2012), which received the AJN Book of the Year Award for Public Interest and Creative Works, 2012; and *Nurses on the Front Line: A History of Disaster Nursing 1879 to 2005* (2010), which received the peer-reviewed 2012 Mary Roberts Book Award from the American Association for the History of Nursing. She has recently completed two other books: *The Nurses of Mayo Clinic*, and, in collaboration with John Kirchgessner, *Nursing Rural America: Perspectives from the Early 20th Century* (2014). Past president of the American Association for the History of Nursing, Dr. Keeling currently serves as cochair of the Expert Panel on Nursing History and Health Policy, the American Academy of Nursing.

Barbra Mann Wall, PhD, RN, FAAN, is associate professor of nursing and associate director of the Barbara Bates Center for the Study of the History of Nursing at the University of Pennsylvania. Dr. Wall received her BS from the University of Texas at Austin and her MS in nursing from Texas Woman's University. She earned a PhD in history from the University of Notre Dame. She has published *Unlikely Entrepreneurs: Catholic Sisters and the Hospital Marketplace, 1865–1925* (2005); and *American Catholic Hospitals: A Century of Changing Markets and Missions* (2011). Her new book, to be published in September 2015, is *Into Africa: A Transnational History of Catholic Medical Missions and Social Change.* Dr. Wall currently serves as cochair of the Expert Panel on Nursing History and Health Policy in the American Academy of Nursing. She also is coeditor, with Dr. Arlene Keeling, of two books on the history of nursing in disasters: *Nurses on the Front Lines: When Disasters Strike, 1878–2010* (2010); and *Nurses and Disasters: Global, Historical Cases* (in press). She is editor-in-chief of the international journal *Health Emergency and Disaster Nursing.* Dr. Wall presents at major international and national conferences and is the recipient of numerous five- and six-figure research and program grants.

Nurses and Disasters

Global, Historical Case Studies

Arlene W. Keeling, PhD, RN, FAAN
Barbra Mann Wall, PhD, RN, FAAN

Editors

SPRINGER PUBLISHING COMPANY
NEW YORK

Springer Publishing Company, LLC
11 West 42nd Street
New York, NY 10036
www.springerpub.com

Acquisitions Editor: Joseph Morita
Composition: Newgen Knowledge Works

ISBN: 978-0-8261-2672-6
e-book ISBN: 978-0-8261-2673-3

15 16 17 18 / 5 4 3 2 1

The author and the publisher of this Work have made every effort to use sources believed to be reliable to provide information that is accurate and compatible with the standards generally accepted at the time of publication. Because medical science is continually advancing, our knowledge base continues to expand. Therefore, as new information becomes available, changes in procedures become necessary. We recommend that the reader always consult current research and specific institutional policies before performing any clinical procedure. The author and publisher shall not be liable for any special, consequential, or exemplary damages resulting, in whole or in part, from the readers' use of, or reliance on, the information contained in this book. The publisher has no responsibility for the persistence or accuracy of URLs for external or third-party Internet websites referred to in this publication and does not guarantee that any content on such websites is, or will remain, accurate or appropriate.

Library of Congress Cataloging-in-Publication Data

Nurses and disasters : global, historical case studies / [edited by] Arlene W. Keeling, Barbra Mann Wall.
       p. ; cm.
Includes bibliographical references and index.
ISBN 978-0-8261-2672-6 — ISBN 978-0-8261-2673-3 (e-book)
I. Keeling, Arlene Wynbeek, 1948- , editor. II. Wall, Barbra Mann, editor.
[DNLM: 1. Disasters—history. 2. Nurse's Role—history. 3. Global Health—history. 4. History, 19th Century. 5. History, 20th Century. 6. History, 21st Century. WY 11.1]
RT108
610.73'49—dc23   2015008674

Special discounts on bulk quantities of our books are available to corporations, professional associations, pharmaceutical companies, health care organizations, and other qualifying groups. If you are interested in a custom book, including chapters from more than one of our titles, we can provide that service as well.

For details, please contact:
Special Sales Department, Springer Publishing Company, LLC
11 West 42nd Street, 15th Floor, New York, NY 10036-8002
Phone: 877-687-7476 or 212-431-4370; Fax: 212-941-7842
E-mail: sales@springerpub.com

Printed in the United States of America by McNaughton & Gunn.

This book is dedicated to all those who suffered or died in the disasters outlined here, and to the nurses, physicians, and other frontline workers who responded.

Contents

Contents

Contributors

Jane Brooks, PhD, RN
Lecturer
School of Nursing, Midwifery
    and Social Work
University of Manchester
Manchester, United Kingdom

Adrienne Byng, BSN, RN
Geriatric Medicine
Humber River Hospital
Downsview, Ontario
Canada

**Maria Gilson DeValpine, PhD,
    MSN, RN**
Associate Professor
Department of Nursing
James Madison University
Harrisonburg, Virginia

Janna Dieckmann, PhD, RN
Clinical Associate Professor
School of Nursing
University of North Carolina at
    Chapel Hill
Chapel Hill, North Carolina

Madonna Grehan, PhD, RN, RM
Honorary Fellow
School of Health Sciences
University of Melbourne
Melbourne, Australia

**Arlene W. Keeling, PhD, RN,
    FAAN**
Director and Professor of Nursing
Eleanor Crowder Bjoring
Center for Nursing Historical
    Inquiry
Chair
Department of Acute
    and Specialty Care
University of Virginia
Charlottesville, Virginia

Victoria LaMaina, BSN, RN
Registered Nurse
New York University Langone
   Medical Center
New York, New York

Anna La Torre, MSN, RN
Professor
Medicina e Chirurgia
University of Milan
Milan, Italy

Emma MacAllister, BSN
School of Nursing
University of Pennsylvania
Philadelphia, Pennsylvania

**Barbara Maling, PhD, RN,
   ACNP-BC**
Assistant Professor of Nursing
Department of Acute and
   Specialty Care
University of Virginia
Charlottesville, Virginia

**Gwyneth Rhiannon Milbrath,
   MSN, MPH, CEN, RN**
PhD Student
School of Nursing
University of Virginia
Charlottesville, Virginia

**Sioban Nelson, PhD, RN,
   FAAN, FCAHS**
Professor
Faculty of Nursing
University of Toronto
Toronto, Canada

Ryoko Ohara
Associate Professor
School of Nursing
Gifu University
Gifu, Japan

Trudy Rudge, PhD, RN
Professor of Nursing
The University of Sydney
Sydney, Australia

**Barbra Mann Wall, PhD, RN,
   FAAN**
Nurse Historian
Associate Professor and
   Associate Director
Barbara Bates Center for
   the Study of the History
   of Nursing
University of Pennsylvania
   School of Nursing
Philadelphia, Pennsylvania

Preface

In October 2014, two registered nurses, Nina Pham and Amber Vinson, both of whom worked at a hospital in Dallas, Texas, contracted Ebola after caring for a patient who eventually died from the same diagnosis. Almost immediately, cable news networks reported the story all over the world. These nurses were the first in the United States to contract the disease. From a global, historical perspective, however, Pham and Vinson were not the first nurses to become infected with Ebola; they were simply—as Americans, and along with two American physicians—the first to be recognized for having risked their lives working on the front lines of the battle against the killer virus. Countless others had already contracted the disease in Kenema, Sierra Leone.[1] As of August 2014, 15 African nurses had died. Yet they remain anonymous, most likely because of their race. Remarking on their deaths and how much these nurses meant to her, Josephine Finda Sellu, RN, the deputy nurse matron at a hospital in Kenema, noted: "It has been a nightmare for me."[2] In spite of the danger, many of Sellu's other nurses "soldiered on," and for their efforts their neighbors and friends shunned them, out of fear that they too would contract the illness.[3] Later in October, as pandemic fear spread faster than the virus, the same reaction would occur in the United States.

The nurses in Sierra Leone were part of a larger frontline response, one that included doctors, janitors, drivers, lab technicians, pharmacists, and "body handlers," all risking their own lives to volunteer in the effort to help. Others, too, had died; in fact, the death toll in Sierra Leone was averaging several thousands a week, most of whom remained nameless in the news reports.

In the United States, Tom Friede, MD, the director of the Centers for Disease Control and Prevention (CDC), initially blamed Pham for "breach of CDC protocol," although he later apologized for making that statement.[4] As the largest union of registered nurses in the country, the National Nurses United demanded increased nurse training in the proper use of equipment for hazardous materials. They demonstrated in the streets, and testified before Congress, calling for the United States to stop the epidemic and stop blaming the nurses on the front lines. Within days, the American Nurses Association supported the nurses, asking for new CDC guidelines, training, and proper protective equipment. The CDC responded with updated guidelines and assurances about the provision of equipment, while public health officials and hospital administrators across the country scrambled to prepare for a possible pandemic.

Fear spread faster than the virus and resulted in federal, state, and local responses that were not coordinated. In late October, a nurse returning from Africa was quarantined in a tent outside a New Jersey hospital for 2 days, despite the fact that she had tested negative for the Ebola virus. After her release, Kaci Hickox, RN, returned to Maine where she was again quarantined, this time in her house for the remainder of the 21-day quarantine mandated by the state. Later, a judge removed the state-mandated quarantine. This episode of quarantine highlighted historic tensions between individual liberty and the protection of the public's health. It also raised questions about ethical dilemmas that nurses face in caring for patients with infectious diseases and the responsibility of local hospitals, states, and federal public health agencies to protect nurses, physicians, and other frontline caregivers.

This book addresses some of those questions from a global, historical perspective, incorporating lessons from nursing history for today. Clearly, nurses work on the front lines of disasters—or right behind the lines in hospital emergency departments, clinics, and wards. Disasters can occur naturally from earthquakes, floods, or hurricanes. They can result from fires, epidemics, explosions, nuclear catastrophes, and human actions during conflicts, such as war.[5] This book describes and analyzes nurses' roles in select cases from disasters that have occurred in areas around the world from the late 19th century to the present. These include an outbreak of typhoid in Tasmania in 1885 to 1887; a devastating earthquake in Italy in 1908; an Ohio (USA) flood in 1913; the Alaskan influenza epidemic of 1918; the World War II bombings of London and Manchester, England, in 1941; the bombing of Pearl Harbor, Hawaii, in 1941; the nuclear bombing of Hiroshima, Japan, in 1945; a destructive wild fire in Bar Harbor, Maine (USA), in 1947; the SARS crisis in Toronto, Canada, in 2003; and the effects of Hurricane Sandy on hospitals in New York City (USA) in 2012. Nurses' actions are situated within local responses, national networks, and international aid.

The book addresses the following questions: How did local, regional, national, and international communities mobilize for emergency care? What was the role of nurses in these responses? How can an examination of nursing during disasters enhance an understanding of how to manage risk? What can be learned about cooperation, conflict, and competition among responders? What was the impact of social and professional expectations on the ways that nurses responded to disasters? What ethical dilemmas did nurses face when they were asked to work on the front lines of disasters? How did preparedness for the disaster or lack thereof affect the nature of the response?

One cannot escape the daily news accounts of disasters occurring throughout the world. Nurses are—and have been—a critical part of disaster response, and this book gives them a voice. Themes that recur throughout the narrative are: the notion of a nurse's "duty to care" versus the need to protect herself or himself; the need for innovation and coordination of the response effort; and cooperation among the responders versus inherent political, racial, and interprofessional conflicts. Thus, the book examines political sensitivities, international conflicts, cultural differences, and societies' varying professional and gendered expectations of nurses. In addition, the book highlights nurses' voices during major World War II bombings, addressing realities that occurred during the war that have long been silenced for reasons of political and social correctness. These case studies document nurses' roles in response to the London Blitz, the attack on Pearl Harbor, and the bombing of Hiroshima, revealing nurses' response to these crises: their dedication to patients, their ability to triage and improvise, and their adaptation to nursing professional norms expected in various cultures. (Doubtless, nurses in other countries involved in the war responded in a similar way, although all those stories are not presented.)

History shows that nurses need to feel that they can protect themselves and their families. With this in mind, the book analyzes risks nurses take and the consequences that result if they do not have the resources, equipment, skills, and knowledge to respond effectively. Nonetheless, the cases demonstrate that time after time, nurses *do* accept risks to their own health in order to fulfill their professional commitments.

STRUCTURE OF THE BOOK

Prelude

The book begins with a Prelude by Barbra Mann Wall, her 2013 Hannah Lecture in Victoria, British Columbia, in 2013,[6] reprinted from the *Nursing History Review*. This sets the stage for the book by starting the discussion on what history can tell us about nurses' roles in disasters. She writes from the stance of a nurse and historian who is concerned with the possibilities as well as the conflicts that occur in nurses' responses to disasters. She frames her discussion on the concept of "emergence"[7] and asks us to consider how knowledge about nursing actions during disasters can enhance an understanding of the notion of "emergent phenomena." This concept, described by sociologists Thomas Drabek and David McEntire, includes the collaboration of interorganizational networks that dedicate themselves to resolving the demands placed on their community in times of disaster. Wall asserts that nurses are part of this multiorganizational network and should be a part of any public response to disaster.[8] Examining nurses' responses as part of a larger whole can help the reader reimagine the possibilities for their action in the public domain.

Chapter 1: Typhoid Fever Epidemic, 1885 to 1887, Tasmania, Australia

Chapter 1 discusses the nursing and hospital politics that occurred in the Australian island colony of Tasmania in the years 1885 to 1887. The sheer persistence of the epidemic taxed Tasmania's nursing workforce, because among those who contracted typhoid and died were six hospital nurses. Other nurses also became ill, resulting in calls for nurses from mainland Australia to assist the ailing colony. The chapter considers the community's confidence, or lack thereof, in the nurses and nursing practice during this public health emergency, evidenced by the arguments over the awarding of 24 hospital nurses with 18-carat-gold "Typhoid Medals" for meritorious service to nursing.

Chapter 2: The 1908 Italian Earthquake

In 1908, a massive earthquake occurred in Messina and Reggio Calabria in Italy, resulting in more than 70,000 deaths. This chapter discusses the collaboration among the military machinery, the Red Cross, and international assistance. The vastness of the destruction shook world opinion and, for the first time, a natural disaster became an event of political significance in the field of international relations. In the nursing response, British, American, and Italian nurses brought their own understandings of nursing and its place in the world order. These beliefs sometimes resulted in praise and, at other times, criticism of each other.

Chapter 3: The 1913 Flood in Ohio (USA)

The American Red Cross response to the 1913 Ohio flood in the United States was the largest of its kind since the 1906 San Francisco, California, earthquake. Between 1906 and 1913, the Red Cross had designed an innovative strategy to expand nurses' work in disaster response, which they activated after cataclysmic flooding in southwestern Ohio. Within days of the massive flooding, Red Cross nurses arrived in Ohio from St. Louis, Chicago, New York City, and Washington, DC, relieving local nurses initially deployed from Cincinnati's Red Cross affiliate. This chapter describes the Red Cross nursing innovations in response to the flood, the professional and gender-based barriers the nurses faced, and the approaches the nurses used to achieve their goals. Emphasis is on the pre-disaster planning by the Red Cross nursing leadership and the nurses' strategic on-site decision making during the crisis. The nurses' experiences in the flooded districts laid the groundwork for a Red Cross nursing response in wartime Europe later in the decade.

Chapter 4: The Alaskan Influenza Epidemic, 1918 to 1919

The lack of access to medical and nursing care in the isolated, remote regions of the territory, a dependence on subsistence living, the freezing temperatures, the Alaskan culture of community, and the severity and virulence of the disease were all part of an "interdependent cascade"[9] of factors that resulted in devastation to indigenous Alaskans in the 1918 influenza epidemic. In particular, more than 22 Inupiat communities of the Seward Peninsula were destroyed; overall, between 4,000 and 5,000 indigenous Alaskans died and several hundred children were left orphaned. The response, which included those of health officials, local government, shipping lines, physicians, nurses, and Red Cross volunteers, relied on well-established patterns of communication already in place in the lower 48 states. Interprofessional collaboration and public–private cooperation were also essential. Clearly, the five to six hospitals throughout the territory, with only eight physicians and 11 nurses, could not handle the epidemic alone, and the local governments could not afford the cost of the response without help from the federal government.

Chapter 5: The Bombing Blitz of London and Manchester, England, 1940 to 1944

Based on data from oral histories, this chapter describes the collaborative response of nurses, physicians, volunteers, Red Cross workers, and local governments to the London and Manchester, England, bombings during World War II. During the Blitz, hospitals, churches, train stations, and homes in both cities were devastated. Many people sought refuge underground during air raids. Meanwhile, nurses remained on duty in the hospital wards, often at great risk to themselves. This chapter focuses on nurses' "duty to care," and the pressures student nurses in particular expressed as they carried out this mandate.

Chapter 6: The Bombing of Pearl Harbor, Hawaii, December 7, 1941

This chapter describes and analyzes the military nurses' roles in the hospitals in Pearl Harbor, Hawaii, in the hours and days after the Japanese attack on the American fleet on December 7, 1941. Themes of emergent behavior, cooperation, and collaboration are identified. Amid the chaos, nurses assumed leadership roles, triaging patients to other hospitals, administering analgesics, immunizing casualties for tetanus, and providing emergency care. Improvisation and innovation became hallmarks of that care, as nurses struggled to meet the influx of burned and injured men while risking their own lives to do so.

Chapter 7: The Nuclear Catastrophe in Hiroshima, Japan, August 1945

With a different perspective on World War II, this chapter relies on oral histories from several Japanese Red Cross nurses who worked in the hospitals in Hiroshima on August 6, 1945—the day the United States dropped the atomic bomb on that city. The chapter examines questions of what happened to those nurses who were already on duty and what they faced in the days immediately following the bombing. It also examines the emergent response of many groups in the context of the overwhelming devastation that included the bombing of the nurses' dorm. This chapter also highlights the risks that the nurses faced in their compelling obligation to give priority to the care of soldier patients. Set amid the chaos of war, the chapter identifies and describes nurses' dedication to patients, their willingness to risk their own lives, and their resilience.

Chapter 8: The Bar Harbor Fire of 1947, Bar Harbor, Maine (USA)

In October 1947, a series of devastating wildfires, fueled by high winds, a buildup of debris in nearby forests, and extreme drought, affected much of the state of Maine on the northeast coast of the United States. Like most towns in the United States, Bar Harbor did not have a plan in place for a massive natural disaster. Located on the edge of Acadia National Park, Bar Harbor was a renowned seaside summer retreat for the wealthy, and home to a local fishing economy. This chapter highlights issues of unpreparedness, the privilege of class, and a state's ability to respond. It also examines the devastating decisions nurses and others had to make as they faced the oncoming inferno.

Chapter 9: The SARS Pandemic in Toronto, Canada, 2003

In 2002, a new disease, severe acute respiratory syndrome (SARS) coronavirus, emerged in south China and rapidly spread across the world, causing a pandemic that resulted in 775 deaths. In Toronto, Canada, between February and September 2003, there were 438 suspected cases and 43 deaths. The pandemic was largely centered in acute care hospitals where patients and health care workers were at the greatest risk of infection and death. Two nurses and one doctor were among those dead. What became clear in the Toronto experience were the tensions between altruistic and service-oriented responses to the risks faced by health workers and the rights of nurses to a safe working environment. This chapter explores those issues. It also identifies a new set of challenges that arose for the public health departments, the government, and the hospitals, including the need to manage mandatory quarantine, the public's stigmatization of health workers, and demands for full access to information.

Chapter 10: Hurricane Sandy, October 2012, New York City (USA)

This chapter focuses on the evacuation of two New York City hospitals during Hurricane Sandy. When the hurricane hit the northeast coast of the United States in 2012, nurses played key roles in responding.

Each New York City hospital had a disaster plan in place, but none had accounted for failed backup generators, a lack of electricity, and flooded elevators. Nurses, physicians, medical students, orderlies, and other staff workers moved hundreds of patients down several flights of stairs during the emergency evacuation, and did not lose a single patient. In this emergent situation, collaboration among many responders was critical to success. Lessons learned from other hospitals, such as those in New Jersey, are also discussed.

Conclusion

The book concludes by returning to the Ebola outbreak in 2014 to examine lessons learned from this global historical perspective on nurses and disaster responses. This concluding chapter examines the roles of hospitals, local health departments, and the state with regard to protecting not only the public's health but also the health of nurses and other caregivers on the front lines. Questions guiding the analysis include: When is it appropriate to quarantine health workers for the protection of the public? What are the issues that emerge related to the nurses' duty to care in a setting that conflicts with their right to protect themselves and their families? What is the role of nursing professional organizations in advocating for nurses' rights during a pandemic? The central conclusion is that the public needs to recognize the importance of nursing and to be able to trust that compassionate and professionally trained nurses will be there to take care of them should the need ever arise. At the same time, nurses have the right to expect the training, skills, knowledge, and resources they need to protect themselves and their families.

Arlene W. Keeling
Barbra Mann Wall

NOTES

1. Adam Nossiter and Ben C. Solomon, "Those Who Serve Ebola Victims Soldier On," *New York Times*, August 23, 2014, http://www.nytimes.com/2014/08/24/woels/africa/sierra-leone-if, accessed August 24, 2014.

2. Ibid.

3. Ibid.

4. "CDC Director Apologizes for Hurting Feelings After Saying Ebola-Infected Care Provider Broke Protocol," October 13, 2014, http://hotair.com/archives/2014/10/13/cdc-director-apologizes-for-hurting-feelings-after-saying-ebola-infected-care-provider-broke-protocol.

5. Definitions of disasters have been debated extensively. See Thomas Drabek, "Revisiting the Disaster Encyclopedia," *International Journal of Mass Emergencies and Disaster* 7 (1999): 237–257.

6. Given at the 2013 Congress of the Humanities and Social Sciences, June 1, 2013, Victoria, British Columbia, Canada.

7. Barbra Mann Wall, "Hannah Lecture" (lecture, Victoria, British Columbia, Canada, June 1, 2013). Barbra Mann Wall, "Hannah Lecture: Disasters, Nursing, and Community Responses: A Historical Perspective," *Nursing History Review* 23 (2015): 11–27. Used with permission of Springer Publishing Company. See also: Thomas E. Drabek and David A. McEntire, "Emergent Phenomena and Multiorganizational Coordination in Disasters: Lessons From the Research Literature," *International Journal of Mass Emergencies and Disasters* 20, no. 2 (2002).

8. Thomas E. Drabek and David A. McEntire, "Emergent Phenomena and Multiorganizational Coordination in Disasters: Lessons From the Research Literature," *International Journal of Mass Emergencies and Disasters* 20, no. 2 (August 2002): 197–224.

9. Louise Comfort, "Risk, Security and Disaster Management," *Annual Review of Political Science* 8 (2005): 335–356 (quoted p. 338).

Prelude

Modern disaster planning has taken on increased importance and urgency in light of the recent dramatic increase in natural and man-made disasters that have resulted in enormous human and economic losses.[1] Such planning is aided by examining the historical role of nurses in disaster responses. Nurses occupy vital positions in disaster care because of their unique roles with patients and their experience in areas such as evacuation, triage, physical and psychological care, screening measures, case findings, vaccinations, monitoring, and disease surveillance and prevention.

What does history tell us about nurses' roles in disasters, particularly their provision of disaster relief during the initial response phase? Why is this important for disaster responses? And how can this knowledge enhance an understanding of the notion of "emergent phenomena"? For this discussion, disaster is defined as a social disruption resulting from natural causes, such as earthquakes and hurricanes; technological causes, such as explosions or nuclear accidents; and conflict situations, such as wartime.[2] Research on the term "emergent behavior" has been a significant feature of disaster studies in sociology, but it has not been examined from the standpoint of the history of nursing. Sociologists Thomas Drabek and David McEntire argue that emergent phenomena include "the appearance of inter-organizational networks after disaster which attempt to fulfill important societal functions made evident by an extreme event." These networks are composed of many organizations that work together to "resolve the demands placed on their community in times of disaster."[3] Drabek and McEntire argue that people become more "cohesive and unified during situations of collective stress, and they work together." Emergent groups often "have no previous knowledge of each other," and they may perform "non-regular tasks." Local communities are particularly important at this time; they are the "first to help themselves."[4] Often, these emergent groups are the most effective and quickest to respond after a disaster.[5]

A history of nursing can contribute to theoretical discussions of emergent behavior. By taking into account nurses' rich heritage in disaster responses, we can learn about which groups should be included in any organizational coordination during disasters.[6] This chapter features case studies of the work of nurses and some physicians situated within a local response and one involving international aid. The aim is to enhance understanding of the social and political forces that informed nurses' actions, and the tensions and inconsistencies that occurred at particular times in particular places.

Doing disaster research has its challenges because records can be lost or destroyed. Some sources are available, however, including newspapers, diaries, letters to family members and other personal correspondence, official histories from organizations, city records, photographs, and oral sources. Problems include memory loss if a letter was written or an oral history obtained some years later. Yet, Joseph Scanlon, who wrote about the 1917 Halifax, Nova Scotia, ship explosion, found that "disasters are so dramatic that many vividly remember what happened even three-quarters of a century earlier."[7]

Another problem is "whose history is recorded? From whose perspective? A gaping hole includes the voices of the silenced, including minorities, the poor, and others excluded from power. This could be because they may have lacked the means to document personal experiences, or archivists and librarians simply did not seek their stories."[8] In my own research, I have had to doggedly piece together different sources and read between the lines of others to get at the silenced voice.

In 2010, Arlene W. Keeling and I edited a book on the history of nursing in disasters.[9] We concluded, based on 13 case studies, that

hx snews

nurses made crucial independent decisions in crisis situations where time was critical to a person's survival. Their senses sharpened as the events at hand took priority. They also often responded with makeshift activities as they helped restore order after extreme social disruption. We also affirmed that disasters unraveled stable geographical boundaries as nurses responded in collaboration with others. For example, nurses from Boston, Massachusetts, assisted in Halifax, Nova Scotia, after the 1917 ship explosion. Nurses from Boston were rewarded a year later when Canadian nurses went to Boston to help during the flu pandemic. From Mississippi to Texas, Boston to Halifax, and New York to Turkey, nurses and others offered to help after disasters in any way they could.[10]

Historically, people have had a sense of obligation to care for strangers during periods of war and devastation. The founding of the International Red Cross in 1863 in Geneva was a milestone in the growth of humanitarian relief based on a position of neutrality. Eventually, several national societies formed.[11]

Historians and sociologists have been saying for decades that health care workers and survivors are resilient in the face of disasters, and our conclusions validate this finding. As an example, after the 1906 earthquake and fire in San Francisco, nurse Lucy Fisher and her companion immediately donned their uniforms and went to a makeshift hospital in a building called the Pavilion. It is interesting that they thought to put on their uniforms; indeed, this gave them legitimacy. The fact that they were nurses allowed them entrance when many others were turned away. In Fisher's firsthand account for the *American Journal of Nursing*, she noted that they faced a chaotic scene of mattresses strewn on the floor, nearly all occupied by patients. An improvised surgery was well equipped and already in operation, however, with operating room tables, dressings, instruments, and hot and cold sterilized water from the destroyed emergency hospital. Patients were constantly being admitted, and Fisher and her friend were told to "pitch in," which they quickly did. Because the surgery area was well staffed, Fisher was particularly concerned about critical cases that might be overlooked in the confusion, and she went around the room with extra blankets, hot water bags, and coffee for people in immediate danger. In the process, she put her assessment skills to work by observing for those "with feeble pulses and blue lips."[12] She and her friend pinned pillowcases to their waists to carry dressings, helped with dressing changes, and gave hypodermic injections for pain. Because of the confusion and the danger of duplication of drugs, the nurses pinned tags onto patients with the name and quantity of the drug and the time it was administered.[13]

Other nurses rode to disaster sites in that new contraption—the automobile. With his father's pistol in hand, Rene Bine, a young San Francisco physician, also responded by commandeering an automobile. He and others broke into hardware and drug stores to get medical supplies and ransacked department stores for pillows and mattresses for the injured. They did not consider this looting—rather, they saw it as a necessity to get the needed supplies. He worked at several makeshift facilities. He later wrote to relatives, "I never felt better in my life. We sleep on the ground & it is better than the country and loads of fun. We have a good supply of rations and are in OK shape all around."[14] Nellie May Brown nursed at a camp in Oakland and wrote to her family telling them that she was "working in the thick of the suffering—at last experiencing the horrors of the field hospital." She was in the first squad sent out to one of the nearby forts. She wrote that she was having the "experience of a lifetime."[15]

Several groups also emerged in 1947 in Texas City, Texas, after a ship loaded with fertilizer exploded in the harbor, killing more than 500 people. The entire local fire department responded, and all its members were killed. More than 3,000 injuries also occurred.[16] Individuals and organizations from the local community immediately responded. One Red Cross administrator noted, "Never in all my days have I seen such response from nurses, doctors, first aid crews, military personnel, law officers, and citizens."[17] One drug store owner opened a first-aid station and, along with some volunteers, began bandaging the injured. Conscious of the racial norms of the day, it was important for him to point out, "We bandaged everyone, whites, Negroes, Mexicans."[18] He knew that doctors used whiskey for shock, and he started passing it out not only to survivors but also to morticians "to keep them going in their horrible job."[19] Search-and-rescue teams were formed. A nurse from a local clinic remembered that men from one of the industrial plants came to help, and they worked "like Trojans."[20]

The city had not prepared for a disaster of this magnitude, and no disaster plan was in place. Without a local hospital, physicians and nurses set up a makeshift clearing station and triaged casualties. Texas City clinics were full, and volunteer physicians and nurses had to work with no water or electricity. Women opened their homes to care for the injured, and even workers at the local radio station got into the act. To maintain a record system for tracking survivors, someone started a file system.[21] Indeed, these residents were the "first to help themselves."[22]

Nurses, surgeons, medical residents, and medical and nursing students from Galveston's John Sealy Hospital across the bay from Texas City were among the responders. After giving emergency first aid to thousands, they sent casualties to 21 area hospitals in cities such as Houston and Galveston. Typical of emergent phenomena, as citizens and organizations took on new tasks, they stepped in and shared their resources.[23] The participants included nursing and medical students who worked both at the disaster site and in hospitals. One nursing student was recruited by her supervisor. At first she resisted going, stating, "I don't have permission from the nursing office." The supervisor cried, "It doesn't matter. I give you permission!" After arriving at the scene, the student administered first aid to severely burned patients, including giving morphine for pain. In fact, in this emergent situation, she had an "open order to administer hypodermics of pain relievers as I saw the need. . . . In a situation like this," she wrote,

> You are oblivious to anything except doing the job at hand. Somehow, everything you have ever learned in this area comes to the surface and you do the best you can. . . . I later realized there was no way that you could take a holistic view of a patient in a situation like this; it's only the immediate needs that are met.[24]

In her memoir, she commented on "what a confident twenty-year-old nurse I was."[25]

A sophomore medical student also responded and was dispatched to John Sealy Hospital's emergency department. In this situation, medical and nursing care blurred. He washed the oil off burned patients and those with severe contusions, set up oxygen tanks, took histories, monitored vital signs, and cleaned wounds. Hospital leaders also drafted medical students to help nurses who worked long shifts on the floors. Thus, for the next 2 days, he cared for patients with suspected gas gangrene until special nurses could take over the care.[26]

One nursing student recalled that she was amazed at how, when she was at the scene of the disaster, "everything began to fall into place and regardless of rank or race we were a team."[27] The medical student wrote,

> For the first time in my life, I didn't care whether a man was white or black. I worked with both equally at ease. It didn't make a bit of difference as both were sick, and all needed to be cared for.[28]

These examples illustrate that nursing and medical students' routine assignments changed, and they found alternative ways to respond as they shared tasks.

The students' stories should not be taken to mean that there were no challenges. Historical research can also add to debates over the impact of race on emergent behavior. Indeed, this study shows that responses were composed of "messy" race struggles. White respondents remembered people pulling together during the emergency period; yet they probably were working from a base of unacknowledged "white privilege": One of the benefits of being White was having the power to ignore race in the situation.[29] A different story was told when Black responders came forward. Black physicians and nurses also rendered aid at the disaster scene, as did morticians and embalmers. Their voices were found through a search of Black newspapers and photographs. Two ministers from local Black churches carried the injured and dying in their cars to hospitals in Galveston.[30] But they reported that "when they began their rescue work, the Negro injured were being walked over while the Whites were being rescued."[31] Although these contrasting accounts were likely true—as they applied to specific situations—the African American newspaper took a different perspective and reported on the continued neglect of Black casualties.[32]

This brings me to a discussion of how photographs can enhance the historical record when few written sources exist on silenced voices. I have written elsewhere about a particular photograph of the emergency room at St. Joseph's Hospital in Houston, where some of the survivors of the Texas City disaster were taken.[33] It reveals a Catholic sister helping an injured woman while several people, both African Americans and Whites, look on. This nun in her white religious garb, being in the center of the picture, lent a settling presence to a chaotic situation. But the photograph can also suggest something about racial relations. One interpretation is that African Americans are working side by side with Whites. This is significant because in 1947, hospitals in Texas were segregated. In showing Blacks and Whites working together, the picture can validate sociologists' claims that disasters often blurred racial boundaries.

Yet, sociologists' disciplinary focus on qualitative and quantitative studies does not include scholarly interpretations rooted in historical analysis.[34] My reading of this photograph is that, although it gives the impression that Whites and Blacks worked together in accord without favoritism, when contextualized with Texas's history of racial discrimination, a different interpretation can be offered. The African Americans are on one side and the Whites on the other. Perhaps, the photograph is staged, as they often are, because no one appears to be actually working. Furthermore, the nun is assisting a White ambulatory woman while a Black woman waits in a wheelchair.[35] This photograph can support what the African American newspapers had reported—that Blacks were ignored, whereas Whites were tended to first.

After the San Francisco earthquake and the Texas City ship explosion, it is also interesting to consider how nurses and physicians described their experiences. They saw themselves as performing meaningful work that was deeply rewarding to them. They turned the disaster into an opportunity (it was exciting for them, in a positive way), and they were proud of their work. What is often overlooked from most contemporary caring models is the personal satisfaction nurses and other health care workers find in actively using their knowledge and skills and being present for patients and their families in times of need.[36]

Yet, what the texts did not reveal is also interesting. They did not mention fear or lack of control. We also do not get the perspective of nurses who did not come to help. During the severe acute respiratory syndrome (SARS) epidemic in Toronto in 2003, for example, some nurses chose not to lend assistance because they were afraid of contagion and of infecting family and friends. Indeed, one study revealed that the attack rates among nurses who worked in emergency departments and intensive care units ranged from 10.3% to 60%.[37] This probably happened in earlier disasters as well.

After 1950, disaster teams expanded with formal state responses that differed from the earlier 20th-century voluntary responses of the Red Cross. At this time, growing world political tensions led to new conceptions of disaster relief. The United Nations had formed in 1945, and the Marshall Plan had succeeded in rebuilding war-torn Europe. This was the context for the growth of international humanitarian aid and, concomitantly, an international disaster relief network that included health care. Rather than private ad hoc initiatives, intergovernmental agencies became more prominent. Among others, these included UNICEF and WHO.[38]

In the 1940s, international nongovernmental organizations, or NGOs, such as Oxford Committee for Famine Relief (Oxfam) and Cooperative for Assistance and Relief Everywhere (CARE) were established. National governments were also taking on greater roles in disaster relief. In the United States, President John Kennedy created the U.S. Agency for International Development (USAID), and in Canada, the Canadian International Development Agency (CIDA) was formed. Nurses and physicians worked in each of these agencies. The organizations expanded their work in developing countries as well, especially in those that had recently won independence from their colonial masters.[39] An Oxfam publication noted that these agencies "could move much more quickly than could governmental and intergovernmental organizations and could often go where governments could not."[40] One sociologist has argued, "The private relief and development organizations, by dressing in 'neutral' clothing, could venture into politically sensitive areas that were out of bounds to governmental agencies."[41]

This happened in the 1967 to 1970 Nigerian civil war. The war led to a public health emergency when a segment of the Nigerian population was displaced and food was cut off to them. Like other disasters, the war generated large-scale displacements of people and resources, and women nurses and physicians played key roles.[42] Yet, little is known about emergence that occurs in conflict situations. Indeed, war complicates the notion of emergent behavior because new groups are constantly being formed.[43]

I analyze this question in my current research on mission physicians and nurses in Nigeria in the mid-20th century. Complex political and religious tensions occurred as Catholic women, working through international networks, attempted to provide medical and nursing care during this period of instability. One important document I found is a diary by Sister Pauline Dean, a pediatrician and a Medical Missionary of Mary who worked at St. Mary's Hospital in Urua Akpan. Sister Pauline wrote her diary from January to September 1968,[44] the period during which her hospital was in the midst of the conflict. At that time, two nurse midwives, Sisters Eugene McCullagh and Elizabeth Dooley; two physicians, Sisters Pauline Dean and Leonie McSweeney; and administrator Sister Brigidine Murphy staffed the hospital. St. Mary's had begun in 1952; at the time of the civil war, it boasted 150 beds, a large surgical clinic, and a training school for midwifery.[45]

The Medical Missionaries of Mary had come to Nigeria from Ireland in 1937 to do both mission and medical work. During this period of violence and upheaval, however, they shifted their understanding of mission from conversion of souls toward humanitarian relief.[46] The Catholic Church was one of the private agencies that played a significant role in the civil war. Although they had made little impact in the northern part of Nigeria, which had a Muslim majority, Catholic missionaries were more successful in the southeastern region, particularly among the Ibo (Igbo). For the Irish missionaries, Nigeria was the centerpiece of their "religious empire," with more Irish missionaries concentrated there than elsewhere in the entire world.[47] By 1965, the eastern area had more than

2 million conversions.[48] The Irish also made great inroads in education and health care, where the British colonial state had not played a large role.

Nigeria was formed in 1914, when Britain joined the two northern and southern protectorates, and it received full independence in 1960. The civil war that began in 1967 was between the eastern region of Nigeria (renamed Biafra) and the rest of the country. Biafra declared itself as an independent state, which the federal military government of Nigeria regarded as an act of illegal secession, and the Nigerian government fought the war to reunite the country. One million people had fled to the East, and by April 1968, Biafrans had flooded into a land-locked enclave entirely surrounded by federal forces that blockaded all the roads. Western nations were unwilling to violate Nigeria's national sovereignty and channel assistance across the border. The 30-month war ended in 1970 when the revolt collapsed.[49]

Cooperation occurred among many groups in Biafra: missionary nurses and physicians, priests, UNICEF volunteers, local people on the ground, and private international and church aid groups. Biafran women helped as nurses and midwives, social workers, caretakers of children, and distributors of relief. The Medical Missionaries of Mary worked out of their hospitals and clinics in the eastern area. Although most Protestant organizations fled, the sisters and many Irish priests made the crucial decision to stay in Biafra.

In her diary, Sister Pauline gave eyewitness accounts of aerial bombardments of her hospital, people being killed, roadblocks established by soldiers, and the disease situation in the refugee camps. The diary provides a vivid account of the most severe health and nutritional problems of the war's effect. Her first entry, on January 23, was an acknowledgment of the food problem: "Food was scarce so we started to farm. Planted pumpkin, melon, and okra." On January 28, she noted the turmoil of the region: "Plane and two thuds in OPD [outpatient department]. I did not hear because of screaming children." Food issues continued to be a problem, and on February 14, she went to Use Abat to get yams.[50] On February 19, she wrote,

> Bad day trying to do Male Ward, Children's Ward, and 2 clinics. Head just doesn't work after 1:30 when working at such

a pace. Continued rounds 4–7:20 and called down again at 7:30 pm. Up at night 1:20–4:45 am. [B]reech delivery and then another delivery by vacuum.

Another "bad day" was February 20; on the 21st, she was "up at night 2–5 am" and the next day faced 108 patients as the only doctor.[51] The hospital was bombed on March 3, after which the sisters treated 21 wounded people. On March 5, Sister Pauline went to a hospital in Aba, where she "begged for some blood giving sets" and received them. The next day she went to Ikot Ekpene to get splints but had to leave quickly because of an air raid there. Throughout the month, in addition to caring for patients, the nuns tended their garden, helped at St. Vincent de Paul's bazaar to get clothes for refugees, and found families for orphaned children. On March 25, Sister Pauline and her colleagues treated 45 outpatients as planes flew over them, and then she and Sister Leonie worked in the operating room all afternoon.[52] Most of the secular nurses had left the hospital to be with their families, and priests began assisting the sisters with feedings and care of babies. On April 3, Sister Pauline wrote, "Father Johnston did well on night duty leaving everything in ship shape. Father Frawley was heard saying to him last night: 'Be sure you have plenty of nappies before you go because I ran short last night.'"[53]

On April 26, Sister Pauline held a huge clinic and gave instructions to the priests on how to put on sterile gloves. The following day, one of them "scrubbed up" to help her in the operating room.[54] In this emergent situation, the existing mission hierarchy blurred: Sister doctors taught priests how to be nursing assistants and even how to change diapers.

In the eastern region, where military operations were the most active, farming could not take place and famine resulted. Although the exact number is unknown, one Irish priest reported that "more than 2 million have died as a result of the blockade set up by Nigeria."[55] Because of the famine, an international ecumenical airlift began operating in violation of Nigerian airspace and without Nigerian authority. In 1968, Protestants and Catholics, with financial support from the American Jewish community, formed the Joint Church Aid organization. These emergent groups were joined by Protestant church agencies in Denmark, Norway, Sweden, and Finland in forming an international Joint Church Aid group. Much of the relief material raised internationally came through these agencies, along with a Canadian group, the World Council of Churches, Africa Concern, and Oxfam. All these agencies proclaimed their neutrality even as they defied the federal blockade, often under gunfire, and flew in medicines and food to Biafra, despite the fact that the Nigerian government had banned outside aid flights.[56]

The International Committee of the Red Cross also had an airlift, but it withdrew after one of its planes was shot down and four of its relief workers were killed. The airlifts were the only remaining lifelines for those in the eastern enclave. The aid agencies used a widened stretch of blacktop road at Uli Airport as a nighttime landing strip for the supply planes that flew in from neutral sites. The airstrip was bombed periodically.[57]

Obviously, the Nigerians were in the majority, but the voices of the people on the ground are silent in missionary archives. Photographs again can be useful. One shows UNICEF and Joint Church Aid workers posing alongside Nigerians who all were rendering service at Uli Airport.

Historians also can read between the lines of written documents. Eventually, the government forced the sisters to evacuate, and they first said goodbye to a Mrs. Hogan, a Nigerian nurse midwife who had trained in England. Sister Pauline mentioned her several times in her diary, although she gave few details of Mrs. Hogan's work and none of her background. When the nuns left in September 1968, Mrs. Hogan stayed behind.[58]

The sisters had another key resource on their side: Nigerian sisters in their congregations and in others who could maintain the hospitals and schools after the expatriates left.[59] One photograph shows a teacher, Sister Joseph Theresa Agbasiere, a Holy Rosary sister, comforting a woman and baby.

This photograph is important in showing the local response of Nigerians caring for themselves. Photographs also reveal that, in this case, emergent groups included a mix of people. Those affected by the disaster included the church workers, local citizens, and international workers who were present to provide relief, shelter, food, and health care—"all important disaster functions."[60]

The Catholic Church's role in the conflict, however, caused considerable political controversy. The Nigerian government was hostile to the priests, sister nurses and physicians, and other relief agencies, arguing that they prolonged the war by feeding the enemy.[61] To the government, this work was illegal, and it became the main reason for its decision to expel 300 priests and 200 sister nurses and physicians from the country. Only a few were invited back later in the 1970s.[62]

The press vilified the Red Cross for not confronting the Nigerian government. Indeed, the international media dwelt extensively on photos of starving Biafran children, which shaped the disaster discourse and grabbed the attention of the public. The French, who had maintained some support for the Biafran government, were especially indignant. What resulted was a new, more "militant" generation of relief organizations, including the French Médicins sans Frontières (Doctors Without Borders) and the group called the Irish Concern.[63] Since then, these groups have been very active in disaster relief.

Although I discussed earlier the role of race in emergent phenomena, research can also inform us about gender. Debate abounds as to "whether men or women are more involved in [emergency responses] and what types of roles they play in disaster."[64] Most results show a gender differentiation, with women's work restricted to domestic duties and the provision of sympathy and psychological support.[65] A history of nursing in disasters, however, shows something different. During the Biafra conflict, for example, it was mainly the men running the airlift who received the media coverage. Yet, my sources illustrate women in the role of nurses and doctors in the thick of the suffering. They performed several tasks that definitely were not restricted to domestic labor and mere provision of sympathy.

To conclude, until the late 1980s, research on emergent phenomena included studies of physicians, nurses, firefighters, and other relief workers who "remained the preferred approach to disaster management." In the 1990s, in addition to disaster assistance, scholarly interest began to include disaster prevention and risk reduction, bringing in engineers, geophysicists, and meteorologists.[66] Rather than strictly reacting to disasters with firefighters, search-and-rescue teams, and emergency medical care, greater attention was paid to anticipating and preventing disasters. For example, in 2005, Portugal took the lead in urging the European Union to put in place a disaster warning system in the Atlantic and Mediterranean regions.[67]

However, as the cases described here reveal, one cannot plan or prevent all disasters. As another example, during the Tokyo subway sarin nerve gas attack in 1995, St. Luke's Hospital received most of the patients. Prior to the attack, the hospital had a disaster plan that focused on conditions from earthquakes, fires, or floods. Officials had never considered a chemical disaster.[68]

So, why is all of this important? Much still needs to be learned about emergent response groups. Sociologists argue that "some groups of people are known for their ability to remain cool and stay clear-headed under pressure, including veteran military officers, [as well as] fire and police commanders."[69] Mayors of cities and others who respond to disasters can also benefit by observing nurses and physicians at their regular work as they cooperate and communicate with many other health care workers daily under extreme pressure. Nurses and physicians are ready for contingencies. They do this every day. After the tsunami in Japan in 2011, 3,000 nurses immediately volunteered to work. They were ready. Likewise, after the Boston marathon bombing on April 15, 2013, a reporter asked a trauma surgeon at Massachusetts General Hospital, which had received many of the injured, about his situation. The doctor replied, "This is work. We just go to work."[70] No doubt nurses were right there with him. These professionals have to gear up for the unexpected and quickly adjust. Policies and protocols may no longer apply as expediency and patients' needs take priority.[71]

To understand and effectively deal with disasters, multidisciplinary approaches are needed, including meteorologists, engineers, anthropologists, lawyers, political scientists, economists, journalists, and others.[72] I suggest that as we study these approaches, it also is important to include historians and nurses in any research on disaster response.

—*Barbra Mann Wall*

Reprinted from Nursing History Review 23 (2015): 11–27. *A publication of the American Association for the History of Nursing. Copyright © 2015 Springer Publishing Company. http://dx.doi.org/10.1891/1062–8061.23.11.*

NOTES

1. Barbra Mann Wall, "Hannah Lecture" (lecture, Victoria, British Columbia, Canada, June 1, 2013).

2. Sociologists have extensively debated definitions of disaster. For an example, see Thomas Drabek, "Revisiting the Disaster Encyclopedia," *International Journal of Mass Emergencies and Disaster* 17, no. 2 (1999): 237–257.

3. Thomas E. Drabek and David A. McEntire, "Emergent Phenomena and Multiorganizational Coordination in Disasters: Lessons From the Research Literature," *International Journal of Mass Emergencies and Disasters* 20, no. 2 (2002): 198.

4. Thomas E. Drabek and David A. McEntire, "Emergent Phenomena and the Sociology of Disaster: Lessons, Trends and Opportunities From the Research Literature," *Disaster Prevention and Management* 12, no. 2 (2003): 99, 101.

5. Russell Dynes, "Community Emergency Planning: False Assumptions and Inappropriate Analogies," *International Journal of Mass Emergencies and Disasters* 12 (1994): 141–158; Drabek and McEntire, "Emergent Phenomena and the Sociology of Disaster: Lessons, Trends and Opportunities From the Research Literature," *Disaster Prevention and Management* 12, no. 2 (2003): 99, 101.

6. Julie A. Fairman and Jonathan Gilbride, "Gendered Notions of Expertise and Bravery: New York City 2001," in *Nurses on the Front Line: When Disaster Strikes, 1878–2010*, Ed. Barbra Mann Wall and Arlene Keeling (New York: Springer Publishing, 2011), 223–230.

7. Joseph T. Scanlon, "Rewriting a Living Legend: Researching the 1917 Halifax Explosion," in *Methods of Disaster Research*, Ed. Robert A. Stallings (Philadelphia, PA: Xlibris, 2002), 267.

8. Philip Fradkin, *The Great Earthquake and Firestorms of 1906: How San Francisco Nearly Destroyed Itself* (Berkeley, CA: University of California Press, 2005).

9. Barbra Mann Wall and Arlene Keeling, *Nurses on the Front Line: When Disaster Strikes, 1878–2010* (New York: Springer Publishing Co., 2011).

10. Ibid. See, in particular, chapters 1, 2, 5, 6, 11, and 13.

11. Caroline Moorehead, *Dunant's Dream: War, Switzerland, and the History of the Red Cross* (London: HarperCollins, 1999); John Hannigan, *Disasters Without Borders* (Cambridge: Polity, 2012); Marian Moser Jones, *The American Red Cross From Clara Barton to the New Deal* (Baltimore, MD: Johns Hopkins University Press, 2013).

12. Lucy B. Fisher, "A Nurse's Earthquake Story," *American Journal of Nursing* 7, no. 2 (1906): 84–98. Aspects of this disaster are published in Barbra Mann Wall and Marie E. Kelly, " 'A Lifetime of Experience': The San Francisco Earthquake and Fire, 1906," in *Nurses on the Front Line*, Ed. Barbra Mann Wall and Arlene Keeling (New York: Springer Publishing, 2010), 43–67.

13. Fisher, "A Nurse's Earthquake Story."

14. Typed copy of Rene Bine to folks, n.d., MS 3640, folder 6, California Historical Society, San Francisco (hereafter cited as CHS). See also Rene Bine to Folks, Monday, April 30, 1906, MS 3540, folder 6, CHS; and "Personal Recollections During the Eventful Days of April, 1906," Online Archive of California, http://www.oac.cdlib.org/view?docId = h b4p3007dw&brand = oac4&doc.view = entier_text, accessed May 6, 2013.

15. Nellie May Brown to Mother, April 20, 1906, CHS.

16. Hugh W. Stephens, *The Texas City Disaster, 1947* (Austin, TX: University of Texas Press, 1997).

17. Ella Tarbell, "Response Impresses Red Cross Leaders: Food, Shelter, Comfort Given Blast Victims," *Houston Post*, April 18, 1947, 6.

18. Aspects of this disaster are published in Barbra Mann Wall, "Healing After Disasters in Early Twentieth-Century Texas," *Advances in Nursing Science* 31, no. 3 (2008): 211–224. See also Elizabeth Lee Wheaton, *Texas City Remembers* (San Antonio, TX: Naylor, 1948), 1–74.

19. Ben Powell, in Wheaton, *Texas City Remembers*, 20.

20. Mrs. J. F. White, in ibid., 18.

21. Mrs. Helen Clough, in ibid., 18 and 20.

22. Drabek and McEntire, "Emergent Phenomena and the Sociology of Disaster," 99.

23. This is seen in Havidan Rodriquez, Enrico L. Quarantelli, and Russell R. Dynes, Eds., *Handbook of Disaster Research* (New York: Springer Publishing, 2007).

24. Luci P. Givin, *Texas City Disaster Memoir* (Galveston, TX: University of Texas Medical Branch Library [hereafter cited as UTMBL], Blocker Historical Collections, 1948).

25. Ibid.

26. Sam to Folks, April 16, 1947, UTMBL. Senior students at the scene in Texas City gave plasma, with one medical student claiming to have given 40 units the first day. They also took medical histories and performed physical assessments.

27. Allie Fay Molsbee, "Students Give Disaster Service in Galveston: A Student Describes Her Part in the Emergency Following the Texas City Disaster," *American Journal of Nursing* 47, no. 6 (1947): 414.

28. Sam to Folks, April 16 and 23, 1947: 1–2, UTMBL.

29. Peggy McIntosh, "White Privilege and Male Privilege: A Personal Account of Coming to See Correspondences Through Work in Women's Studies," in *Race, Class, and Gender: An Anthology*, Ed. Margaret L. Andersen and Patricia Hill Collins (Belmont, CA: Wadsworth, 1992), 147–160; David Roediger, *The Wages of Whiteness* (New York: Verso, 1991).

30. "Many Negroes Killed, Scores Injured in Texas City Blast," *Informer*, April 19, 1947, 1; and "Employee of Texas City Tells of His Escape," *Informer*, April 19, 1947, 10.

31. "Baptist Ministers Risk Lives to Evacuate Injured," *Informer*, April 19, 1947, 1, 10.

32. These issues are noted in Alice Fothergill, JoAnne DeRouen Darlington, and Enrique G. M. Maestas, "Race, Ethnicity and Disasters in the United States: A Review of the Literature," *Disasters* 23, no. 2 (1999): 156–173.

33. Barbra Mann Wall, "Looking Back: Celebrating Nursing History," *American Journal of Nursing* 108, no. 6 (2008): 26–29.

34. For an interesting analysis of the disciplinary focus of nursing history, see Patricia D'Antonio, "Toward a History of Research in Nursing," *Nursing Research* 46, no. 2 (1997): 105–110.

35. Barbra Mann Wall, "Looking Back: Celebrating Nursing History," *American Journal of Nursing* 108, no. 6 (2008): 26–29.

36. Julia Hallam, "Ethical Lives in the Early Nineteenth Century: Nursing and a History of Caring," in *New Directions in the History of Nursing: International Perspectives*, Ed. Barbara Mortimer and Susan McGann (London: Routledge, 2005), 25.

37. Monali Varia et al., "Investigation of a Nosocomial Outbreak of Severe Acute Respiratory Syndrome (SARS) in Toronto, Canada," *Canadian Medical Association Journal* 169, no. 4 (2003): 285–292; Robert Maunder et al., "The Immediate Psychological and Occupational Impact of the 2003 SARS Outbreak in a Teaching Hospital," *Canadian Medical Association Journal* 168, no. 10 (2003): 1245–1251.

38. Hannigan, *Disasters Without Borders*.

39. Ibid.

40. Frederick C. T. Cuny, *Disasters and Development* (New York: Oxford University Press, 1983), 18.

41. Hannigan, *Disasters Without Borders*, 49.

42. Ndubisi Obiaga, *The Politics of Humanitarian Organizations* (Dallas, TX: University Press of America, 2004); Olukunle Ojeleye, *The Politics of Post-War Demobilisation and Reintegration in Nigeria* (Burlington, VT: Ashgate, 2010).

43. Drabek and McEntire, "Emergent Phenomena and Multiorganizational Coordination."

44. Sister Doctor Pauline Dean, MMM, Biafra War Diary, Urua Akpan 1968 (hereafter cited as Diary), Archives of the Medical Missionaries of Mary, Drogheda, Ireland (hereafter cited as MMM).

45. "Article by Sister Doctor Margaret M. Nolan," MMM.

46. Ottavio Velho, "Missionization in the Postcolonial World: A View From Brazil and Elsewhere," in *Transnational Transcendence: Essays on Religion and Globalization*, Ed. Thomas J. Csordas (Berkeley, CA: University of California Press, 2009), 36. See also Jose Casanova, "Religion, the New Millennium, and Globalization," *Sociology of Religion* 62, no. 4 (2001): 415–441; Deborah Gaitskell, "Missions by Other Means? Dora Earthy and the Save the Children Fund in the 1930s," in *Protestant Mission and Local Encounters in the Nineteenth and Twentieth Centuries: Unto the Ends of the World*, Ed. Hilde Nielssen, Karina Hestad Skeie, and Inger Marie Okkenhaug (Leiden: Brill, 2011), 233–258.

47. Enda Staunton, "The Case of Biafra: Ireland and the Nigerian Civil War," *Irish Historical Studies* 31, no. 124 (1999): 513. See also Fiona Bateman, "Ireland's Spiritual Empire: Territory and Landscape in Irish Catholic Missionary Discourse," in *Empires of Religion*, Ed. Hilary M. Carey (New York, NY: Palgrave Macmillan, 2008), 267–287.

48. Laurie S. Wiseberg, "Christian Churches and the Nigerian Civil War," *Journal of African Studies* 2 (1972): 297–331.

49. Staunton, "The Case of Biafra"; Ojeleye, *The Politics of Post-War Demobilisation*.

50. Diary entries for January 23 and 28, 1968, and February 14, 1968.

51. Ibid., February 19, 20, 21, and 22, 1968.

52. Ibid., March 3, 5, 6, 12, 19, 23, and 25, 1968.

53. Ibid., April 3, 1968.

54. Letters to "mother" dated April 1969, MMM.

55. Father Kilbride, "Genocide, 1969," Clearing House for Nigeria/Biafra Information Records, 1968–1970, Collection: DG 168, Swarthmore

College, Swarthmore, PA (hereafter cited as Clearing House). The Clearing House for Nigeria/Biafra Information was established to provide information about the Nigeria/Biafra War. The organization was headquartered in New York and was in operation from October 1968 to February 1970.

56. The dates for the formation of Joint Church Aid-USA conflict, with some sources saying it was formed in December 1968 and others January 1969. See News Release, Joint Church Aid-USA, Inc., October 1 and 17, 1969; DG 168, Acc. 81A-120, Box 3, folder 1.8: Africa Concern and Joint Biafra Famine Relief (Ireland), Clearing House.

57. Wiseberg, "Christian Churches."

58. Ibid., July 7, 1968.

59. Sister Agnes Maria to Mother M. Reparatrice, September 11, 1968, 11/FOU/6(H)/183, MMM.

60. Drabek and McEntire, "Emergent Phenomena and Multiorganizational Coordination," 200.

61. Edd Doerr, "Nigeria's Civil War, the Untold Story," Secular Perspectives (blog), November 22, 2011, http://secularhumanist.blogspot.com/2011/11/nigerias-civil-waruntold-story.html. See also Wiseberg, "Christian Churches."

62. Bengt Sundkler and Christopher Steed, *A History of the Church in Africa* (Cambridge: Press Syndicate of the University of Cambridge, 2000).

63. Hannigan, *Disasters Without Borders*, 56.

64. Drabek and McEntire, "Emergent Phenomena and Multiorganizational Coordination," 202.

65. Elaine Enarson and Betty Hearn Morrow, Eds., *The Gendered Terrain of Disaster: Through Women's Eyes* (Westport, CT: Praeger, 1998).

66. Hannigan, *Disasters Without Borders*, 58.

67. Katherine Worboys, "The Uses of History in Disaster Preparedness: The 1755 Lisbon Earthquake and the Construction of Historical Memory," *Journal of the International Institute* 13, no. 2 (2006).

68. Tetsu Okumura et al., "The Tokyo Subway Sarin Attack: Disaster Management, Part 2: Hospital Response," *Academic Emergency Medicine* 5, no. 6 (1998): 618–624.

69. Rodriquez, Quarantelli, and Dynes, *Handbook*, 49.

70. Peter Fagenholz, interview on MSNBC, April 15, 2013.

71. Tener Goodwin Veenema, "When Standards of Care Change in Mass-Casualty Events," *American Journal of Nursing* 107, no. 9 (2007): 72A–G.

72. David A. McEntire, "The Importance of Multi- and Interdisciplinary Research on Disasters and for Emergency Management," in *Disciplines, Disasters and Emergency Management: The Convergence and Divergence of Concepts, Issues, and Trends in the Research Literature*, Ed. David A. McEntire (Springfield, IL: C.C. Thomas, 2011).

CHAPTER 1

Typhoid Fever Epidemic, 1885 to 1887, Tasmania, Australia

Madonna Grehan

The nursing is everything in bringing persons successfully through typhoid, the hospital is the place to get that nursing....I was struck by their painstaking industry and the risk they ran of contagion.[1]

Mr. Thomas S. Willison, the author of a letter published in Hobart's *The Mercury* newspaper in 1887, was one of the numerous grateful individuals and families who publicly lauded nurses of Hobart General Hospital (HGH) for their care during a lengthy epidemic of typhoid fever in the Australian colony of Tasmania. Willison wrote that the nurses' efforts were so extraordinary during the crisis that they deserved an honorarium. In his 6 weeks as a typhoid patient, Willison observed that the nurses' focus at all times was "the comfort, happiness, and ultimate recovery of the patients under their charge, their duties frequently being of the most patience-trying character." His remarks struck a chord. A campaign of support for bedside nurses at HGH culminated in a celebratory public function held in August 1887. At that event, 25 nurses were awarded medals for meritorious services in nursing. The specially minted, 18-carat-gold, Maltese crosses were gifts from a grateful Tasmanian public.[2]

The medals were presented in recognition of the "great and good work performed during the past half-year by the nursing staff."[3] The evening's proceedings at the Tasmanian Hall included a performance of Thomas Williams's 1866 one-act farce, *Pipkin's Rustic Retreat*, and a dance. The HGH nurses and the lady superintendent, Miss Harriet Munroe, provided the supper. At the ceremony, the 19 nurses present stood on the stage in a semicircle, dressed in their nursing uniforms, looking "appropriate, pretty and effective."[4] Lady Felicia Hamilton, wife of Tasmania's governor, pinned the decorations to each nurse's breast. Scotsman Dr. Thomas Smart, honorary surgeon and chairman of HGH's Board of Management (BoM), was effusive in his praise. He noted that it was a common occasion to award men with medals for sporting; yet it was "a comparatively untrodden path" in the history of Tasmania to distinguish nurses for merit, but as Smart saw it, many Hobartians owed their lives to "a trained, educated, and zealous nursing staff, acting in unison with the medical officers" because the nurses were unafraid of typhoid and selfless in the face of this most potent of enemies.[5] Speeches at the August festivities pronounced that a fraternal plinth supported the nurses' labors during the crisis. According to Smart, success in battling the protracted epidemic was the result of harmony: harmony between the nurses and harmony between the nurses and the medical staff.[6] A correspondent to a local newspaper underscored this spirit of fraternity in the nurses' battling of the epidemic. He declared the nurses to be "the Florence Nightingales of our time."[7]

The 1887 awarding of the medals for meritorious services was a significant milestone in Australian nursing history. It is thought to be the first time in Australia that civilian nurses, as a group, were decorated for their work in a public health emergency.[8] Reporting of this congratulatory occasion gave the impression that HGH was a collegial workplace. As this chapter shows, however, the collegiality that characterized nursing at HGH during the 1887 epidemic was entirely new. Right up to February 1887, and for years previously, HGH was plagued by a crisis of professional tensions and deep disharmony.

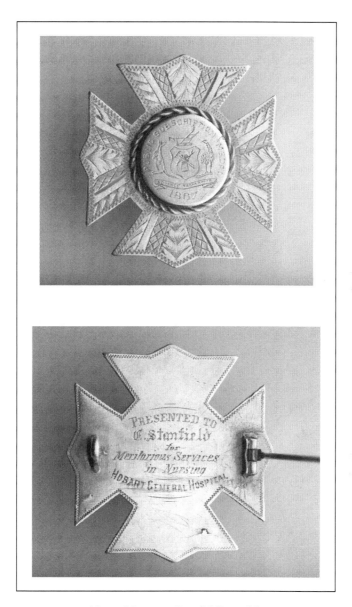

Nurse Margaret Stanfield's medal.

Reproduced with permission from the Collection of the Tasmanian Museum and Art Gallery.

On the surface, these conflicts seemed to be little more than acrimonious spats between individual nurses, yet they involved doctors, patients, and the Tasmanian government. In what was a toxic workplace, animosities festered throughout 1885, exploded in late 1886, and then lingered throughout 1887 as the typhoid epidemic raged.

Drawing on administrative records and detailed newspaper reporting of events, this chapter teases out the tensions and ambiguities around the awarding of medals for meritorious services in nursing. It examines what was at the heart of HGH's problems, and how the hospital's toxic climate was transformed into one of collaboration during the typhoid epidemic. The chapter is presented in two parts. The first part introduces the disease typhoid. It describes the intensive nursing that was so necessary in cases of typhoid and explains how the epidemic impacted the HGH. The second part addresses the crisis in the nursing administration at HGH in the 2 years preceding the typhoid epidemic and its subsequent resolution during the year of the epidemic.

TYPHOID IN TASMANIA

In the 19th century, Tasmania, an island 300 miles to the south of the Australian mainland, was one of Australia's seven colonies. With many ports in this island colony, Tasmania was no stranger to infectious diseases. Since the early 1880s, typhoid had been on the rise in most parts of Australia. Geographical analysis by Roger Kellaway points to a coalescence of climatic and social conditions as responsible for typhoid's transition from an endemic to an epidemic: A 5-year weather cycle of hot, dry summers in a row that reduced water quality, less water for street cleaning, a parallel increase in the population, the continued existence of cesspits, use of unhygienic "pails" for night soil, and illegal distribution of that waste (what the newspapers euphemistically referred to as "nuisances"). Household slops thus mixed with human and animal excreta in open drains and gutters or soaked into the soil.[9] In Tasmania, endemic typhoid transitioned to an epidemic status in the northern city of Launceston in 1885 and persisted there until 1886.

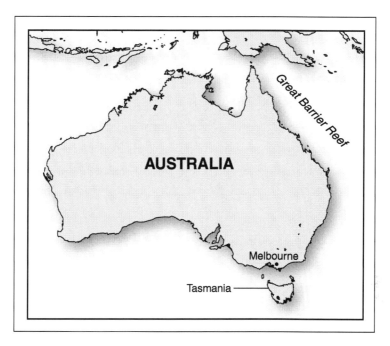

Map of Tasmania, Australia.

In late 1886 and 1887, epidemic typhoid emerged in Tasmania's southern capital, Hobart.

Cases of typhoid were often managed at home in the late 19th century, but both HGH and Launceston General Hospital (LGH) had fever wards and accepted a range of patients. Unlike the many charity-based hospitals in Australia, HGH and LGH were government-run institutions, established early in the 19th century. Tasmania at that time was the convict colony of Van Diemen's Land. HGH and the forerunner of the LGH accommodated regimental soldiers and other personnel of the civil administration. These early hospitals consisted of tents and temporary structures, but permanent buildings eventually replaced them, in Hobart (1820) and in Launceston (1863).[10] After transportation of convicts ceased, the general public was able to gain admission to both institutions. Some people were accepted as charity cases; some were paying patients. Both hospitals played a significant role in the management of typhoid in Tasmania.

In the 1880s epidemic, the majority of the individuals with the disease were adults aged 15 to 45 years.[11] Unsurprisingly, typhoid was described as an "insidious foe,"[12] because it was rather different from a natural disaster or other such calamity of scale. It was an extremely taxing disease for those afflicted and difficult to treat in a pre-antibiotic age. Caused by the bacterium *Salmonella typhi*, its early manifestations are diarrhea, pyrexia, general debility, abdominal pain, and rose-colored spots on the belly and chest. The disease can progress rapidly, manifesting in complications that include agitation, delirium, and ulceration of intestinal linings. These tissues become fragile and hemorrhage, and eventually the bowel perforates.[13] What care patients received in the 19th century is hard to gauge without extant medical records, but some indication comes from advice articles written by a trained nurse, Frances Gillam Holden, matron of the Sydney Children's Hospital. Holden's articles were published in *The Launceston Examiner* newspaper under the banner "Typhoid or Ignorance?" and in *The Mercury* as "What Typhoid Is and How to Nurse It."[14]

In 1875, Holden was working as a nurse at HGH with two of her sisters when she contracted typhoid.[15] Clearly she was speaking from professional and personal experience when she wrote that "all the skill and resources of the most experienced nurse" were necessary in cases of advanced typhoid. Holden described typhoid as "an invisible, intangible enemy" with two main elements leading to fatalities: "first, from not knowing the salient points of the disease which require very special care and second, from not beginning this special care from the outset." She believed that if basic steps were followed "steadily, perseveringly, quietly, cheerfully and hopefully," the patient had every chance of recovery. As she put it, the means to recovery were "not difficult, mysterious or vague."[16]

THE IMPORTANCE OF NURSING CARE

Holden explained typhoid as "intestinal inflammation." Using metaphors, she conveyed the fragile condition of a patient with typhoid. She likened Peyer's patches to angry red ulcers on a piece of damp blotting paper, which the slightest breath of air threatened to tear. She emphasized that moving a patient from his bed required three people to do it safely, and recommended that the nurses carry the patient as if he or she were a "dishful of liquid diamonds." The fundamentals in nursing typhoid cases were

> perfect cleanliness of the room, person and linen; frequent [three-hourly] changes of bedclothes and airing of blankets, frequent sponging in high temperature; steady and quiet lifting when moving...good liquid nourishment, good beef tea, mutton broth or chicken broth, or Ice Company's milk...weak acid drinks and ice to suck...plenty of fresh air.[17]

Aside from frequent sponging, a hydropathic treatment called "packing" emerged in the 1880s. Packing acted as "a cooling poultice," using wet sheets insulated by blankets to lower a patient's temperature. To pack a patient, the nurse placed several blankets on a bed, in layers. On top of the blankets, she placed a cold wet sheet with the water wrung out of it. Nurses then placed the patient on the wet sheet and wrapped him or her in it, and wrapped the sheet in the blankets. Every 10 to 15 minutes, and depending on the degree of fever, the nurses undid the entire bundle, renewed the wet sheet, and replaced the swaddling blankets, continuing the whole process for an hour. After that, the nurses put the patient in a tepid bath, or bathed him or her in bed until the temperature dropped.[18] This was a time-consuming process, which involved several people and their labor. An alternative was a cold compress. This worked in the same way as packing but saved time, caused fewer disturbances to the patient, and required fewer people to apply. The cold compress consisted of two separate pieces of soft flannel. One piece measured 14 by 18 inches, and the other 2 by 18 inches. The larger piece formed an outer "compartment," which held a wet compress in place. The smaller flannel was the cooling wet pack. To apply the compress, the nurse folded the smaller cloth in half and dampened it with cold water. With safety pins, she secured the wet flannel to the larger dry piece and then placed the whole compress under the patient's back. When the cooling effect diminished, the nurse undid the safety pins, removed the wet cloth, and applied a fresh compress.[19] Another specific intervention Holden advised was to clean the patient's mouth several times a day. To do this at home, she explained how to make a "mop" for the mouth by tying strips of lint to the end of a small paintbrush. This could then be used to moisten and wipe out the mouth.[20]

On top of these essential tasks, another was changing soiled linen. At HGH, nurses changed the bed linen of typhoid patients up to seven times a day when there was high fever. Other patients had their beds made twice a day and the drawsheets reversed. The nurses changed the linen on these beds once per week.[21] The level of industry that typhoid generated can be seen in supply statistics. In the month of April 1887, at which point HGH had 68 inpatients with typhoid, the laundry washed and dried 1,147 bed sheets, 1,002 drawsheets, 540 shirts, and 775 night gowns.[22] These figures do not include compresses, bandages, dress- ings, uniforms for the nurses, and other items processed by the laun- dry. How the nurses managed the delicate subject of patients' excreta is unclear. For those nursing typhoid cases at home, Hobart's local board of health recommended disinfection of all bowel motions, but gave no instructions on the disinfection process. Notably, Miss Holden's pub- lished advice did not refer to excreta either, but she did recommend disinfection of soiled linen, first by placing it in a tub of water with carbolic added, and second by thorough cleaning and exposure to fresh air.[23] Deaths demanded a different regime of practice from the nursing staff. When a typhoid patient died, the nurses and wardmaids at HGH removed everything from the bed and the surrounding area. They took off the mattress and left it to air for at least one day. Likewise, the empty bed frame aired for a minimum of 24 hours.[24]

In an era before intravenous therapies, hydration by mouth was critical. What the typhoid patients were given at HGH depended on the status of an individual's intestine. Milk was available, but it tended to sour easily in the hot summer weather. The main source of liquid nutrition was beef tea, a strained form of beef stock. Every day dur- ing the epidemic, the cook at HGH made 50 pints (28 L) of beef tea.[25] The nurses also dispensed prescribed forms of alcohol referred to as "stimulants." There was some dispute between Tasmania's doctors about the wisdom of giving stimulants to typhoid patients, but at HGH, these were a foundation of treatment. The daily allowance consisted of 12 fluid ounces of brandy (350 mL) plus a bottle of champagne, supplemented with wine, ale and stout, and cordials if the doctor ordered them.[26] Crushed ice was another valuable therapeutic agent, but its supply was never guaranteed. From late 1886 to January 1887, HGH used 32 pounds of ice during what was the summer typhoid season. These volumes could not be produced in Tasmania; therefore, the ice was made on mainland Australia and shipped to Tasmania by sea. Just as the epidemic escalated in early 1887, Tasmania's supply of ice ran out, owing to a severe drought in southern Australia.[27]

When typhoid was endemic in Hobart, mortality stood at around 15 cases per year.[28] With the onset of the epidemic in January 1887, and a rapid spread, death numbers increased. From January to mid-April, 111 cases of typhoid were admitted to HGH, 17 (15.3%) of which ended fatally.[29] In March alone, there were 68 admissions for typhoid.[30] In this demanding environment, staffing the hospital was a challenge. HGH had a daily average of 80 inpatients in nonepidemic times, although it had a capacity for 140 beds. In 1887, 22 nurses were employed for the entire hospital, something that *The Launceston Examiner* newspaper judged as "wanton extravagance."[31] This critique was unfair because the 22 nurses covered daytime and nighttime shifts and the one day off that the nurses were entitled to. Even when wards were not full of inpatients, the nurses were fully occupied while on duty, sewing and mending, padding splints, preparing other equipment, and sometimes cleaning.[32] During the epidemic, head nurses worked particularly long hours, usually 7:00 a.m. to 6:00 p.m., 6 days per week, with 45 minutes for dinner and 30 minutes for lunch.[33] They had to supervise their subordinates, too, including the wardmaids who cleaned the kitchen utensils and cooking pots used for preparing and serving the patients' food and drink. Each ward had its own supply of this equipment.[34]

The nursing care of typhoid patients was constant; it required regular sponging, compressing, hydration, feeding, and recording the various treatments and stimulants given. Going by Miss Holden's advice on the number of nurses needed just to move a serious patient, it is easy to see how intensive this whole nursing effort was. It is hard to know exactly what the staff-to-patient ratio at HGH was during this period.

At the epidemic's peak, 14 of the 22 nurses were working in the fever wards, assisted by five wardmaids.[35] Taking April as an example, while 14 nurses managed the 68 typhoid inpatients, the other 8 nurses managed the rest of HGH's patients. It did not help matters that, around this time, some of the nurses fell ill. In April 1887, advertisements placed in *The Mercury* newspaper called urgently for two or three probationers to join the hospital's staff because of the number of fever cases. The lady super-intendent sought applications from "Earnest, educated girls, with good health and free from fear."[36] Good health and a lack of fear were useful attributes for nurses who would care for patients with typhoid, given that HGH was called "the headquarters of death" by one newspaper and LGH a "fever breeding establishment" by another.[37] This advertisement underscores the enormous risk that bedside nurses faced in caring for typhoid cases. They dealt with highly infectious bodily fluids as a mat-ter of course, and it is hard to know how they protected themselves, if at all. It seems likely that doctors faced a reduced risk of infection because, although they examined patients, their exposure was intermittent.

Ensuring Safety

Even with the arrival of the cooler months, the epidemic continued unabated. In June 1887, HGH accepted 66 new cases of typhoid, in what was the first month of winter. Every fever bed was occupied "and extem-porized accommodation" was in use.[38] In many cases, the patients were moribund on admission after being managed at home for weeks. Under these circumstances, the confusion that presented in advanced typhoid added a particular complexity to bedside nursing care. Delirious patients moaned, cried out, and disturbed recovering patients. Some could be violent while seeming lucid. On occasion, the nurses restrained patients for safety's sake. To do this, the nurses placed the patient on the bed in a supine position. They then applied restraints

> in the gentlest way that can be effectual. Cotton wool having been laid over the ankles, calico bands are fixed around them and firmly attached to the bottom of the bed. In this way the

feet are kept secure. The upper part of the body is held down by a sheet extending from the throat to the knees, which is fastened down to each side of the bed.[39]

Even this level of restriction was not always sufficient to restrain confused patients. Right at the peak of the epidemic in June 1887, the hospital was under enormous strain. A strong and fit local footballer was an inpatient at HGH, suffering from advanced typhoid. The nurses had restrained him in the usual way, but he managed to escape when the nurse left to help in a nearby ward. With brute force, the man tore off the calico bands and sheet, ran out of the ward, leapt over a cleaner working in the corridor, mounted the hospital's stone wall, and walked along its perimeter until he found a spot to jump down. He landed just outside the hospital grounds where he was stopped. After just 7 minutes of freedom, this rambling patient was returned to the ward by the porter. The nurses placed him immediately into the straight waistcoat; he was only the second case in 6 months to be confined to that extent.[40]

Individuals with advanced typhoid could muster enormous reserves of strength, despite their delirium and underlying weakness. In August 1887, another delirious typhoid patient escaped. This occurred when a senior nurse went for her meal, having left a junior nurse in charge of a ward that housed two patients. One patient was recovering from typhoid and the other was seriously ill. The junior nurse completed her work and went to help her colleagues elsewhere. She put the recovering patient in charge of the ward, as was usual practice, and told him to ring for help if it was needed. No sooner had this nurse left the ward than the seriously ill patient, a profoundly deaf 30-year-old man with delirium and a history of mental illness, declared that he wanted to destroy himself. He squeezed through a partly open window, jumped to the ground, and made his way out of the hospital grounds. Soon after, a policeman retrieved him from the street and returned him to the ward. The nurses isolated this distressed man in a special room where the walls and floor were padded with mattresses to minimize the risk of self-harm. Every 30 minutes, nurses checked on these isolated patients. This patient died a week later from typhoid complications. A coroner's inquiry into his death revealed that he had attempted escape before, but the senior nurse on duty that day judged that restraint was not necessary because the patient's delirium was transient. The inquiry also revealed typhoid's effects on the nursing staff. On the day that the escape occurred, HGH operated on skeleton staff because several of the nurses were seriously ill with typhoid. This meant that work done normally by four nurses had to be done by two. Junior nurses, not usually placed in charge, also had to take on more responsibility in these circumstances.[41]

Nurse Recamia Graves with medal on a chatelaine.
Collection of the author, c. 1887–1888.

The intensive nursing that Holden described became crucial in the 6 months from January to June 1887, when HGH admitted more than 210 typhoid patients. The unrelenting workload inflicted a heavy toll on the nurses. According to one of the doctors, the nurses were "in a low state of health from the strain and anxiety of the past three months," and desperately needed rest.[42] In April 1887, the BoM had declared that the conduct of the nursing staff warranted the "highest commendation," given the large influx of typhoid cases. Acting Lady Superintendent Sarah Wane reported, "Nothing could be more satisfactory than the spirit with which the work of the nursing staff had been attended to during the present trying time."[43]

DUAL CRISES OF TYPHOID AND DYSFUNCTIONAL RELATIONSHIPS

The BoM was proud of its nurses working together under these crisis conditions, for good reason. For some time, the whole nursing staff, and indeed the hospital, had been laboring under the strain of dual crises: the typhoid epidemic and an atmosphere of crisis. This latter predicament was characterized by disharmony, antipathy, and dysfunctional relationships. In fact, *The Launceston Examiner* described HGH and its ongoing crisis-ridden atmosphere as "a kind of social volcano with its peculiar attendant eruptions." In this social volcano, mud was not thrown. It was a toxic environment where, as the newspaper put it, "mud springs" burst forth.[44] The origins of this poisonous climate had little to do with disease, but they manifested in a lengthy crisis nonetheless. In the second part of this chapter, the long-standing crisis at HGH preceding the months of epidemic is examined.

NURSING ADMINISTRATION AT HGH BEFORE THE EPIDEMIC

It is fair to say that HGH had its fair share of administrative concerns during infectious disease challenges in the 1870s and 1880s, because the hospital failed to keep up with community expectations of health care.[45] The functioning of HGH was overseen by its BoM, a committee of a dozen men, including the honorary medical officers, the house surgeon and his assistant, and several prominent gentlemen of Hobart. There were yearly elections, but the honorary doctors were long-standing board members. Until 1880, rules of the institution decreed that the BoM controlled the finances of the institution. Day-to-day decisions about nursing at HGH, including the hiring and firing of staff and organizing clinical care, were the remit of the lady superintendent. That arrangement changed after an incident in which the lady superintendent fired a senior nurse for insubordination. The nurse appealed to the BoM and she was reinstated, against the wishes of the lady superintendent. Subsequently, the BoM assumed responsibility over appointments and dismissals because, as one BoM member put it, "it was undesirable that any such power should vest in the lady [superintendent] at all. It was an invidious responsibility which ought not to devolve on her."[46]

In 1883, this rule was reversed when Mrs. Essie Ann Wilson, at that time a head nurse at HGH, was appointed the lady superintendent. An English woman, Wilson had taken up nursing after the death of her husband, reputedly a high-ranking civil servant in Ireland. She had nursed at St. Bartholomew's and St. Luke's Hospitals in London for about 2 years. Wilson had neither certificate nor diploma from either of the London hospitals, but did have testimonials from reputable doctors. Wilson was well liked and selected from 33 applicants. It seems that the BoM had great faith in Mrs. Wilson's management potential. Under the rule change, she was given control over all of the nursing staff, with power to suspend or dismiss a nurse or servant in cases of disobedience to order, misconduct, or neglect of duty. But it came with a caveat: The lady superintendent was to report these incidents to the BoM for them to deal with. She was also to work with HGH's house surgeon and his assistant on a committee to deal with "selection, appointment and distribution of the nurses."[47] Changing rules about who selected the nurses did not ameliorate a fundamental and ongoing problem that all HGH administrators faced: attracting and maintaining an ongoing supply of nurses to do the work of the institution. Not only that, the loosening of the rules created confusion in the following months.

Staffing was a perennial problem, and of course was not unique to Tasmania. Colonial hospitals throughout Australia, both charitable institutions and government-run institutions like HGH and LGH, used apprentice nurses as the backbone of staffing because they were cheap to employ. Hospitals offered "training" in nursing for these apprentices. Even by the 1880s, however, there was no universal agreement on the fundamentals of training: what it consisted of, how it should be delivered, or by whom. This guaranteed a lack of uniformity in the "trained" nurse as a product of training schemes.[48] At HGH in the early 1880s, teaching of probationers was the responsibility of the lady superintendent, and her experienced senior nurses were expected to undertake instruction at the bedside. At HGH, generally a 2-year apprenticeship was served, without a curriculum, without any examinations, and without the issue of certification or a diploma. When a nurse wanted to leave, she simply asked the hospital's doctors for a testimonial that affirmed her qualifications and skills.[49]

Between January 1883 and June 1885, 22 of the hospital's apprenticed nurses abandoned their term of service before completion. According to one of HGH's doctors, 18 of these probationers "bettered" themselves in mainland Australian colonies, courtesy of testimonials provided by HGH doctors.[50] It is not surprising that probationers sought to improve their lot by leaving Tasmania, because wages were higher on mainland Australia. Senior nurses also could earn more money outside Tasmania. Toward the end of 1884, shortages of staff at HGH were evident, with too few probationers attracted to train. Even if new probationer nurses joined the hospital's ranks, there were not enough senior nurses in place to teach them how to nurse, because five positions for senior nurse had been vacant for most of the year. HGH could manage with fewer staff while diseases, such as typhoid, were not flourishing. But the deficit in nurses became pressing when admissions with typhoid increased, usually during the summer months.[51]

In late 1884, after Wilson had been a lady superintendent for a year, the staffing situation was dire. Wilson advised the BoM that she could not fill the five vacant positions for head nurses, despite advertising in mainland Australia. She recommended that "two trained head nurses from the Mother Country" be secured at once.[52] Given that Wilson was English, it is possible that she expected English nurses to be recruited. But Dr. Smart assumed responsibility for hiring new nurses. He was a Scot and so asked his brother in Edinburgh for help. Dr. Andrew Smart subsequently secured the services of three trained, certified, experienced, and highly recommended head nurses from the Edinburgh Royal Infirmary. They were contracted to work at HGH each for a period of 3 years, and on the understanding that they were to introduce a system of nurse training. Many Australian hospitals at the time were yearning for the uniformity in training that appeared to be emerging in Britain's modern hospitals. The Edinburgh Royal Infirmary was one of them, with a reputation of producing skilled and disciplined nurses under the tutelage of Angelique Pringle, a protégé of the Nightingale School, and reputedly "one of the best nurses in the world."[53] Smart told the BoM that the new recruits were about 30 years of age and had excellent testimonials. With substantial experience as head nurses in charge of large wards, and accustomed to the instruction of probationers,[54] they seemed to be just what HGH needed. A month before the nurses from Scotland were due to arrive in Tasmania, Wilson appointed an English nurse named Julia Ayres. Ayres had trained at St. Bartholomew's Hospital, as had Wilson.[55] Although this appointment filled a vacancy, Wilson engaged the new nurse without consulting the BoM first. This act later had implications for the lady superintendent and the nurse, because she was deemed to have contravened HGH's rule on hiring staff.

Six months passed from the time of Smart's request for nurses to their arrival in March 1885. The nurses from Edinburgh were referred to collectively as the "Scotch Sisters" in BoM discussions, in communications with the lady superintendent, by the newspapers, and later by the Tasmanian Parliament. Three months after the trio's arrival, the BoM reviewed the workings of the hospital's nursing staff to ascertain "its cost and state of efficiency."[56] The result was a new set of regulations for nurses in training, along the lines of schemes "in the old country." Introduced in June 1885, the regulations included a probationary period of 3 months with 2.5 years' apprenticeship to complete training, binding contracts, lectures, examinations, the issue of formal certification on completion, and the cessation of individual doctors giving nurses-in-training a testimonial. It was some cause for celebration. For the first time in its history, HGH had a concrete framework for the engagement and education of trainee nurses. The expectation was that, under the guidance of the Scotch Sisters, the new regulations would attract a better class of probationers to HGH and improve the nursing generally through a system of training.[57] These recommendations likely proved effective in improving nursing care by the time the typhoid epidemic raged 2 years later.

Still, within weeks of the BoM's 1885 announcement that the new regulations would apply, serious discord manifested among the nurses. In October of that year, the BoM decided to reduce the number of staff employed because the fever wards were empty. Disengaging staff occurred from time to time, the convention being that the most recently appointed employee should go. But the newest employees were the three Scottish nurses and they were under contract to serve for 3 years. This meant that Ayres, Lady Superintendent Wilson's appointee, had to relinquish her position. Ayres had served HGH with satisfaction for 9 months and, not surprisingly, demanded an explanation for what she believed was her "dismissal."[58] From that point on, relations between Wilson and the Scotch Sisters unraveled. Over the next 14 months, the BoM, and later the Tasmanian Parliament, conducted at least five formal inquiries to ascertain the root of this disharmony.

A CRISIS IN INTERNAL MANAGEMENT JUST PRIOR TO THE EPIDEMIC

The first investigation was conducted in August 1886 by a subcommittee of the BoM. It followed Lady Superintendent Wilson's suspension and dismissal of Margaret Turnbull, another of the Scotch Sisters. Wilson charged Turnbull with eight wrongdoings, some dating back to months. Among them were leaving her post without asking permission and without leaving someone in charge, not supervising the cleanliness of tins used to store the patients' beef tea, leaving empty medicine bottles on the ward, not teaching the nurses, having an untidy ward, and neglecting the patients. The inquiry uncovered numerous issues, including hostilities between Wilson and the Scotch Sisters. The subcommittee found all charges against Turnbull unsubstantiated and reinstated her.

At the heart of the Scotch Sisters' complaints was that they were unable to put into place a system of training, owing to Lady Superintendent Wilson's deliberate obstruction.[59] But the Scotch Sisters also felt unwelcome. They claimed to have received only a cursory introduction to HGH and its practices from Wilson before being sent to work on the wards.[60] They felt that Wilson deliberately and frequently moved the nurses from ward to ward, which prevented any consolidation of teaching, and that she corrected the sisters in front of the probationers. Allegedly, Wilson isolated the Scotch Sisters by placing them on night duty and then on fever duty. Purportedly, Wilson also sent the probationers working in the wards to ask frivolous questions of the Scotch Sisters who were off duty. Jeanetta Milne, one of the Scotch Sisters, vented her wholesale discontentment with HGH. Not only was she placed on night duty, contrary to her engagement agreement, but Milne claimed that Wilson interfered in the management of Milne's ward by speaking with the house surgeon about the patients' care. Milne sent the lady superintendent a firm letter demanding that she desist.[61] In essence, the Scotch Sisters felt that Wilson was undermining their every effort to improve the HGH.[62]

The investigating committee's assessment of the disharmony was that Lady Superintendent Wilson had erred. In engaging Ayres and suspending and dismissing Turnbull, Wilson had not consulted the BoM.[63] She was judged not to have cooperated with the Scotch Sisters in implementing the system of nurse training. Furthermore, Wilson had not cooperated with the BoM, or the medical staff. The subcommittee concluded that Mrs. Wilson's employment should be terminated, a controversial recommendation. News of Wilson's impending dismissal emerged soon enough. In response, 17 of HGH's 21 nurses signed a testimonial in her support. Just 6 months before the onset of the 1887 typhoid epidemic, the mood of HGH was adversarial.

Antipathy was not just pervading the nursing staff at HGH. It manifested at the monthly meetings of the BoM as well. There, Drs. Smart and Edward L. Crowther locked horns on aspects of hospital management, particularly the management of the disputes between the nurses.[64] Daily newspapers reiterated these unsavory disagreements because reporters recorded verbatim the BoM's meetings. Thus, the literate Tasmanian public was well aware of the crises of confidence brewing at HGH. Crowther was an established member of the BoM and an honorary doctor at HGH. He was also a member of Tasmania's Parliament. Crowther took issue with the BoM investigation that judged Lady Superintendent

Wilson the guilty party while exonerating the Scotch Sisters of any blame. Unable to gain traction within the BoM, Crowther used his parliamentary position to air grievances about Smart's handling of the investigation. That forced another investigation by a different subcommittee of HGH's BoM, conducted during September and October 1886. Controversially, the investigating committee excluded reporters from taking a record of interviews, on the basis that the proceedings were confidential.[65] Their investigation, subsequently, was referred to by detractors as "the miserable secret inquiry."[66]

Throughout the confidential inquiry, nurses, domestic staff, doctors, and BoM members again offered their opinion on the beneficial or detrimental influence of the Scotch Sisters, and vice versa of Lady Superintendent Wilson. Crowther accused Smart and his BoM allies of favoring the Scotch Sisters to Wilson's detriment. Smart retaliated by accusing Crowther and his factional allies on the BoM (one of whom was Crowther's father-in-law) of blatant partisanship against the Scotch Sisters. Most of the evidence was hearsay. Several witnesses, for instance, alleged that Turnbull, one of the Scotch Sisters, used opium because she appeared rather pale at times and often "in a very nervous condition."[67] A junior nurse claimed that she had put Turnbull into bed in the nurses' quarters because of Turnbull's emotional state.[68] Another head nurse, Rebecca Mackay, who was not one of the Scotch Sisters, was said to be "flushed with drink" while on duty.[69]

This second investigation identified that HGH's numerous woes stemmed from a lack of discipline, structure, and reporting lines. It recommended that an adequate system of training for nurses be introduced with three categories: theoretical training from the matron and staff nurses, professional training from the doctors, and practical training at the bedside from the house surgeon and staff nurses. The inquiry upheld the termination of Wilson as the lady superintendent, concluding that HGH had been plagued by "considerable disorganization...and a want of harmony between the officers which was detrimental to the interests of the institution."[70] The confidential nature of this inquiry, however, was its undoing. Allegations soon emerged of a cover-up and a conspiracy. The Tasmanian government stepped in to investigate the investigation.

Three weeks later, in January 1887, the government sanctioned Wilson's dismissal. At the same time, Crowther lost his seat in the BoM in the yearly election.[71] With Crowther's and Wilson's departures, it seemed that a major eruption of this simmering social volcano was averted, just as typhoid began its insidious spread around Hobart. But ill will pervaded HGH. At the end of February, when Wilson finally left her position at HGH, Smart asked Isabella Rathie, one of the Scotch Sisters, to supervise the nursing department until the appointment of a new lady superintendent. Rathie's elevation was the last straw for head nurse Mackay and she resigned immediately. Mackay, according to a correspondent to *The Mercury* newspaper, was "the oldest and best sister of the hospital."[72] The situation was inflamed further when Smart declined to issue Wilson with a testimonial of her 5 years' service at HGH. The institution seemed to be mired in chaos, with a toxic climate, dysfunctional personalities, and irreparable differences. Right at this point, typhoid began its insidious assault on the community of southern Tasmania.

A TOXIC CLIMATE CONTINUES DURING THE EPIDEMIC

Crowther, although no longer a member of HGH's BoM, was a member of the Tasmanian Parliament. At the end of February 1887, he staged a public meeting at Hobart's Town Hall to air his mounting grievances. Among these were negligence by HGH nurses, mismanagement of HGH, theft of alcohol from the HGH store, and treachery by the BoM. Crowther laid blame for the situation firmly at the feet of the BoM and Smart's chairmanship. The most spectacular allegation Crowther made was that, under Smart's management, HGH operated a "Scotch ring" of exclusion, a "little clique within a clique," as he put it. Crowther told the meeting that

> in the annals of Tasmania there was no more contemptible thing
> than the persecution of the matron of the hospital and orchestrat-
> ing her dismissal....There were some nurses introduced from
> Scotland, no doubt very able women, but from the moment they
> came to Tasmania there had been a sort of antagonism between

them and the matron, the result was that there had never been any harmonious working in the institution.[73]

Going by Crowther's version of events, the Scotch Sisters were to blame for the lack of collaboration at HGH. Most of HGH's nurses appeared to agree with Crowther. Seventeen signed the testimonial in support of former Lady Superintendent Wilson, and several declared their views earlier to the confidential inquiry.[74] But the simple fact was that HGH's climate was toxic and the potential for discord was high. The BoM had to do something to arrest any further enmity. As the search for a permanent replacement for Wilson continued, the BoM made a strategic temporary appointment of an emergency administrator. This act relieved Miss Rathie of oversight of the nursing at HGH and dampened the prospect of an eruption in this social volcano. A member of the BoM later reported that "within a very short time after the engagement of Mrs. Wane" the entire hospital was working harmoniously.[75]

Wane, a 30-year-old English woman, took up the position of acting lady superintendent at HGH on March 24, 1887. She knew HGH well, having been a probationer in training there and then a head nurse in the early 1880s. In 1884, she was an unsuccessful candidate for the job of lady superintendent at HGH, the role to which Wilson was appointed. Wane instead took up the position of lady superintendent at LGH. It was not an easy role. During her term in office, in the space of just 18 months, three nurses and a wardmaid died from the effects of typhoid. Nurse Charlotte Pitman was the first nurse to succumb in April 1885. Pitman was a "great favorite" at the LGH and her death poignant, given her upbringing as an orphan in Hobart.[76] In March 1886, wardmaid Kate J. James died.[77] Twenty-three-year-old nurse Frances Anna Briant died 8 weeks later, in May 1886. She ailed for 77 days with the sequelae of typhoid.[78] Ominously, *The Launceston Examiner* newspaper declared that nothing short of martyrdom awaited nurses as they went about their bedside work.[79] Next, Nurse Elizabeth M. Delaney, afflicted for 5 months with typhoid, died in September 1886. Delaney had spent months at LGH in charge of 14 beds, which were occupied solely by typhoid patients.[80] The three trained nurses were formerly probationers in training at HGH.

When Wane relinquished her position at LGH in August 1886, after 2 years' service, she explained to the LGH's BoM her reasoning. Wane declared an overwhelming responsibility for the welfare of LGH's nursing staff. She considered that the Tasmanian government had done little to improve the nurses' living arrangements there, despite her numerous repeated requests for building and drainage works.[81] Wane's advocacy for her nurses was public knowledge because the business of the LGH, like that of HGH, was reported verbatim in the newspapers. Her temporary employment by HGH was a triumph. Wane had substantial experience in Launceston's typhoid crisis throughout 1885 and 1886 and regarded the nurses working under her management as assets worth protecting. It seems likely that selection of this skilled and humane administrator facilitated a fresh start for nurses at HGH at a pivotal juncture, and for the hospital generally, just as the typhoid epidemic surged in Hobart. In the social volcano that was HGH, a sense of calm and harmony was reached so quickly that it contrasted sharply with the disputes and disharmony of previous years.

COLLABORATION AND CRITICISM DURING THE EPIDEMIC

Acting Lady Superintendent Wane immediately began building collaborative relationships at HGH; yet the scrutiny of the nursing continued unabated, courtesy of the Crowther family. In April 1887, Dr. Bingham Crowther, Edward's son, used a public lecture about typhoid to repeat allegations that the nursing at HGH was inferior. He then reiterated those allegations in a letter to the head of Tasmania's government. The complaints were flimsy: that nurses did not change a patient's bed linen for 10 days even though it was soiled with excrement, that the nurses gave preferential treatment to patients of higher class and those who paid for their care, and that the nourishments nurses prepared were unfit to consume.[82] Bingham Crowther claimed that he had witnesses to prove that the allegations were true. His communication to the Tasmanian government forced yet another investigation conducted by members of Parliament. This inquiry was held in May 1887 at the peak of the epidemic. It necessitated two of the nurses and Acting Lady Superintendent Wane to give testimony about the nursing care at a time when the hospital was strained with typhoid cases. Ten patients gave their impressions of care. Caroline Budd experienced "every kindness night and day," as did P. F. Macfarlane, who was a typhoid patient for 5 weeks. Eliza Carrier had no complaints, and Eva Watts said that "nothing could be greater than the cleanliness of the hospital." John Langdon, 4 weeks in the hospital, was thoroughly satisfied with his treatment, while Thomas Newton and Thomas McKinley Willison agreed on the "excellence of the arrangements in the hospital."[83] Bingham Crowther's witnesses were unconvincing, however, having been coached in what to say. The investigation concluded that his allegations were baseless.

SERVICE IN THE FACE OF RISK

At the end of May 1887, after just 3 months at the helm, Wane's acting term concluded when Harriet Munro from Sydney was appointed the lady superintendent.[84] In one of her last reports to HGH's BoM, Wane commended, "the zeal and unanimity displayed by the nursing staff in carrying out their duties."[85] The crisis in personnel and their management seemed to be resolved, but the typhoid crisis was far from over and the terrible effects of the epidemic on the nurses' health became apparent. Nurses Victoria and Margaret Gourlay, siblings from Melbourne, were both unwell. They resigned and returned home to recuperate. Another nurse resigned "owing to ill health," while yet two more nurses contracted typhoid.[86] In early June 1887, and despite Tasmania's cooler winter weather, the number of typhoid cases surged again. Several of HGH's nurses became seriously ill.[87] The urgency to replace the sick staff was so great that nurses were recruited from mainland Australia at a salary of 2.5 guineas. Because HGH was a public institution, the lady superintendent of the trained nurses' home in Melbourne, who supplied the nurses, reduced the fee to 2 guineas per week.[88] In July, more of the staff fell ill. Four of HGH's nurses were declared as having typhoid, while 10 others had "ailments." Two more nurses were engaged hastily from mainland Australia at a salary of 1 guinea per week. At least one came from the Victoria Trained Nurses

Association Home in Melbourne, while another nurse was supplied from Sydney. In a deviation from convention, her traveling expenses were paid for by HGH.[89]

The Tasmanian government had to absorb these extra costs. It is not known how much money the relief nurses earned or how much was paid to the nurses' home superintendent. Still, the salaries of these emergency staff were more than what HGH nurses usually received. In late 1887, it emerged that nurses' pay at HGH throughout this period varied enormously. One nurse had worked primarily in the fever wards for 6 years, at some risk to her health it has to be said. Her salary, static for these 6 years at £45 per annum, was raised to £50 after her circumstances became public knowledge.[90]

ACKNOWLEDGING NURSES' SERVICE IN THE EPIDEMIC

Under these conditions, and in the face of so much publicly aired critique, it is not surprising that nurses at HGH were held in high esteem by many among the Tasmanian public. During 1887, at the same time as the supporters of Dr. Crowther voiced their ire toward Dr. Smart and his Scotch Sisters, former patients and families of former patients extolled the nurses' selflessness and their exceptional efforts in letters and notices placed in *The Mercury* newspaper.[91] What they had to say marked a stark contrast to the severe criticism of nursing at HGH. "A Late Female Patient," for instance, wrote:

> The old nurses were too big for their boots...both the nurses and wardmaids were quite indifferent as to those who would be over them, as they are all too sick of the petty squabbles that have been going on to trouble their heads about it. They went on with their duty the same as ever....Sister Rathie always has a clear head and never forgets that she is a lady, as well as a head nurse, so that all the patients love her, and also respect her. I, as a late female patient of five months standing, can say the greatest kindness I received was from the two Scotch [S]isters and the two youngest nurses, whose example ought to be a little copied by the oldest staff nurses.[92]

Similarly, Henry Coulson, a licensed publican of the Angel Inn hotel in Hobart, wrote to *The Mercury* after hearing a number of "very unkind and illiberal remarks passed upon the hospital, its doctors, and its nurses." He went on to say:

> Of the lady attendants, I cannot find words strong enough in the English language to express my gratitude I feel for the unremitting kindness and attention towards myself and others during my long illness and although it is invidious to particularise, I must name Sister Lucas and Nurse Forrester as the saviours of my life, for had it not have been for their sisterly kindness and care, I feel confident that I should not have been now to express my heartfelt thanks for my deliverance, through the agency of the doctors and nursing staff of the General Hospital, from that terrible scourge—typhoid fever—of which so many of our fellow colonists have become victims.[93]

"A Late Female Patient" and other correspondents highlighted a significant point. Although inquiries and endless disputes continued in 1887 within the BoM, nurses at the bedside carried on the skilled care for the patients, washing, feeding, administering stimulants, applying compresses, and occasionally restraining patients for their own protection. This work continued during the epidemic, as the reputation of the hospital was tarnished, and as individuals were criticized without recourse.

In early May 1887, Mr. Willison, an ex-typhoid patient, suggested an honorarium for the hospital's nurses, but as officers of a government institution, nurses were not permitted to accept rewards or gifts.[94] Dr. Smart recommended that "a token of merit," such as a silver medal suitably inscribed, would be a fitting gesture to commemorate "alike the jubilee year of Queen Victoria and the esteem of their fellow citizens."[95] Others, however, argued that the nurses needed a holiday to "recruit their health" and that any money gathered should pay for nurses to replace them.[96] Hobart's *The Mercury* newspaper actively supported Smart's idea. An editorial claimed, "The band of sisters in the hospital have worked in unity and in faith, with an earnestness and sense of duty, knowing no halt or falter."[97]

A subscription fund established to pay for the medals was a public one, but, in practice, the idea originated at HGH, specifically via Dr. Parkinson, the house surgeon, and Dr. Smart, sparking yet more criticism and claims of nepotism. Smart believed that the hospital's "own staff who bore the heat and burden of the day from January last" were worthy recipients. Another honorary surgeon and member of the BoM felt that others should receive medals. He argued in favor of the nurses who had traveled from Melbourne and Sydney to assist in the epidemic at their own peril and the wardmaids and cleaners who worked well outside of what was expected of them.[98] Next, a correspondent to the newspaper appealed for the hospital's porter to receive one.[99] With the £128.15.0 pledged by the Tasmanian public, Mr. W. P. Golding, a jeweler of Liverpool Street, was commissioned to craft the 22 medals. These decorations were placed on display in a chemist's shop. Their awarding was postponed until the end of August because at least seven of the nurses remained ill from typhoid and the rest were still recuperating.[100]

By the end of September 1887, HGH had treated 260 inpatient cases of typhoid. Thirty-one (11.9%) of them died. In October, just 2 months after receiving her medal, nurse Ella Gertrude White died from the effects of typhoid. She was a "young, faithful, and most promising nurse." Her family surely worried that two of her siblings, who also were nurses at HGH, would become ill.[101] The hospital's BoM finally acknowledged the toll of the epidemic on the nurses' health. With most of them bearing "a jaded appearance and impaired physique," the BoM reported to the government that:

> Considerable anxiety is felt with regard to the impaired health of the nursing staff generally. Typhoid still lingers in the wards, and a fresh outbreak early in the ensuing year is much to be dreaded, moreover a marked increase of diphtheria has taken place, and [with] scarlet fever…added to the list of infectious diseases, a heavy strain on the nurses therefore continues, and several of them have suffered in health in consequence.[102]

To help the nurses regain their health, the BoM permitted two nurses at a time to have leaves of absences in the country. After some debate, the Tasmanian government eventually agreed to cover the cost of this convalescence.

CONFLICT PERSISTS

Eight weeks after the medal-awarding ceremony, Edward Crowther succeeded in forcing another parliamentary inquiry into the management of HGH, with himself as the chair of the "Report of Inquiry Into Mrs. Wilson's Claim for a Testimonial." *The Mercury* insisted that the inquiry was nothing less than "a private *vendetta*" and a gross waste of money.[103] Nonetheless, Crowther reinvestigated every dispute at HGH, dating back to the arrival of the Scotch Sisters in 1885. He pursued the suspension, dismissal, and reinstatement of Sister Turnbull, Sister Milne's terse communications with Lady Superintendent Wilson, and the chain of events that led to Wilson's dismissal. Throughout, Crowther successfully dredged up enmities that had pervaded HGH's staff relations.

With evidence from 23 witnesses, including nurses, the inquiry placed on the public record the underlying prejudices, challenging personality traits, personal agendas, and simple misunderstandings that had combined to produce disharmony and conflict at HGH in the 2 years leading up to the typhoid epidemic. Wilson submitted, for example, that the Scottish nurses should never have been recruited because they "were not ladies at all...only common women...lowering the tone" of the hospital.[104] A member of the BoM argued that "the real secret of the trouble" was the favoritism shown to the Edinburgh nurses and Smart's encouragement of their "rebellious spirit."[105] Another blamed Wilson's "coercion practiced on the nurses from Edinburgh which caused all the trouble."[106]

The inquiry unearthed the salient fact that there had been little teaching of probationers. It confirmed that Wilson was passively resistant to this object and had impeded the Scotch Sisters' capacity to instruct the probationers for almost 2 years. The Scotch Sisters could not teach when on night duty, and after Wilson left, the extent of the typhoid epidemic made teaching impossible. Remarkably, despite all of the turmoil in personnel, and the deficit in teaching probationers, one witness told the inquiry, "The nursing went on as well as ever. The service was not affected."[107] Julia Ayres, the English nurse disengaged in October 1885, echoed this assessment. She told the inquiry, "I think the Scotch Sisters had some little troubles, but it did not interfere with the harmonious working of the Hospital."[108] This parliamentary inquiry concluded in November 1887. By that time, in Tasmania, HGH seemed to be operating effectively. During 1887, 1,000 cases of typhoid were reported to Tasmania's Board of Public Health. Of these, 112 (11.2%) died.[109] A third of those fatalities occurred at HGH, giving an indication of the workload experienced by its nurses. By the end of 1887, criticism of this government institution had waned and public concern about typhoid gave way to another looming health crisis, that of smallpox.

CONCLUSION

The awarding of medals to nurses for meritorious services demonstrates the Tasmanian public's support for the nurses who cared for patients affected by the 1887 typhoid epidemic in Hobart. Without doubt, the reported collaboration between the nurses and the broader hospital staff during the epidemic marked a watershed. Nursing during the epidemic was indeed a triumph, but that triumph was not a product of the epidemic itself, nor did it result from cooperation among all practitioners. Rather, it was a coalescence of several factors.

First, the antipathy that exemplified interactions between Lady Superintendent Wilson and the Scotch Sisters dissipated with Wilson's departure in February 1887. The animosity within the BoM dissipated with Crowther's departure; although he was able to criticize HGH in Parliament, he was not able to interfere in the day-to-day management of the institution. This dual change in senior personnel at HGH made it possible to conduct the care of patients without Crowther's previously unrelenting internal critique, and without Wilson's disobliging behavior. Second, it is likely that the new nursing regulations announced in June 1885 made some difference. Their implementation was planned just after the Scotch Sisters arrived; however, even by August 1886, they had not been introduced because of intransigence. It seems likely that they were operational by early 1887. Under these new arrangements, HGH had a degree of certainty about its workforce as the epidemic surged. For the first time in its history, probationers could not leave on a whim and expect to obtain a testimonial of their skills written by a doctor associated with HGH. In complete contrast to past practice, probationers had contracts based on a fixed term. They had to sit for an examination and earn a certificate. These rules guaranteed staffing levels, at least of the apprenticed nurses. The rules enabled roles and responsibilities to be defined more clearly. Senior nurses were employed with the expectation that they had to teach probationers; probationers were expected to learn and complete the term of training. These factors, independent of any camaraderie that may have developed during the typhoid emergency, helped to address the long-standing crisis in the management of nursing at HGH.

Third, and perhaps most important, the appointment of an emergency administrator to lead the nursing staff was a critical factor in arresting the ill will among the nursing staff. After years of disunity and a crisis of confidence in HGH's management, Acting Lady Superintendent Wane provided effective leadership in the difficult, early phase of the 1887 epidemic. Interestingly, hospital reports during her short appointment do not feature issues about the nursing department other than the effect of the epidemic on the nurses' health. Wane was a fine administrator who lent experience and maturity in overcoming HGH's dual crises of typhoid and dysfunctional relationships. Wane's publicly declared respect for nurses may have been the catalyst that enabled a spirit of collaboration to emerge at HGH after so much hostility had prevailed. It seems likely that the nurses' confidence in her ability to steer HGH enabled them to work beyond what was expected of them. It is possible to speculate that, had Wilson remained in her position as the lady super-intendent, the exigencies of the typhoid epidemic may have trumped the prevailing disharmony, but this seems unlikely given the depth of animosities.

When seen within the broader context, right up to the onset of the 1887 epidemic, nursing management at HGH was in crisis for 2 years, without any sense of collaboration whatsoever. These long-standing professional tensions were unsustainable. Something, or at least some-one, had to give. The Scotch Sisters were more change agents than they were "rebellious spirits" in the "social volcano" that was the HGH. But their challenge to the existing, undefined arrangements at HGH created management uncertainty. Because their sponsor, Dr. Smart, was a fellow Scot, and because the nurses from Edinburgh had been expressly selected by Smart's brother, it is not surprising that he actively supported their path at HGH. It is also possible to see this from Lady Superintendent Wilson's perspective, that HGH was a partisan in favoring Scotch nurses over English nurses. What is hard to fathom is Dr. Crowther and his allies' mordant criticism of nursing at HGH. After all, concerns about its nursing and the teaching of probationers had persisted since the 1870s, during which Crowther was a member of the BoM. The fact remains that the BoM had proved unable or unwilling to implement a basic structure for the training for nurses, at least until Smart recruited the Scotch Sisters.

Just as the success in nursing the typhoid cases was ultimately a coalescence of several factors, the hostility that reigned at HGH before the epidemic also arose through a coalescence of contested issues, including how to manage a hospital in the face of staff shortages and ideas about training nurses. At the heart of HGH's troubles were pro-fessional and personal jealousies between nurses from different back-grounds and with different expectations. Power relationships in public office were also on show, with the contest between two forceful and forthright medical practitioners: Drs. Smart and Crowther. In light of these toxic relationships, the project of commissioning and awarding of medals for meritorious services in nursing was a strategy driven by Smart to muster support for his management of HGH.

Last, this account of a 19th-century hospital in an infectious disease crisis offers a sobering reminder of the risks that work posed to nurses' lives in this pre-antibiotic era. Four of LGH's staff died as a result of typhoid in that city during 1885 and 1886. One of HGH's nurses died as a result of the 1887 epidemic. The difference in staff death num-bers between HGH and LGH may have resulted from a more virulent strain in Launceston or, perhaps, because HGH's higher staff numbers, derided as extravagant, were actually protective to the staff. Even so, more than 30 of HGH's nurses were adversely affected in health during the typhoid epidemic, necessitating substantial convalescence and, possibly, resulting in long-term sequelae. Sarah Wane, the emergency acting lady superintendent, was one of those whose health failed. She died in 1890, just 34 years of age. Wane was not a recipient of the typhoid medal.

NOTES

1. "Hospital Treatment: A Patient's Perspective," *The Mercury*, May 12, 1887, 2.
2. "Letters to the Editor: Crosses v. Medals?" *The Mercury*, August 27, 1887, 3.
3. "Presentation of Medals to the Hospital Nurses," *The Mercury*, August 31, 1887, 3.
4. Ibid. The Maltese cross has four arrowheads meeting at the points, with eight angles. See http://orderofmalta.org.au/about-the-order-of-malta/prayer-of-the-order-eight-pointed-cross. Lady Hamilton knew most of the nurses. Reportedly, she took those who were convalescent to Government House where she nursed them to recovery.
5. Ibid.
6. Ibid.
7. "Letters to the Editor: Crosses v. Medals?" *The Mercury*, August 27, 1887, 3.
8. Three histories refer to this event with limited analysis. See Beatrix Kelly, *A History to the Background of Nursing in Tasmania* (Moonah, Tasmania: Davies Brothers, 1975); Cheryl Norris, *In My Day: A History of General Nurse Training at the Royal Hobart Hospital 1803–1993* (Hobart: Cheryl Norris, 2011); Bartz Schultz, *A Tapestry of Service: The Evolution of Nursing in Australia, Volume I, Foundation to Federation 1788–1900* (Melbourne: Churchill Livingston, 1991).
9. Roger Kellaway, "The Hobart Typhoid Epidemic of 1887–88," *Social Science and Medicine* 29, no. 8 (1989): 953. Dumping of night soil avoided collection fees.
10. Kelly, *A History to the Background of Nursing* 28, 100.
11. Kellaway, "The Hobart Typhoid Epidemic of 1887–88," 953.
12. "An Insidious Foe," *The Launceston Examiner*, February 27, 1886, 3.
13. Typhoid Fever Factsheet, New South Wales Department of Health 2012, accessed December 3, 2012, http://www.health.nsw.gov.au/Infectious/factsheets/Pages/Typhoid.aspx.

14. "Typhoid or Ignorance?" *The Launceston Examiner*, March 6, 1886, 1; *The Mercury*, March 9, 1887, 4. Holden first published "Plain Directions for Nursing Typhoid" in 1883 in the *Australian Women's Magazine*, under the pen name Australienne. In 1884, she added more material for a pamphlet titled "What Typhoid Is and How to Nurse It." Holden was a prolific author, also publishing *Woman's Ignorance and the World's Need: A Plea for Physiology* (Sydney: George Robertson, 1883) and *Plain Words to Mothers and Temperance Reformers on Food and Health* (1883). She gave papers entitled "Trained Nursing" and "The Root of Hospital Reform" at the Victorian Social Science Congress in 1882.

15. B. E. Briggs, "Frances Gillam Holden (1843–1924)," *Australian Dictionary of Biography*, National Centre of Biography, Australian National University, accessed March 3, 2012, http://adb.anu.edu/biography/holden-frances-gillam-6702/text11567, published in hardcopy 1983.

16. "Typhoid or Ignorance?"

17. Ibid.

18. "A Cure for Typhoid: Dr. Steiger's Method," *The Mercury*, May 18, 1887, 4.

19. "Typhoid or Ignorance?," 1.

20. Ibid.

21. "Hospital Management: Resumed Enquiry[sic]," *The Mercury*, May 31, 1887, 4. A drawsheet was a smaller piece of sheeting placed across the bed at its middle. Sometimes combined with a rubber underlay, the drawsheet protected the larger bed sheeting from soiling.

22. Ibid.

23. "Typhoid or Ignorance?" *The Mercury*, March 9, 1887, 4.

24. "Hospital Management," 1.

25. Ibid.

26. "Stimulants in Typhoid," *The Mercury*, September 9, 1887, 2.

27. "Hospital Board," *The Launceston Examiner*, August 27, 1887, 1.

28. Kellaway, "The Hobart Typhoid Epidemic of 1887–88," 953.

29. "Hospital Board," *The Mercury*, April 16, 1887, 1.

30. "Central Board of Health: Typhoid at Hobart," *The Mercury*, March 30, 1887, 3.

31. "Editorial," *The Launceston Examiner*, June 16, 1885, 2.

32. "Hospital Board," *The Mercury*, June 13, 1885, 3.

33. "Coroner's Inquest," *The Mercury*, August 24, 1887, 3.

34. *Journals and Printed Papers of the Parliament of Tasmania* 1887, Volume XII, Paper No. 145 (hereafter, "Report of Inquiry Into Mrs. Wilson's Claim for a Testimonial"), 5.
35. "Letters to the Editor: Typhoid Cases in the Hospital," *The Mercury*, April 5, 1887, 2.
36. "General Hospital Hobart: Probationers Wanted," *The Mercury*, April 11, 1887, 1.
37. "Editorial," *The Launceston Examiner*, April 17, 1885, 2; April 8, 1885, 2.
38. "Letters to the Editor: The Hospital Nurses," *The Mercury*, June 17, 1887, 4.
39. "A Runaway Fever Patient," *The Mercury*, June 11, 1887, 3.
40. Ibid.
41. "Coroner's Inquest," 3.
42. "Hospital Board," *The Mercury*, June 11, 1887, 1.
43. "Hospital Board," *The Mercury*, April 16, 1887, 1.
44. "Editorial," *The Launceston Examiner*, December 8, 1886, 2.
45. Norris, *In My Day*, 23–24.
46. "Hospital Board," *The Mercury*, October 9, 1880, 2. Head nurse Madame Gleichen was reinstated by the BoM. The lady superintendent resigned some 6 months later, in 1881, and the next one resigned after 2 years.
47. "Hospital Board," *The Mercury*, December 15, 1883, 2.
48. Madonna Grehan, "Visioning the Future by Knowing the Past," in *Contexts of Nursing: An Introduction*, Eds. John Daly, Sandra Speedy, and Debra Jackson (Sydney: Elsevier, 2014), 4th ed., 15–37.
49. "Hospital Board," *The Mercury*, June 13, 1885, 3.
50. "Hospital Board," *The Mercury*, June 29, 1885, 4.
51. "Hospital Board," *The Mercury*, August 18, 1885, 3.
52. "Hospital Board," *The Mercury*, September 13, 1884, 3.
53. "Hospital Meeting," *The Mercury*, August 21, 1886, 2. The Nightingale model had two tiers of pupil: lady probationers who trained for shorter periods and regular probationers who trained for longer. For more on the development of nurse training in 19th-century Australia, see Madonna Grehan, "Professional Aspirations and Consumer Expectations: Nurses, Midwives, and Women's Health." PhD dissertation, University of Melbourne, 2009.
54. "Hospital Board," *The Mercury*, March 14, 1885, 3.
55. "Report of Inquiry Into Mrs. Wilson's Claim for a Testimonial," 21.

56. "Hospital Board," *The Mercury*, June 13, 1885, 3. This was subsequently published as "Report of the Board of Management, General Hospital Hobart, on the Working of the Hospital," *Journals and Printed Papers of the Parliament of Tasmania* 1887, Volume XII, Paper No. 105.

57. "Hospital Board," *The Mercury*, August 18, 1885, 3.

58. *The Mercury*, November 17, 1885, 3. It is not clear who identified Miss Ayres as the employee for release.

59. "Report of Inquiry Into Mrs. Wilson's Claim for a Testimonial," 23.

60. Ibid., 22. The Scotch Sisters had been engaged on the understanding that they would not serve any night duty.

61. "Hospital Board," *The Daily Telegraph*, September 17, 1886, 3. In August 1886, Sister Milne accepted the position of lady superintendent at Launceston, after being released from her contract with HGH. Her position at HGH had been complicated by the fact that she brought with her to Australia an adopted niece, Elizabeth Hutchinson Milne. She was 8 years old and an orphan. See "Report of Inquiry Into Mrs. Wilson's Claim for a Testimonial," 4.

62. "Report of Inquiry Into Mrs. Wilson's Claim for a Testimonial," 10. One such question put to Miss Margaret Turnbull was what should a nurse do if a man in the bush was ordered poisonous medicines by a doctor.

63. "Hospital Meeting," 2. Mrs. Wilson did not tell the BoM that she intended to dismiss Sister Turnbull.

64. Edward Lodewyk Crowther was born in Hobart in 1843. Tasmania had no medical school. Crowther began medicine as an apprentice to his surgeon father, after which he took formal education at Guy's, Moorfields, and Birmingham Hospitals, and study at Edinburgh and Aberdeen Universities. Crowther was a member of Tasmania's Parliament, in the House of Assembly (MHA). See http://adb.anu.edu.au/biography/crowther-edward-lodewyk-3347.

65. "House of Assembly," *The Mercury*, October 28, 1887, 3.

66. Ibid.

67. These details were reiterated in a Select Committee of Inquiry held the next year in 1887, which produced the "Report of Inquiry Into Mrs. Wilson's Claim for a Testimonial." The initial inquiry in 1886 took more than 530 foolscap pages of evidence from 32 witnesses who offered partisan and hearsay evidence.

68. "Report of Inquiry Into Mrs. Wilson's Claim for a Testimonial," 2.

69. Ibid., 16.

70. "Summary of News for Home Readers," *The Mercury*, December 11, 1886, 1.

71. "Hospital Board," *The Mercury*, January 19, 1887, 2.

72. "Letters to the Editor: The Hospital," *The Mercury*, February 28, 1887, 3.

73. "The Hospital Management: Public Meeting in the Town Hall," *The Mercury*, February 25, 1887, 3.

74. The nurses placed their view on the public record in November 1887, at the Select Committee of Inquiry.

75. "Report of Inquiry Into Mrs. Wilson's Claim for a Testimonial," 24.

76. "Launceston General Hospital," *The Launceston Examiner*, April 8, 1885, 2.

77. "Hospital Board, Thursday March 18," *The Launceston Examiner*, March 19, 1886, 3.

78. "The Late Nurse Briant," *The Launceston Examiner*, May 25, 1886, 2.

79. "Hospital Board," *The Mercury*, July 18, 1885, 3. The Launceston Hospital's BoM decided to erect a memorial tablet to Nurse Pitman in her ward, recognizing that she "died through exposure to dangers incidental to her calling." As a government-funded institution, the Tasmanian government's approval was necessary for such an undertaking. The government rejected the plan on the basis that it was too costly and it would upset the nurses for them to be reminded of Miss Briant by the memorial tablet. At the same time, the government did assent to a memorial tablet for a generous benefactor, Mr. Henry Reed.

80. "Tasmanian Intelligence," *The Launceston Examiner*, September 13, 1886, 1.

81. "Hospital Board," *The Launceston Examiner*, May 28, 1886, 3.

82. "Dr. B. Crowther on Typhoid Fever," *The Mercury*, April 22, 1887, 3.

83. "Hospital Management."

84. Munro was sometimes spelled Munroe. Mrs. Wane retired from nursing and initially established a boarding house for boys.

85. "Hospital Board," *The Mercury*, May 14, 1887, 4.

86. "Tasmanian Intelligence," *The Launceston Examiner*, June 13, 1887, 3.

87. "Letters to the Editor: The Hospital Nurses," *The Mercury*, June 17, 1887, 4.

88. As an annualized sum, this usage was more than twice that of staff nurses employed at HGH in 1887.

89. "Hospital Board," *The Mercury*, July 9, 1887, 4.

90. "Hobart Hospital Board," *The Mercury*, November 12, 1887, 3.

91. The following thanks were placed in *The Mercury* during 1887: Mrs. Cotton for her late daughter, February 17, 1; Miss Wall on behalf of her late brother, February 23, 1; Mrs. Dixon for her late husband, May 10, 3; Mr. J. Dunn "for their unremitting care and attention" during his dangerous and severe illness, May 30, 1; Mr. J. Turner for "their unremitting skill and attention" on his wife, June 21, 1; Mrs. Babington for herself, June 29, 2; Mrs. Meyers for herself, July 5, 3.

92. "The Hospital," *The Mercury*, March 4, 1887, 4.

93. "Letters to the Editor: The Hospital," *The Mercury*, July 2, 1887, 2.

94. "Hospital Treatment: A Patient's Experience," *The Mercury*, May 12, 1887, 2.

95. "Letters to the Editor: The Hospital Nurses and the Jubilee," *The Mercury*, June 14, 1887, 3. The only other medal awarded to nurses in the British Colonies at that time was the Royal Red Cross, introduced by Queen Victoria on St. George's Day, April 27, 1883. The Queen's Jubilee was celebrated on June 21 and 22.

96. "Nurses and Sanitation," *The Mercury*, June 16, 1887, 4.

97. "Editorial," *The Mercury*, June 15, 1887, 2.

98. "Hospital Board," *The Mercury*, July 9, 1887, 4.

99. "Hospital Medals," *The Mercury*, July 19, 1887, 3. The nurses from mainland Australia received medals, but not the ward maids or the porter.

100. "Tasmanian Intelligence," *The Launceston Examiner*, August 15, 1887, 3.

101. "Hobart Hospital Board," *The Mercury*, November 12, 1887, 3.

102. Ibid.

103. "Editorial," The Mercury, September 8, 1887, 2.

104. "Report of Inquiry Into Mrs. Wilson's Claim for a Testimonial," 2. In December 1883, when Mrs. Wilson was selected to be lady superintendent, the BoM endorsed her testimonials. She had taken on nursing after the death of her husband, who was in a senior position in government service in Ireland.

105. Ibid., 14.

106. Ibid., 24.

107. Ibid.

108. Ibid., 19. Julia Ayres was by then matron of the New Norfolk Asylum, to the northwest of Hobart. She later moved to Melbourne on the Australian mainland.

109. Kellaway, "The Hobart Typhoid Epidemic of 1887–88," 953. Typhoid retained its epidemic status until 1891.

CHAPTER 2

The 1908 Italian Earthquake

Anna La Torre

> *His Majesty Victorio Emmanuel, Rome:*
> *With all my countrymen, I am appalled by the dreadful calamity which*
> *has befallen your country. I offer my sincerest sympathy. The American*
> *National Red Cross has issued an appeal for contributions for the suf-*
> *ferers and notified me that it will immediately communicate with the*
> *Italian Red Cross.*[1]

On December 29, 1908, President Theodore Roosevelt sent this cablegram to the king of Italy, Vittorio Emanuele III, after receiving the notice about the fatal earthquake in Messina, Sicily, and Reggio Calabria. The notice had arrived after 5:21 a.m. on December 28, when a violent earthquake had shaken southern Italy. The epicenter occurred along the Strait of Messina between the island of Sicily and mainland Italy.

People felt the ground shaking not only in Sicily but also in Naples and Campobasso on the Italian mainland, on the island of Malta (south of Sicily), and as far away as Montenegro, Albania, and the Ionian Islands off the west coast of Greece.[2] The shaking lasted only 38 seconds, but the earthquake remains the deadliest event in Europe with an

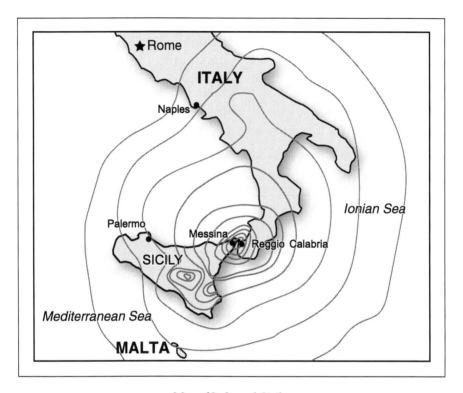

Map of Italy and Sicily.

estimated 60,000 to 120,000 fatalities.[3] The devastation was amplified by a tsunami that occurred shortly thereafter. Less than 10 minutes after the initial shock, the tsunami hit the coastlines on either side of the Strait of Messina and consisted of at least three major waves that destroyed the harbor.

This chapter focuses on a disaster that resulted in international cooperation at a time of political conflict. The rapidity with which the news spread, especially in the international press, was unprecedented and resulted in a worldwide response. The vastness of the destruction and the number of persons who remained under the rubble shook the world's public opinion; for the first time, a natural disaster emergency became an event of political significance in the field of international relations. What historically is known as the "Bosnian Crisis" or the

"First Balkan Crisis" had occurred just 2 months earlier when Austria–Hungary annexed Bosnia and Herzegovina. This led to protestations from Russia, Great Britain, France, and Italy. In spite of the tensions existing in the relationships between these major European powers, which eventually led to World War I (WWI), many nations would, for a time, share in the misfortune that hit the Italian nation, giving a striking example of human solidarity.[4] Even American women joined in the rescue efforts. Significantly, nurses were among the responders, and they came as volunteers alone, with the military, or as members of the Italian Red Cross.

THE EARTHQUAKE'S SCENARIO

Italy has a lengthy history of catastrophic earthquakes; in fact, it is one of the most earthquake-prone areas in Europe. In the past 2,000 years, more than 400 destructive earthquakes have been documented in Italy. Seismic activity has varied considerably across the country due to the complex tectonics of the region.[5] Sicily is especially earthquake prone, because it is situated near the spot where the European and African continental plates collide. In 1783, the island endured a horrible earthquake in which an estimated 30,000 people died. In the 125 years following, there were another 20 major earthquakes. None of these subsequent quakes was particularly deadly, however, and the population of Sicily grew to about 3.8 million people by 1900. Of these, 158,000 resided in Messina, a port city across the strait from Reggio on the Italian mainland.

During the evening of December 27, 1908, Messina was celebrating; the city was crowded with tourists because of the opening of *Aida*, an opera by Giuseppe Verdi, in the new theater. Tourists and residents also came to view the new electric lighting on the promenade along the sea.[6] Early the next morning, the earthquake hit. Seismographs all over the world went wild; the shock was so powerful that the Mercalli scale, used at that time to calculate the power of an earthquake, appeared inadequate. The employees of the observatory Ximenian in Florence noted, "This morning at 5:21 the instruments of the observatory began an impressive, extraordinary recording: the widths of the tracks were so large that they have not entered into the cylinders, measuring over forty centimetres. Somewhere something serious is going on."[7]

The worst hit areas were Messina, on the northeast Sicilian coast, and Reggio in the province of Calabria on the Italian mainland. From all accounts, both cities were completely destroyed. The ground shook so intensely in the port area of Messina that the stone paving was permanently displaced in a wave-like pattern.[8] Describing the damage, one reporter wrote: "The enormity of the destruction of Messina is really beyond one's imagination. All the buildings in the city were, with a very few exceptions, considerably cracked or absolutely reduced to masses of ruin."[9] Around 90% of the buildings in Messina were destroyed, with the worst damage in the central and northern parts of the city where the soil was especially soft.[10]

Less than 10 minutes after the initial shock, a tsunami hit the coastlines on either side of the Strait of Messina, with waves exceeding 20 feet (6 m) in some locations. The tsunami originated in the Strait of Messina and consisted of at least three major waves. In most locations, the second and third waves were higher than the first.[11]

Although the precise number of casualties resulting from the Messina earthquake remains unknown, historical accounts place the number of fatalities between 60,000 and more than 120,000.[12] The tsunami was estimated to have caused 2,000 deaths in coastal areas along the eastern shores of Sicily and the Calabria coast.[13] Populations of the cities of Messina and Reggio Calabria were 150,000 and 40,000, respectively; thus, casualty estimates indicate that nearly half of Messina's population died from the disaster. Written and pictorial records reveal that the majority of the casualties resulted from the collapse of unreinforced masonry buildings.[14] The large number of damaged buildings highlighted the vulnerable nature of the building stock in Messina at the time. The use of poor-quality construction materials, often rubble stones, poor-quality mortar, and delicate stone facades was blamed for the widespread collapse of many buildings. Buildings constructed with better quality materials were less prone to collapse during the earthquake.[15]

FIRST RESCUERS

On the afternoon of December 28, a telegraphic message came to the Italian Ministry of the Navy: "Messina completely destroyed."[16] It was sent by the Scorpio torpedo boat from Nicotera. Initially, the Italian government thought the city had been bombed by the Austro-Hungarian fleet,[17] certainly not that it had been at the center of a natural disaster.[18] In this tense atmosphere, there were numerous naval units near the Sicily Channel, ready to intervene at the first emergence of a crisis. However, it was not an international political crisis, but a natural disaster that suddenly required the commitment of many units to prepare a relief operation. Although the local response would be quick, on the morning of December 29 British and Russian ships were the first to arrive on the scene.[19] Despite a language barrier, sailors immediately started rescue work.[20] For several days, men of different nationalities worked side by side, engaging relentlessly to liberate the survivors from the rubble, carrying and treating the wounded, and alleviating the suffering.[21]

On the morning of December 29 in La Valletta, Malta, officials knew something terrible was happening because a tidal wave shook the small boats docked in the port and warehouses along the water. By that afternoon, various nations had intercepted the news from the telegraph station. On hearing the earthquake, the British commander of the Mediterranean fleet, His Royal Highness (HRH), the Duke of Connaught, sent personnel and provisions for a field hospital. On December 29 at 7:16 a.m., local time, British Colonel Military Attaché Sir Charles Delmè Radcliffe was the first foreign officer to arrive in Messina and offer help. According to one source:

> The first foreign ships to arrive at Messina after the disaster were His Majesty's ship, *Sutlej*, and His Majesty's destroyer, *Boxer*, from Syracuse, with civil doctors and relief stores. The same day other British men-of-war ships were ordered to Messina, and His Royal Highness the Duke of Connaught at once offered tents, blankets, stores, and any other help that might be required. The *Sutlej* landed 400 men and a fire

brigade and established a dressing station on the quay where many hundreds of people had their injuries dressed; also a depot where food and water were issued to the unfortunate inhabitants.[22]

One writer described the arrival of the British ship:

The *Sutlej's* commander ordered to anchor a half mile wide of the main pier. Immediately the ship was stormed by numerous small boats packed with survivors, many of them wounded, hysterical and without clothes. They all wanted to be taken on board.[23] For a few moments it was a total chaos until ways were found to proceed with order. Children and injured adults were boarded first. Messina was all a pile of rubble, with bodies without life scattered everywhere along with the furnishings of the destroyed homes. Everywhere was an echo of groans and cries of those who remained buried alive, asking for help. Hundreds of survivors of all ages and walks of life were collected in small groups or wandered along the harbour among the ruins, in the incessant rain, complaining and crying without hope.[24]

To the crew of the *Sutlej*, it appeared to be a scene from the end of the world. These were men no older than 17 years, who were completing their sea training before joining the British Navy.

The *Sutlej* was one of the eight British ships that responded. The Royal Navy transported a field ambulance section of the Royal Army Medical Corps to Messina, and this included nurses of Queen Alexandra's Imperial Military Nursing Service (QAIMNS). Sir Delmè Radcliffe reported:

On the 1st January His Majesty's ships *Duncan*, *Euryalus*, and *Philomel* arrived, and also proceeded to the Calabrian coast opposite Messina. These ships brought the Military

Field Hospital, with 200 beds, thirteen Nursing Sisters, and the Military Bakery, consisting of five field ovens, sent by His Royal Highness the Duke of Connaught from Malta. They also brought a large stock of provisions and medical stores, besides seven naval and thirteen civil surgeons from Malta. The Military Field Hospital was established at Catona on the 1st January, where it remained till the 15th January, and where about 1,200 wounded were treated. All the British ships had every available man on shore engaged in rescue and relief work, and they landed an immense quantity of stores of all kinds or transferred them to the ships of other nationalities where they were needed. About 1,000 wounded were conveyed by His Majesty's ships to Syracuse or transferred to other ships for transport to Naples and Palermo.[25]

He specifically noted that a female physician and female nurse were also part of the team in the field hospital:

Dr. Douglas arrived at Messina with the Lady doctor Miss Mary Flint-Taylor, the nurse Miss Niesigh, and Mr. Edwardes, on the 1st January. As soon as the Duke of Connaught's field hospital arrived at Catona, Dr. Douglas with his party joined it and all rendered invaluable services in the hospital until its departure on the 15th January. After the hospital [ship] had left, Dr. Douglas's party continued their medical work, and were also formed into the local Catona committee for the distribution of relief.[26]

Writing from gendered assumptions that women were delicate and unaccustomed to hard labor, he noted:

Dr. Mary Flint-Taylor and Miss Niesigh remained at Catona in camp till the end of February, and when their services being no longer required, they returned to Rome. The devotion of these Ladies, and their cheerful endurance of discomforts and even hardships, cannot be praised too much. They were in camp the whole time, and at first under the roughest and most primitive conditions, without any camp furniture or convenience of any kind, and having to do their own cooking. All this time the weather was cold, wet, and abominable in the extreme. Besides attending to a great number of sick in the camp, they made journeys into the mountains with mule caravans to carry relief to the people in the ruined villages, where the snow and exposure made the conditions even worse than they were on the shores of the Straits.[27]

In the context of this disaster, however, gender roles blurred as women experienced working conditions that society assumed applied only to men.

A Baltic Russian naval squadron that had been in the Mediterranean Sea for war training also sailed into the port of Messina. Instead of planning for war, however, the sailors intervened in rescue and relief operations. Three modern warships, each with a crew of nearly 800 men, had a strong impact on the events of the day as they brought bread and blankets. Although one ship took 550 survivors to Naples, the medical staff of the two other Russian ships organized an emergency relief operation and set up operating tables. Meanwhile, the bulk crews, composed of small groups led by a young lieutenant or an ensign, immediately began to search through the rubble of collapsed houses checking for bodies. Each group managed to save an average of seven lives per hour. The police force had not yet been organized, and the young officers had orders to shoot if they spotted anyone looting.[28] Others transported the wounded to the public garden where the medical staff of the English ship had organized another basic first-aid station.[29]

The Russian sailors were an example of military courage and efficiency. Even the British military attaché wrote in his diary: "The work done by the crews of the Russian vessels from the moment of their first arrival was beyond all praise and excited the warmest admiration of the British officers and seamen present."[30]

44

ITALIAN GOVERNMENT AND MILITARY RESPONSES

Local responses to the earthquake augmented external assistance. Because the tsunami rendered the Messina harbor unusable, Italian Royal Navy torpedo boats could not immediately be used for helping the population. Thus, the council of ministers and the Italian Prime Minister Giovanni Giolitti issued the first directives of the government. The army mobilized most of its units and the minister for the marine contacted three battleships and one cruiser off the Sardinia coast to head to the disaster area.[31] The Minister of Public Works Piero Bertolini immediately departed for Naples as did Italian King Vittorio Emanuele III and Queen Elena del Montenegro, who departed on December 29.[32]

The warships became hospitals and transports, shuttling the wounded between Naples and other coastal towns. Naples became the center for refugees, and its hospitals were filled with the wounded.[33] The influx of people and army units continued into Messina, where fires burned for several days. In addition, the Italian Royal Navy mobilized at Reggio Calabria. Commander Cagni temporarily assumed command of the rescue operations, and sailors disembarked the ship to organize assistance and establish the first field hospital.[34] The sailors also assisted police patrols with the goal of providing public safety and preventing episodes of profiteering.

The navy provided 69 units of various types and tonnage ships for the transportation of troops, food, supplies, hospital units, work equipment, field materials, and kitchens to help in the rescue action. Several civil steamers were needed as well, and operational commands based in Messina and Reggio Calabria divided the towns into blocks and coordinated aid. Men and materials were located in the areas most affected by the disaster; from there, they were dispatched to other suburbs, smaller towns, and villages in the vicinity. The first troops arrived the day after the quake and other troops continued to come until April 1909. More than 20,000 men from the army participated in rescue operations. More than 12,000 worked in Messina, while others were employed in Reggio Calabria and its surroundings.[35] Joining these groups were departments of policemen and a finance corps. In order to protect civilians and to prevent looting, soldiers, police, and sailors provided night patrols.

RESPONSE OF THE ITALIAN RED CROSS
AND VOLUNTEER ORGANIZATIONS

The Italian Red Cross, officially founded in 1875, also responded to the crisis. The Messina earthquake was the first disaster in which its members were actively involved, especially the female volunteer nurses or ladies, as they were called.[36] On the evening of December 28, a rescue team was established in Rome and in Palmi (Calabria) with a 20-tent hospital, an ambulance from the mountain, blankets, and food. With strong support from the government and military, the nurses and other Red Cross workers were extraordinarily fast and efficient. The doctors and nurses, who had trained in caring for the wounded during wartime, were ready for mobilization. The first school of nursing of the Italian Red Cross had opened in Milan and Florence in 1906; by the end of 1908, 737 volunteer nurses were ready for duty.[37] In rescue operations, 252 officers, 781 soldiers, and 730 volunteer nurses deployed, and they served in 10 hospitals, 30 infirmaries, several hospital ships, and 10 ambulances.

For the first time, the Italian Red Cross tested the use of special trains as hospitals. These proved useful for the care of persons with light wounds and for transportation over short distances. A hospital train consisted of 16 wagons, each containing 16 stretchers. One was a pharmacy and dressing room, another was a kitchen, and two accommodated the staff. The train was under the command of a first-class administrative inspector, and a physician had the task of overseeing the entire health service on the train. Other Red Cross crew included 10 junior officers (six doctors, two pharmacists, one commissioner, and one chaplain), 42 military workers, and nine female volunteer nurses. On board the steamer *Taormina*, they admitted 214 injured people and either treated them immediately or transported them to hospitals in Naples, Livorno, and Florence, where major reception centers were set up. Outside the earthquake zone, in Naples and Rome, other temporary emergency hospitals were established.[38]

After the initial rescue work, the priority became disease control and vaccination of the entire population of southern Italy. Among other activities, the Italian Red Cross was also in charge of the children, trying to reestablish a normal life for them. It created itinerant family counselling with health education activities for mothers and children, distributed food, provided vaccinations, controlled the spread of infectious diseases, and created a registry and a method of reporting any disease outbreaks. Elementary school teachers were recruited to organize recreational and educational activities for the children. The Italian Red Cross organized some "field" schools in the disaster zone and established an office to locate missing children and to arrange for adoption of the many orphans.[39]

Nelda Bertone, Italian volunteer nurse.
Used with permission of Giancarlo Celeri Bellotti.

47

The Red Cross Volunteer Nurses Corps provided an opportunity for many women to be useful in public roles. At the time, public opinion held that women did not have the psychological maturity and physical stamina to assist the wounded in war zones. Yet, Messina's earthquake became a test for women as nurses to demonstrate their commitment and skill. As an example, during the earthquake, Nelda Bertone was a preschool and elementary school teacher. She stayed in Messina and Reggio Calabria from February 15 to March 16, 1909, and became a nurse in 1915 before Italy went to war.

In the face of this disaster, Italians rediscovered the sense of brotherhood and cooperation, even though Italy had just been established as a nation and the differences between the north and the south were very strong. In addition to the interventions organized by the Italian Red Cross, the Order of the Knights of Malta and other relief committees

Croce Verde Genovese responders to Il Terremoto di Messina del 1908 (Green Cross of Genoa responders to Messina and Reggio Calabria earthquake, December 28, 1908).
Used with permission of Giancarlo Celeri Bellotti.

formed in every Italian province to collect money, food, and clothing. Despite the difficulties of transferring people to the disaster area, volunteer teams consisting of nurses, doctors, engineers, technicians, workers, priests, and teachers provided their assistance to survivors in the earthquake zone. As an example, even though it was a long distance from the earthquake site, the Green Cross from Genoa responded.[40] The Green Cross was a volunteer organization established in 1899 to help harbor workers, who had no health care. In case of occurrence of occupational accidents, the workers themselves decided to obtain training in first aid and organize aid in case of need.[41] These men lent support in Messina and in Reggio Calabria by helping to dig through the rubble and ruins to find the injured or dead.

INTERNATIONAL AID

On becoming aware of the magnitude of the disaster, many countries pledged to provide emergency aid. The dire disaster and the sufferings of the survivors raised expressions of sympathy from Europe, the United States, Canada, and countries in South America. Rulers and presidents expressed their condolences, and people spontaneously provided funds and aid. One hundred ships, both military and civilian, brought supplies as they quickly headed to the desolated region; and rulers, ambassadors, and ministers hastened to express their deep sympathy with Italy in her affliction.[42]

Many nurses volunteered to help the survivors. Several groups from the International Red Cross reached Italy. On December 31, 1908, a team of French nurses headed by a nursing major was quickly sent to serve in Naples's largest medical center and in the Sicilian and Calabrese rural areas. Although Italy and Germany were embroiled in territorial disputes at that time, the German Red Cross delegation contributed in bringing help to the areas hit by the earthquake. Baroness Elisabeth von Keudel led the delegation, and later the Nightingale Foundation recognized her dedication and support.

Other humanitarian organizations sent their nursing staffs: the Congregation of Mutual Aid in Vienna from the Austro-Hungarian

Empire, the Congregation of Mutual Aid from Spain and Portugal, and several religious congregations around the world. The common language spoken is unknown, though it seems most likely it was French at that time; if ever there was one it is unknown if the nurses, other than Fitzgerald, spoke Italian. The documents that were left do not indicate any evidence that they had been circulated to international teams: each one is written in the language of the institution that prepared it.

ALICE FITZGERALD'S EXPERIENCE

Alice Fitzgerald was a young American nurse who had graduated from the nursing school at Johns Hopkins Hospital, Baltimore, Maryland, in 1906; she was working in Italy at the time of the earthquake.[43] In 1908, she became a member of the Florence branch of the Italian Red Cross. When she heard about the earthquake, she quickly wrote to the president of the Women's Branch of the Red Cross of Florence and volunteered her services for the Messina and Calabrian sufferers. She wrote about her adventure in an article titled "My Experiences in Naples After the Messina Disaster" that was eventually published in *The American Journal of Nursing*.[44] This important manuscript became an essential report on the events surrounding the natural disaster, the types of treatment nurses provided, as well as the status of Italian nursing at the time.

Initially, Fitzgerald faced a bureaucracy that prevented her from immediately leaving for the disaster scene. Indecision as to when to send nurses to Naples, where many survivors were taken, led her to leave for the city on her own. She was particularly critical of the Italian Red Cross in general, for its "lack of general unity and co-operation."[45] On her arrival, she discovered that one of the Red Cross hospitals was at the new Excelsior Hotel, whose proprietor had offered the fourth floor for a hospital. Because she had left so quickly and without official documentation as a Red Cross nurse, she had to convince the authorities of her desire to help by offering to do whatever she could. She knew international cooperation required trained nurses, which she could provide, but it was especially important that she could speak Italian.[46]

One of the Red Cross officers allowed her to work, and she described the international situation she found:

> I found a staff composed of Neapolitan ladies, two of whom were wives of doctors; three Russian women medical students; and three Americans, all women of good common sense, and possessed of the true charity and tact which at all times can accomplish more than training.... We also had one lady of the Milanese[47] Red Cross, which had come to Naples with its own doctors, aids, etc., and had started a hospital of its own.[48]

Fitzgerald described the types of cases she encountered and the specific nursing care she gave. She mainly cared for patients with fractures, "all with pathetic stories of being caught under the ruins and kept prisoners from two to four days and nights, suffering from their wounds, thirst and hunger!"[49] She also described a little boy, badly bruised; a poor reserved old man, who "had a fractured arm, but rarely spoke, and never complained of his pains or troubles"; [and] a church sexton with scalp wounds that eventually led to his death, presumably from infection. "One patient had a bad sore on her back, and as we had no rubber rings I took some cotton and a bandage and started to make her a ring. She watched me carefully, not understanding what my object was, but keeping up a steady stream of protests that she did not need or want the thing I was making! After it was in place, and she felt so much the better for it, she confessed that she had feared that I was going to try and squeeze it around her in some way!"[50]

Fitzgerald demarcates her work from physicians. While physicians and medical students took temperatures and gave medicines, nurses provided nutrition and applied splints and soft dressings to fractures and wounds. As a nurse, she massaged the fractured area but not until after several days, because only physicians and their students could do it initially. Fitzgerald also provided comfort to the patients by rubbing their backs with some cologne, made pillows with clothes, and constructed bed cradles by taking a piece of cardboard bent into a semicircle and held together with a piece of string that was passed through the cardboard from one end to the other. The provision of personal hygiene was also a nurse's task. She described trying to comb a woman's hair after it had not been touched for 10 days. The woman had been buried in the ruins for 3 days, and other caretakers had ignored her hair. As she noted, "I worked for several hours daily as the patient begged not to have it cut, and after many days the remains of the Messina disaster were banished from that hair, at least."[51]

Fitzgerald was sympathetic with her patients, but her cooperation with Italian workers was filtered through her own ethnocentrism. She strongly criticized orderlies who slept while on night duty and described Italian people in general as "simple people," as if she was speaking of a child. She considered peasants as "primitive" in that they were not accustomed to clean linen. In her opinion, Red Cross Italian nurses deserved the worst criticism, because, although they were willing to work, they had received no professional preparation.[52] In some cities, such as Milan and Florence, they received a course of lectures and had the opportunity for some practical work, but physicians gave the lectures and, in the process, completely missed the nurses' point of view. Fitzgerald astutely pointed out the importance the physician gave to theoretical teaching that was rarely balanced with daily practical training:

> Not a scientific term was spared us. One whole lecture was devoted to the names and uses of some familiar and many unfamiliar surgical instruments, sutures, etc., but we were not shown how to make a bed!...The practical work consisted in spending a few hours, for a few mornings, in the wards, watching the doctor make one or two hypodermic injections or a few dressings, and occasionally watching operations.[53]

By contrast, Fitzgerald pointed out the nursing implications that she deemed important for disaster nursing: "Could any one of those ladies say that she had learned to make a bed, wash and feed a sick or wounded patient, change an under sheet, comb a patient's hair, etc. though she may have learned the name of every bone and articulation of the body, and also how to make a surgical knot?"[54] Her belief in the absurdity of the physician's lectures for nurses during periods of war and disaster was clear.

Fitzgerald suggested that Italian nurses were not trained in the nursing profession as other European colleagues because of a fear that the trained nurse may want to claim some of the work, privileges, or financial gain that had always belonged to physicians. Yet, particularly in disaster nursing, "there will always be plenty of work for both to do if the patient is to be well cared for."[55] Drawing on American ideas about social class that separated trained from untrained nurses as well as her own status as a graduate from the elite Hopkins program, she noted that in Italy, "the question of training the right kind of women for nursing is not even in its infancy. The average doctor is not even thinking of it and much less wanting it."[56]

Fitzgerald also criticized the Italian hospitals' decision to entrust care and supervision to Catholic nuns, reporting that "the Sisters do no nursing and very little supervising, except of meals and linen."[57] At the same time, she held up American nurses as the standard. She praised a hospital run by another Hopkins graduate, a Miss Baxter.[58] "Though just as crowded and busy as the others," she wrote, "it was such a pleasure to see the pupil nurses in the wards, in their neat blue uniforms, white aprons, and caps, instead of the slouchy, slovenly 'Inserviente'[59] of both sexes who do the nursing in most Italian hospitals."[60] Clearly, the "right kind" of nurse for disaster responses was the trained, disciplined worker who could respond efficiently with skill and precision. Despite Fitzgerald's criticism, she did speak of hardworking "co-workers," including the male director of her hospital who made it "a temple of harmony and good will."[61] This was not easy, because many nationalities, various conditions, and different people from all over the world had congregated there.

AMERICAN COLLABORATION

In addition to Fitzgerald's response, the humanitarian and economic aid from the United States to the Sicilian and Calabrese population was impressive. By the early morning of December 29, the *New York Times* had already published a passionate article titled "Shaken Italy; Thousands Die."[62] American aid was immediate and direct in the form of ships from the Great White Fleet, the popular nickname for the U.S. Navy battleship fleet sent to tour the world from December 1907 to February 1909. At the time of the earthquake, the fleet was on its 43,000-mile trip with 16 modern warships and 15,000 men. The fleet was in Egypt when its crew received news of the Messina earthquake. The flagship *Connecticut* arrived in Messina on January 9, 1909, with thousands of pounds of food, medicine, and temporary shelter for survivors.[63]

There were many reasons for such a prompt response from the United States. A high number of immigrants had come from Italy to settle in the United States in that period and more would come afterward. Additionally, the 1906 San Francisco earthquake and fire were still fresh in Americans' memories. Assistance may also have been used as a cover to achieve a specific foreign policy objective: to establish a strong American presence in the Mediterranean Sea. Although politics may have blurred with humanitarian intervention, nonetheless, on January 4, 1909, the U.S. Congress voted to donate funds to Italy in response to the following message from President Roosevelt: "The immense debt of civilization to Italy; the warm and steadfast friendship between that country and our own; the affection for their native land felt by great numbers of good American citizens who are immigrants from Italy; the abundance with which God has blessed us in our safety; all these should prompt us to immediate and effective relief."[64] American crowds were eager to contribute, and funds raised in New York totaled nearly half a million dollars. Other cities added their donations and the final total surpassed a million dollars.[65]

Timber transported by U.S. Navy ships led to the construction of 3,000 houses in Moselle, an area within the city of Messina. What became known as the "American Quarter," named by the Italian government in gratitude to the United States for its help, included this post-earthquake reconstruction site where all the main activities of the city of Messina started again. Messina's major schools, the barracks of the fire department and police department, the main churches, the Chamber of Labor, and the Court of Assizes all were located among the wooden buildings of this district. Furthermore, the greatest ice cream artisans and the best local bakers carried out their activities among the barracks of the

American Quarter.[66] Although the American Red Cross officially sent no nurses to Italy, Italian Red Cross records report that at least three or four American nurses who were already working in the country, similar to Fitzgerald, volunteered in Italy.[67]

On July 27, 1909, the *New York Times* reported on President Roosevelt's visit: "The impression produced by Mr. Roosevelt's visit to Naples and Messina is still so vivid as to form the subject of general conversation. The highest tribute paid to the illustrious visitor was possibly contained in the cry of welcome of the destitute population of Messina, which greeted him by shouting: 'Long live our President!' " The article continues, "The first baby born in a new house in Messina was named Theodore Roosevelt, Lloyd Belknap Palmieri!"[68] This was another tribute to the American diplomats and health professionals who brought relief to the city of Messina.

CONFLICT

At the same time, some organizational activities were not very efficient. William Bayard Cutting, Jr., U.S. vice consul in Milan, after having received the tragic news, immediately departed for Sicily to reopen a U.S. consulate in the city that would serve as a Special Representative American Red Cross. His official reports were loaded with tragic descriptions and were duly published every day by the *New York Times*, which, like most of the newspapers in the world, devoted considerable space to the news about the earthquake. Cutting sent daily letters to the American ambassador in Rome, Lloyd C. Griscom, in which he reported his sharp criticism on the way Italy managed aid operations, and how materials and money sent from the U.S. government, the Red Cross, and other spontaneous collections born on American soil were used. On January 2, 1909, he wrote: "The organization here is inexcusably deficient with regard to the general preparations. Telegraph of the Italian system works so poorly that the government's messages must be sent from the *Minerva* English ship. We need a lot of sterilized milk, not condensed." They also needed drinks that were immediately ready for use. "It's all you can give to women and children who almost starve. Bread is the other most important thing, and then the pasta, olive oil.

Cans of butter and sugar. Even the corned beef would be very helpful. Linen, sheets, socks and wool sweaters."[69]

On January 3, Cutting noted, "Our group of Red Cross, formed by excellent doctors, is operating especially in hospitals, on ships and in Naples, where they are greeted with most difficult cases."[70] Yet, he also faced the problem of the broad masses of emigrants who wished to go to the United States. The decision he had to make proved extremely difficult. In 1906, American legislation had refused entry into the United States to those who were classified as "assisted." Although most of the survivors of the 1908 earthquake had received a monetary allowance from the Italian authorities, some American officials might consider them "assisted" persons. Cutting wrote:

> Normally we discourage those who had the intention to immigrate to America and say that you do not have the funds, but it is only a delaying strategy....If we have the money, if the law allows it, and if we are able to defend ourselves from the pressures indiscriminate, we should help them.[71]

Although no reliable quantitative data are available, it is known that the Italian ambassador in the United States obtained a list of potential emigrants who wanted to join either family or friends in Boston, New York, and San Francisco.

CONCLUSION

Europe's most powerful earthquake shook southern Italy; as the disaster made worldwide headlines, international relief efforts mobilized. These included Red Cross personnel and British and Russian sailors; Italian civilians; Green Cross workers; American, Italian, and British nurses, physicians, and journalists; and leaders of nations. On July 5, 1910, the Italian royal official journal published a decoration list of more than 46 countries who sent help to the Italian survivors. President Roosevelt and the American Red Cross received a gold medal for the enormous aid they provided. More than 17 American states from Massachusetts to California received a special thank-you for their generosity and altruism. Many in the world expressed solidarity toward those who were suffering.

However, the feeling did not last. Warning winds of war were blowing in Europe. Just a few years later, nationalist and imperialist tensions in Europe that had escalated since the second half of the 19th century would drag 28 countries into the tragedy of WWI. By the time the war ended, all of Europe was weakened by destruction and debt. Eight million people died and 20 million were wounded.

Yet, the history of nursing in periods of war and other disasters is full of episodes of everyday gestures of care and attention. Fitzgerald's article, despite its ethnocentric criticism, showed how nursing was an essential part of the disaster response. Having left her home in the United States, she noted the need for cooperation between different people and different cultures, albeit with her distinct American vision. She strongly believed in the importance of education for nurses for disaster responses, and this ideal eventually became the standard for her homeland and abroad. Specifically, nurses needed two main qualities: to be well aware and to be well trained. Other lessons became evident after the earthquake. The Italian Red Cross's special trains had been so successful after the earthquake that hospital trains were adopted again during WWI.

ACKNOWLEDGMENT

Special thanks to Barbra Wall Mann and Maria Cristina Bertoni.

NOTES

1. Special to *New York Times*, December 30, 1908: Robert Pear, "Dead in Quake May Be 100,000," *New York Times*, December 30, 1908, accessed February 28, 2014, http://spiderbites.nytimes.com/free_1908/articles_1908_12_00000.html

2. Maria Serafina Barbano, Raffaele Azzaro, and Daniel Emilio Grasso, "Earthquake Damage Scenarios and Seismic Hazard of Messina, North-Eastern Sicily (Italy) as Inferred From Historical Data," *Journal of Earthquake Engineering* 9 (2004): 805–830.

3. Walter Coburn Arwin et al., *Factors Determining Human Casualty Levels in Earthquakes: Mortality Prediction in Building Collapse* (Madrid: Proceedings of the 10th World Conference on Earthquake Engineering, 2004), 5989–5994.

4. Giorgio Boatti, *Messina 28 Dicembre 1908. I Trenta Secondi che Cambiarono l'Italia, Non gli Italiani* (Milano: Le Scie Mondadori, 2004), 102–103.

5. Antonio Billi et al., *On the Cause of the 1908 Messina Tsunami, Southern Italy* (Rome: Geophysical Research Letters, 2008), 35.

6. Andrea Giovanni Noto, *Messina 1908: I Disastri e La Percezione del Terrore nell'Evento Terremoto* (Rome: Rubettino, 2008), 67–69.

7. Luigi Lombardo, *Messina Risorgerà. Il Terremoto del 1908 Nelle Storie del Popolo* (Reggio Calabria: Bonanno, 2010), 25.

8. Francesco Mulargia and Enzo Boschi, "The 1908 Messina Earthquake and Related Seismicity," in *Earthquakes: Observation, Theory and Interpretation. Proceedings of the International School of Physics, Enrico Fermi* (1984): 493–518.

9. Levi Holbrook, "Bulletin of the American Geographical Society," *American Geographical Society* 42(1910): 115–128.

10. Maria Serafina Barbano, Raffaele Azzaro, and Daniele Emilio Grasso, "Earthquake Damage Scenarios and Seismic Hazard," 824–825.

11. Galcinto Platania, "I Fenomeni Marittimi che Accompagnarono il Terremoto di Messina del 28 Dicembre 1908," *Riv. Geogr. Ital.* 16 (1909): 16, 154–161.

12. Guiseppe Mercalli, "Atti R," *Instituto d'Incoraggiamento* 7 (1909): no pages found.

13. Many original documents were lost in the confusion following the Italian earthquake, and it was difficult to assess the accuracy of various estimates. Prior to the Messina earthquake, only the 1775 Lisbon earthquake has caused similar levels of fatalities. Estimates of death ranged from 65,000 to 100,000.

14. S. Tinti and D. Giuliani, "The Messina Straits Tsunami of December 28, 1908: A Critical Review of Experimental Data and Observations," *Il Nuovo Cimento*, Luglio-Agosto 6 (1987): 6429–6442.

15. G. Restifo, "Local Administrative Sources on Population Movements After the Messina Earthquake of 1908," *Annali di Geofisica* 38 (1997): 5–6.

16. Eleonora Iannelli, *Messina Reggio 1908 2008: un Terremoto Infinito: Storia di una Città Tornata Alla Vita ma Rimasta Incompiuta* (Messina: Kalos, 2008), 27.

17. In fact, in 1908, the crisis in the Balkan Peninsula heralded the political tensions before World War I.

18. The captain of an Italian battleship on duty on the strait had reported to the British military lieutenant Delmè-Radcliffe, who had forwarded the information in his interim report to Ambassador Sir Rennell Rodd.

19. Roger Perkins, *Angels in Blue Jackets. The Navy at Messina 1908* (Chippenham, London: Picton Publishing, 1985): 95–102.

20. Franz Riccobono, *Il Terremoto dei Terremoti* (Rome: Edas, 2008), 57–58.

21. Rosa Maria di Stefano and Vittorio di Paola, *1908 Marinai Russi a Messina* (Messina: ETHOS, 1988), 76–77.

22. John Fisher and Antony Best, *On the Fringes of Diplomacy: Influences on British Foreign Policy, 1800–1945* (London: Ashgate Publishing, 2013), 84–85. See also "The Messina Earthquake," *Manawatu Standard* XLI, no. 8774 (January 15, 1909): 5–6.

23. Albrect Carrie, *Storia Diplomatica dell'Europa* (Rocca di S.Casciano: Cappelli editore, 1964), 34–37.

24. Ibid., 42.

25. Maria Teresa Di Paola, "L'Emergenza Come Fatto Politico: l'Intervento Della Marina Inglese nel Terremoto di Messina del 1908," *Archivio Storico Messinese 64. Società Storica di Messina* 64 (1974): 154–164.

26. Ibid., 64, 157.

27. Ibid.

28. Tatiana Ostakhova, *Abbiamo Visto Messina Ardere Come una Fiaccola. I Marinai Russi Raccontano il Terremoto del 28 Dicembre 1908* (Moscow: Leonida, 2008), 87–92.

29. Benjamin Reilly, *Disaster and Human History: Case Studies in Nature, Society and Catastrophe* (Jefferson, NC: McFarland, 2009), 90.

30. Maria Teresa Di Paola, "L'emergenza Come Fatto Politico: L'intervento Della Marina Inglese nel Terremoto di Messina del 1908," *Archivio Messinese Storico* 67 (1994): 64, 163.

30. Giovanni Giolitti (1842–1928), an Italian political leader, was the prime minister of Italy five times between 1892 and 1921. He is the second longest serving prime minister in Italian history, after Benito Mussolini.

32. The participation of the royalties, King Vittorio Emanuele III and Queen Elena del Montenegro, was much publicized and magnified by the newspapers. Italy was a very young nation, having been unified in 1861, and it needed to create a nationalism through strong propaganda.

33. Maria Teresa Di Paola, "L'emergenza Come Fatto Politico: L'intervento Della Marina Inglese nel Terremoto di Messina del 1908," *Archivio Messinese Storico* 64 (1994): 64, 174.

34. Charles Morris, *Morris's Story of the Great Earthquake of 1908, and Other Historic Disasters* (Memphis, TN: General Books LLC, 2010): 174–182. Umberto Cagni Conte di Bu Meliana (1863–1932) was an Italian admiral and explorer. He held the office of senator of the kingdom and the consortium independent commissioner of the port of Genoa.

35. Ornella Fiandaca and Raffaella Lione, *Il Sisma. Ricordare, Prevenire, Progettare (Atti ARTEC). Con CD-ROM* (Rome: Alinea Editrice, 2009), 78–81.

36. Costantino Cipolla and Paolo Vanni, *Storia Della Croce Rossa Italiana Dalla Nascita al 1914: I. Saggi* (Milano: Franco Angeli, 2013), 120–125.

37. Ibid., 132.

38. Ibid., 140–147.

39. Booklet 34 (*Fascicolo n. 34*), Italian Red Cross National Archive, via Bernardino Ramazzini, 31. Rome.

40. Genoa is a maritime city in Northern Italy, almost a straight-line distance of 600 miles to Messina. At the time, it took 5 or 6 days by boat to get to Messina. Many cities in the Genoa region, including La Spezia and others, had Green Cross organizations. Genoa's was the first to be established.

41. Pubblica Assistenza Croce Verde Genovese, Una Parola ai Lettori. *Bolletino Mensile Della Società*, July 1908. Historical Archive, Genoa. Thanks to Daniele D'Angelo, secretary and volunteer.

42. Università di Messina, *Dipartimento di Scienze Giuridiche, Storiche e Politiche. Il Disastro è Immenso e Molto più Grande di Quanto si Possa Immaginare: il Sisma Calabro-Siculo del 1908: Atti del Convegno Organizzato dal Dipartimento di Scienze Giuridiche, Storiche e Politiche Dell'Università di Messina: Messina, 4–5 Dicembre 2008* (Messina: Aracne editore, 2010), 54–57.

43. Alice Louise Florence Fitzgerald was born March 13, 1874, to a Baltimore family and raised in Florence, Italy. She was educated in France, Switzerland, and Germany. She entered the Johns Hopkins Hospital Training School for Nurses in 1902 against her family's wishes. During her life, she was a war nurse and teacher. She retired from active nursing in 1948. She lived the remainder of her life at Peabody Nursing Home in New York City where she died on November 10, 1962.

44. Alice Fitzgerald, "My Experiences in Naples After the Messina Disaster," *The American Journal of Nursing* 9, no. 7 (1909): 482–492.

45. Ibid., 482.

46. Ibid., 483.

47. Ibid. Milanese (from Milan, in Italian in the original text) was a very active humanitarian association that cooperated with the Red Cross.

48. Ibid.

49. Ibid., 483.

50. Ibid., 485.

51. Ibid., 484.

52. Ibid., 487.

53. Ibid., 488.

54. Ibid., 488–489.

55. Ibid., 490.

56. Ibid.

57. Ibid., 489.

58. Grace Baxter was born in Florence, from an English family. She graduated at the Johns Hopkins Hospital Training School for Nurses. With Amy Turton, she is considered the nonreligious nurses' training school pioneer in Italy. She opened the first Italian nurses school in Naples in 1896. Despite fascist autarchy laws, she was a teacher in the Italian Red Cross nurses school in Florence and she wrote a famous nursing textbook in 1932.

59. Hospital attendant, in Italian in the original text.

60. Fitzgerald, "My Experiences," 7, 488.

61. Ibid., 486.

62. Robert Pear, Rome reporter, "Italy Shakes: Thousands Died," *New York Times*, December 29, 1908, accessed February 28, 2014, http://query.nytimes.com/mem/archive-free/pdf?res=F10B16F93C5D16738DDDA00A94DA415B888CF1D3.

63. Richard T. Arndt, *The First Resort of Kings* (Sterling, VA: Potomac Books, Inc., 2005), 123.

64. Salvatore J. Lagumina, *The Great Earthquake, America Comes to Messina's Rescue* (Youngstown, NY: Teneo Press, 2008), 97.

65. Julia F. Irwin, *Making the World Safe: The American Red Cross and a Nation's Humanitarian Awakening* (London: Oxford University Press, 2013), 62–63.

66. The District was devastated by a fire in 1924 and later on, ironically, by the Allied bombing during WWII.

67. Vincenzo Tomeo, *Il Diritto Come Struttura del Conflitto: una Analisi Sociologica* (Milano: Franco Angeli, 1981), 147–148.

68. Long Branch, "Roosevelt Square for a New Messina," *New York Times*, July 27, 1909, accessed February 28, 2014, http://spiderbites.nytimes.com/free_1909/articles_1909_07_00000.html.

69. United States, *Dept. of State Register of the Department of State U.S. Government Printing Office, 1908* (Princeton, NJ: Princeton University e-book, April 29, 2010), 54–57.

70. Ibid., 72.

71. Ibid., 75.

CHAPTER 3

The 1913 Flood in Ohio (USA)

Janna Dieckmann

A city street, river mud and debris piled breast high on either side, houses off their foundations or entirely washed away; a very different looking "Red Cross lady" serenely picking her way around wrecked furniture, sodden mattresses, ruins of porches and sheds, wearing rubber boots, skirts kilted high, wet nearly to the waist, sending sick people to hospitals, inspecting plumbing, backyards, and cellars, superintending all sorts of work from feeding the baby to the digging of trenches. Through all parts of the flooded city, nurses going on similar errands, inspecting nearly nine thousand houses and reporting conditions found.[1]

In June 1913, Mary Gladwin, RN, wrote these words, describing what Red Cross nurses had done during the flood that had devastated Ohio earlier that year. Red Cross nurses had been critical to the response, going from house to house, in some instances, to provide relief and doing whatever needed to be done. Compared to other types of disasters, floods are complex: The number of persons affected is usually much larger than that in other disasters; property losses are significant; and problems of sanitation are challenging and interlaced with

63

Map of the state of Ohio, USA.

the problems of sustaining public health. In Ohio, in 1913, all of these challenges occurred.

This chapter examines the American Red Cross response to the 1913 floods in the Ohio–Mississippi river basin through the events that occurred in the cities of Dayton, Hamilton, and Cincinnati. This response was the largest relief task for which the Red Cross had assumed sole responsibility up to that time,[2] and "the greatest disaster relief problem" it faced until 1918.[3] As part of the response, the Red Cross Nursing Service deployed in large numbers for the first time; between 234 and 260 nurses were in the field at some point. Their availability and organized arrival, their resourcefulness and perseverance, and their skills and successes were intended to demonstrate the potential of the enrolled Red Cross nurse. Within the context of the overall local and national disaster response, this chapter describes and explains these Red Cross innovations in disaster response, the professional and gender-based barriers the nurses faced, and the approaches the nurse–responders used to achieve their goals.

THE OHIO FLOOD IN DAYTON

Beginning on Easter Sunday, March 23, 1913, unprecedented heavy rains fell over Ohio and surrounding states onto soil already saturated from winter rains and melting frost. The rains fell in a pattern familiar in earlier, less severe spring storms that had led to significant flooding during the 19th century.[4] The March storm began in northern Ohio, and moved slowly southward over 5 days. Dayton, located at the confluence of several rivers, was particularly at risk: the Great Miami River "twists like a snake as it winds its S-shaped curves through the city," joining with the Mad River, Wolf Creek, and Stillwater River to create "four great torrents."[5] About 4:00 a.m., "the ringing of bells and the blowing of whistles" notified residents of increasing dangers as levees built after previous floods were overwhelmed and fractured. On Tuesday morning, March 25, raging water inundated the flood plain on which Dayton's central city was built.[6] Flood danger was at 18 feet; at 29.3 feet, the 1913 high water measure was 8 feet over the previous record.[7] "The water poured into houses, ruined furniture, undermined foundations, wrecked walls, floated many wooden buildings from their sites, overflowed privy vaults and cesspools, and deposited a mass of mud and wreckage over the whole flooded area."[8] Almost two thirds of Dayton was completely inundated; water, electricity, and gas were cut off; and railroad, telephone, and telegraph service were interrupted extensively.[9] Fires from broken gas mains erupted in the business district, adding to stranded residents' fears and destroying whole blocks of buildings as nothing could be done.

Some residents stayed at home and their homes swept away; others left their homes and drowned during their search for safety, yet their homes remained dry. Many of those who stayed at home were marooned for days on the top floors or in their attics—desperately seeking refuge from the depth of the floodwater. For those people who left their shelter, strong water currents and whirlpools swept them off their feet and swamped their small boats. Many evacuated their homes with only the clothes on their backs, and with nothing to protect them from the cold—well below 30° Fahrenheit. Those who lost their lives in the flood were primarily women and children; relatively few were adult, wage-earning men.[10] Loss of life in the flood was difficult to determine; very early reports feared 600 had been killed in Dayton. As the flood ebbed, estimates fell to about 100; later, sources set deaths at 361.[11] Likely more were lost in the waters and never found, while others died of sickness following the flood. Others succumbed to overwhelming stress; 32 survivors were admitted to psychiatric care at the Dayton State Hospital. Thus, human losses from the flood in Dayton alone were well more than 400 individuals.[12] Across Ohio, losses in property, land, and highways and bridges totaled almost $97 million[13] ($2.33 billion in 2014 dollars). To respond to the Ohio floods, the National Red Cross assembled "a greater number of trained agents than had before been brought together by the Red Cross in any single disaster."[14]

Ultimately, the Red Cross disbursed $2.5 million ($60.6 million in 2014 dollars) within Ohio, from joint contributions of the Red Cross and the state of Ohio.[15] In the weeks after the flood, 65,000 families, totaling 256,000 individuals, left their homes and relied on others or voluntary and government agencies for housing, with more than 300,000 people depending on relief supplies.[16]

Panoramic view of the flood in Dayton, Ohio, March 1913.
Source: Library of Congress.

BACKGROUND: STRENGTHENING THE AMERICAN RED CROSS CAPACITY FOR DISASTER RESPONSE

In order to understand the nursing response to the 1913 Ohio flood, it is helpful to place the nurses' innovation within the organizational context of the American Red Cross in relation to changes in leadership, national status, and programs. With Clara Barton's departure from the American Red Cross in 1904, and following the arrival of Mabel T. Boardman as national director, the organization began a purposeful series of changes to strengthen disaster response through increased financial stability, as well as political and organizational linkages. In 1905, the U.S. Congress approved a new federal charter for the American Red Cross that reflected organizational changes and also gave the Red Cross status as a quasi-governmental agency, with expectations that the Red Cross would continue to meet expectations in peace and during war. The U.S. secretary of war and Red Cross board member, William Howard Taft, gave his full support to the emerging structure of the renewed Red Cross, as well as to its increased alliance with the U.S. government.[17]

The next year, the unexpected nature and jarring severity of the 1906 San Francisco earthquake and fire caught the entire country's attention. In asking that all donations for the people of San Francisco be directed toward the American Red Cross, President Theodore Roosevelt signaled the organization's singular place in protecting the nation. Yet, the missteps of the Red Cross response to the 1906 San Francisco disaster provided a "major impetus" to reform relief operations through securing increased financial resources and improved response coordination.[18]

As director of Chicago's Bureau of Charities (a charity organization society), Ernest P. Bicknell gained disaster response experience in San Francisco, and with much persuasion from Red Cross leaders, he gradually increased his alliance with its work. In 1908, he joined the Red Cross full time, yet clearly retained the value and centrality of scientific charity (the central principles of the charity organization movement). At the Red Cross, he introduced the concept of institutional membership to provide a national reservoir of trained relief workers who would be available during a disaster. His goal was to avert many of the challenges of the San Francisco response. He gradually developed an array of strategies to promptly respond to any emergency with a practical relief program.[19] But in 1913, these innovations had not yet been tested.

Meanwhile, with the formulation of an effective structure for the Red Cross Nursing Service in 1909, Jane Delano became its part-time chairman. In 1912, Delano received a personal financial bequest of sufficient size that she was able to resign from her position with the U.S. Army to work full time with the Red Cross. Under her leadership, the Red Cross sought nurses who were best qualified for its nursing service, and created guidelines for selecting individuals. The effect was to increase standards of training in many nursing schools.[20] Many qualified trained nurses were able to enroll and receive their cherished Red Cross pin. Most were White. Qualified African American nurses were accepted and enrolled into the Red Cross Nursing Service after significant advocacy and negotiation in 1917. However, due to the societal norms of segregation, these nurses received Red Cross nurses' pins numbered in a separate series (recorded as "A pins") to reinforce the nurses' separate status.[21]

Just the year before, the Red Cross Nursing Service, the American Nurses Association, and staff of the *American Journal of Nursing* jointly paid for an "interstate secretary" to conduct a 6-month outreach and recruitment tour across the United States. Isabel McIsaac, the highly respected former superintendent of the Illinois Training School for Nurses, visited 54 cities and spoke to 81 groups of nurses. In early 1912, she continued these activities through a southern route from Tennessee to Texas.[22] Another Red Cross committee, chaired by Mary E. Gladwin of Ohio, developed a lecture series to educate nurses in the traditions of Red Cross service, including the roles of the Red Cross in disaster preparation and response for wartime or civil disasters, charitable relief and other humanitarian movements, and the experiences of deployed Red Cross nurses since the 1906 San Francisco earthquake.[23] By 1912, the Red Cross Nursing Service had established 32 state committees and 92 local committees, with 3,461 enrolled nurses,[24] and with more than 4,000 nurses in 1913.[25] These enrolled nurses would form the core of the disaster response to the 1913 Ohio floods, which the Red Cross Nursing Service leadership deemed "a test of the efficiency"[26] of the nursing service, and a demonstration that "Red Cross nurses can be quickly mobilized and relied upon... in the chaos following storm and flood."[27] Delano understood the hazards of disaster response; only when the Red Cross nurses "had been called to the field could she be sure that her organization would work as it should."[28]

THE MILITARY IN DISASTER RESPONSE

The military began its response to the Dayton flood shortly after the adjutant general (its chief officer) saw floodwaters flowing through the city immediately after the levees were breached, and telephoned Governor James M. Cox for approval. Brigadier General George H. Wood had nearly 3,000 soldiers from the Ohio National Guard under his command, to "prevent looting and disorder and to assist in purchasing, transporting, and distributing supplies."[29] The strictest martial law was enforced, with orders to shoot to kill any looters; unconfirmed accounts, possibly based on the many rumors then circulating, reported that 10 men were summarily shot. Yet, this step reassured residents in severely flooded neighborhoods where all utilities had been lost, and where night brought great isolation and fear. In Dayton, as elsewhere during the flood, local authorities also closed saloons, hoping to mitigate "lawlessness and disorder."[30]

With the military presence established, it coordinated disaster responses from the U.S. Navy, which provided material goods, such as blankets, tents, and sanitary supplies.[31] The U.S. Army detailed 60 medical corps members to sanitary duty; provided two fully equipped field hospitals; and supplied large quantities of vaccine, as well as medical and surgical dressings sufficient to last a division of 20,000 men for 1 month.[32] Both U.S. military branches also set up supply bases for continued support in Cincinnati and Columbus,[33] as transportation in and out of Dayton was at first impossible and later limited.

The Red Cross nurses worked parallel to the military, their major interface being the use of martial law passes so that they could travel when and where they were needed, given the nighttime curfews. They

69

also acquired supply cards to denote families requiring certain assistance or items. The military sometimes provided transportation, especially in crossing rivers by boat or pontoon bridge, as few bridges had survived the flood. Coordination between the military and the Ohio Red Cross nurses benefited from previous collaborations. Army Major James Edward Normoyle, who had been responsible for Mississippi River flood relief from Hickman (in southwestern Kentucky) to New Orleans during 1912, coordinated efforts with 13 Red Cross nurses serving at relief camps[34]; received the national director, Mabel T. Boardman; and worked closely with Ernest Bicknell.[35] Thus, Major Normoyle's involvement with flood relief during the Ohio flood (March 26–May 2, 1913)[36] gave the city a military leader familiar with the focus of the Red Cross nurses' work, and experience with meeting their needs. Both would prove essential to the Red Cross nursing response in Dayton.

DAYTON'S CIVIC LEADERS: SUPPORT AND COLLABORATION

Dayton's civic leaders supported rescue and response efforts beyond what was expected. John H. Patterson, founder and president of the National Cash Register Company (NCR), the largest industry in Dayton and one that escaped the flood waters, opened his entire office and factory complex to meet the needs of flood survivors and responders.[37] As the flood threatened, even before failure of the levees, NCR's woodworking shop made seven boats an hour to assist in rescue efforts. The NCR offices soon sheltered a hospital, a canteen, and a distribution center for food and clothing. The NCR became the center for the Red Cross nurses' relief efforts.

FIRST RESPONSE FROM CINCINNATI AND ITS NURSES: EMERGENT BEHAVIOR

Cincinnati, located 55 miles south of Dayton, was the largest departure point for nurses bringing assistance to the city of Dayton. Nurses from Cincinnati as well as nurses from the East Coast and Midwest gathered to prepare for departure to the flooded area. The Cincinnati Red Cross Chapter, which coordinated the movement of these nurses, had just established a physical headquarters; during the meeting of enrolled Red Cross nurses on Tuesday (the first at the new headquarters), word of flooding in Cincinnati and Dayton arrived from Washington and news was reported in the local newspapers.[38] All of the nurses present immediately agreed to respond to the local disaster in Cincinnati.[39] The Cincinnati Visiting Nurse Association and other local social service organizations provided telephone access and meeting rooms to organize the response, including many enrolled Red Cross nurse volunteers. A card catalog organized nurses, volunteers, and autos and trucks. Other organizations offered assistance, and college students and women's clubs provided volunteer workers. Immediate goals were to render first aid; promptly staff emergency hospitals, relief stations, and dispensaries set up by the Red Cross in schools and churches; and coordinate material relief distribution.[40]

Volunteers and material relief were donated from many sectors of Cincinnati residents. At the University of Cincinnati, the president called on male students to respond to the needs in Dayton. Most of the young men who were physically able went immediately with the relief trains. Only after the departure of the men was a mass meeting held with female students, from whom money, food, and clothing donations were requested. The young women then assisted the Cincinnati Red Cross in packing donated food and materials for shipment to Dayton.[41]

Other women outside the flood zones also offered donations. Members of the Ohio Woman Suffrage Association sent money and supplies individually. In Canton, the Woman Suffrage Party gave the entire $50 contents of their treasury; in Cleveland, the Woman Suffrage Party made 1,400 children's garments, sending these through the local Red Cross Society. Acknowledging Governor Cox's support of flood relief, an association representative encouraged members of the group to write to the governor to advocate for his formal support for woman's suffrage, because "the suffragists had responded nobly to the Governor's call for help and he ought to be feeling rather kindly to us now."[42]

RED CROSS NURSE DEPLOYMENTS
FROM CINCINNATI TO DAYTON AND HAMILTON

The lead Red Cross nurses in Cincinnati, Mary Hamer Greenwood (chairman of the Nursing Committee) and Annie Laws (secretary of the Chapter),[43] conferred with the Cincinnati mayor and Dr. Landis, the health officer, on Wednesday morning, but plans for sending nurses who were not enrolled in the Red Cross (from City Hospital) to Dayton were already underway. Five Board of Health nurses were then added. At Greenwood's nomination, Mary Blythe Wilson, an enrolled Red Cross Nurse and super-intendent of social service work at City Hospital, took charge of the entire group. On their arrival in Dayton, a request for 25 more nurses quickly followed, and soon still more nurses were needed. An enrolled Red Cross nurse led each party of nurses. On her arrival in Dayton, Mary Gladwin relieved Wilson. Clearly, the Red Cross was in control. This assertion of the right and importance of the Red Cross, given its Federal Charter, to determine who responded and how they responded to the disaster was critical in establishing the fact that everyone followed Red Cross proto-cols and adhered to the highest nursing standards.

Some conflict did occur. On Wednesday, March 26, nine nurses left Cincinnati for Hamilton, under the leadership of Abbie Roberts, founder and superintendent of the Cincinnati Visiting Nurses' Association. A man recorded only as "Mr. White," in charge of a portion of the relief work in Hamilton, immediately sent seven of the nine nurses back to Cincinnati, as in his opinion, nurses were not needed. (Although his reasoning is not known, he may have believed that female nurses would be more in danger than of aid.) Abbie Roberts insisted on remaining in Hamilton and opened a relief station at the Mosler Safe Works. Her tele-gram to the Cincinnati Red Cross office on Thursday morning urgently requested 10 nurses: "Words cannot tell of the terrible tragedy and dis-tress everywhere and each hour it seems to grow worse." The additional nurses were sent and proved critical to addressing health needs and nursing care. Perhaps, White reconsidered the severity of local needs; however, it is likely that he could not resist the Ohio governor's and the Ohio Flood Commission's political persuasion to accept help from Red Cross nurses. As the only endorsed organization in disaster response,

72

the Red Cross had the power to be effective and the ability to implement skilled interventions where they were needed.[44]

Late on Friday, March 28, the city of Hamilton remained in crisis. Mary Hamer Greenwood wrote of her arrival from Cincinnati, and what she saw as her driver tried to locate the temporary hospital established by Abbie Roberts:

> As long as I live the sight of that principal street of Hamilton on that Friday afternoon will remain with me. A long bread line, a long clothes line, waiting in silent patience in the bitter cold, with no rich, no poor, all class distinction leveled by a great disaster to a common need. Wrecked homes, muddy streets, the gruesome tales of our guide, told a story of catastrophe so great that the imagination was staggered.[45]

Breadline during disaster response, Dayton, Ohio, 1913.

Dayton and Hamilton were not the only cities that needed nurses, however. On Thursday, March 27, rapidly rising waters in Cincinnati were of such concern that city officials requested 100 more Red Cross nurses for assignment there. The next day, Jane Delano telegraphed that 25 nurses would arrive from St. Louis and 25 from Detroit, while 50 nurses would be sent from Chicago. Delano herself arrived from Washington, DC, by the "Post Special" train on Sunday with 10 Red Cross nurses, Mabel Boardman, U.S. Secretary of War Garrison, and others.[46] By this time, due to the difficulty and time necessary for travel, the flood was abating in Cincinnati, and the arriving nurses were sent to Dayton or Hamilton, as both cities remained in crisis.

The arrival of Jane Delano, chairman of the National Committee on Red Cross Nursing Service, with other Red Cross nursing leaders gained the only locally published notice of the nurses' activities.[47]

Jane Delano, American Red Cross nurse.
Courtesy of the Library of Congress.

Delano inspected work in the flood-impacted cities, to an extent achieving her desire to do the "actual work," of which she longed to be part.[48] In Dayton, the chief nurse (likely Mary Gladwin) "apologized because she was not able to make her distinguished guest as comfortable as she would have liked. [Delano] pushed aside the apology, exclaiming, 'Comfortable, why should I be made comfortable when there is so much suffering and you are all working under such a strain?' "[49] On Tuesday, April 1, Delano met in Cincinnati with the Red Cross Nursing leaders from the disaster-response area, and then departed for Columbus to meet with Red Cross and Ohio officials.[50]

RED CROSS NURSES' RESPONSE IN DAYTON

One key to the successful disaster response in Dayton was the coordinating role played by Ella Phillips Crandall, then secretary of the National Organization for Public Health Nursing and a faculty member at Teachers' College, New York City.[51] Important to her role, Crandall was native to Dayton where she had recently been administrator (1899–1908) of its Miami Valley Hospital, before her public health nursing work with the Henry Street Settlement.[52] Her personal knowledge and family connections within the city, and her ability to get resources, leaders, and people to help, meant that the nurses' efforts could be specifically targeted. Indeed, Crandall led the Red Cross nurses' public health nursing outreach and education efforts.

The nurses' response in Dayton was varied and one of coordination, education, outreach, sanitation, and much more. One striking example describes some of the wide variety of tasks the nurses undertook, from the viewpoint of Mary Gladwin, of Akron, Ohio:

> Up the sticky, muddy steps of sanitary headquarters, [one goes] to find a little nurse in brown, well known in Teachers College, New York [likely Crandall], dispensing the most varied assortment of knowledge as to mattresses, shoes, rubber boots, baby clothes, contagious ambulance, the obligations of landlords, the cleaning of cellars. At a table on one

side, a nurse in the well-known garb of the Chicago Visiting Nurses Association [likely Miss Phelan], with pencil poised, is answering questions, directing nurses, and making valuable and unique records.[53]

In both Dayton and Hamilton, the Red Cross nurses began by establishing hospitals; although the cities' own hospitals continued their work, more care was required.[54] The nurses' hospitals were located in schools or churches, but most buildings lacked heat, meaning that the nurses provided care in subfreezing conditions. These hospitals might have a first-aid room, or it might be tucked in elsewhere, with drugs and dressings provided by a Red Cross nurse. Nurses also staffed temporary shelters, tending to flood victims, helping with meals, finding new clothes, or simply providing comfort.

Outside, long bread lines and endless clothing distribution lines provided nurses with opportunities to assess survivors' status and to fill out the important family cards that authorized immediate and long-term relief provisions. Nurses offered assistance to those waiting in line; hurrying up and down the length of the long lines, they helped those too weak or tired to stand, and sometimes handed out a small card that allowed a fragile individual to move up to the front of the line.

Sanitation and disease prevention were serious challenges during disaster response; the loss of sanitary disposal facilities combined with the large numbers of refugees created ideal conditions for diseases to spread. Broken sewers, befouled water supplies, scattered garbage, and dispersal of the contents of broken privy vaults and cesspools only complicated the flood devastation.[55] In addition, 1,500 horse carcasses and uncountable dead dogs, cats, and chickens[56] all had to be removed.[57] Led by Ella Phillips Crandall, Red Cross nurses conveyed to residents the most important public health sanitation measures: first, to boil drinking water, and second, to spread disinfectants over all flood deposits that could not be "buried, burned, or removed."[58] They encouraged residents to clear their houses and yards of flood detritus, and reestablish sanitary conveniences. Although the Ohio State Board of Health provided printed bulletins to the local press,[59] it was essential for the nurses to provide interpretation household-by-household to convey the importance of action and application to that particular home and family.

Going to the people and making house-to-house inspections enabled the Red Cross nurses to become more effective; overall, 9,000 houses were inspected.[60] Prior to the flood, a serious epidemic of small-pox and spinal meningitis had affected parts of the Dayton area, but the post-flood incidence was cut in half.[61] Dayton authorities attributed the absence of flood-related epidemic conditions to the nurses' work. They labeled their work a "triumph of preventive medicine," as nurses educated the survivors, thus preventing "sanitary breakdowns" and other health hazards that frequently occurred following a disaster.[62] Major Rhoades, U.S. Medical Corps and chief sanitary officer for the military response in Dayton, wrote: "The nurses rendered a service which calls for the highest commendation and have given invaluable assistance to the District Sanitary officers."[63]

AMERICAN RED CROSS AND CHARITY: THE FAMILY AS "THE UNIT TO BE SERVED"

The charitable principles of the Red Cross were shared with the charity organization movement. During disaster response, the Red Cross gave charity based on three principles. First, the unit of relief was the family, as addressing family needs "meets and advances the welfare of both the individual and the community." Second, relief was to be apportioned according to need, rather than losses, supporting the belief that "not infrequently those who lose least, need most."[64] Strategies for addressing post-disaster need must be individualized. Third, it was thought that the Red Cross, the stricken communities, and the families should cooperate to assure "the fullest possible utilization of the resources for self-help in each community and each family."[65]

Early in the response, the Red Cross assisted the affected families with the most "elemental," common, and urgent needs. As a result, there was little differentiation for individual circumstances and differences.[66] Recognizing the impossibility of restoring residents' losses during "reconstruction" or "rehabilitation," families were helped back to a normal standard of living based on securing comprehensive information about their needs, leading to various types of aid, such as financial, counseling, or other services directed toward their individual circumstances and requirements.[67] For this purpose, the Red Cross nurses collected information about families through interviews in relief stations, in private rooms, or at temporary shelters, and recorded what they found on small cards.[68] In Hamilton alone, more than 6,500 cards were collected and separated by the character and immediacy of the needs.[69] For example, in Dayton, more than 5,000 families required furniture. They were then supplied with furniture ordered from a local furniture store, to promote recovery of the local economy. The supplied furniture was utilitarian, rather than the equivalent of replacing what they had before the flood.[70]

Bicknell applied "scientific charity" to the American Red Cross disaster response and strategies. Scientific charity suggested that continuous temporary, post-disaster financial assistance would "pauperize" or encourage lost self-respect and personal initiative, as well as encourage disaster survivors to have long-term dependence on charities. Because disaster relief committees were "responsible for conserving and promoting the welfare of the family,"[71] they decided that funds contributed to the Ohio Flood Relief Commission and the American Red Cross in response to a disaster were best provided to families during the emergency period. Yet, the period of immediate response might be extended for those returning late from refuge outside the area.[72] The expected longer term, continuing "rehabilitation" following disaster should be addressed within the communities themselves by establishing mutual aid organizations that follow the principles of scientific charity in controlling and shaping aid given to families and individuals.[73] Although the Ohio floods were a disaster, the greater tragedy would be to "deprive any family of its proper self-respect, or halt in any degree its desire for self-help and independence... [and] a much greater misfortune if that should result to any community as a whole."[74] Yet, some principled exceptions were considered.

To an extent, Bicknell used what he had learned from a plan of assistance developed as part of disaster recovery following the 1909 mine fire in Cherry, Illinois, and applied it to the 1913 Ohio flood.[75] If families lost the wage earner, they might need assistance for the rest of their lives, or until children were old enough to earn a wage to help the family. If so, sometimes, substantial amounts were set aside in their names, to be administered and overseen by the local associated charities. For example, a Dayton mother who lost a son, her main support, was granted $250 to establish herself in the rooming house business. In another example, an African American widow with two school-age sons (8 years and 12 years old) "fatherless by flood" received $600, also to be supervised by associated charities to supplement the mother's earnings.[76] Supervision of the allowance, especially by a responsible social agency, was preferred because these agencies were considered "more flexible," and "because it assures an active, friendly interest in the family."[77] This element of "moral supervision" embedded in the Cherry Plan and used to guide post-flood assistance in Ohio established long-term family oversight by the charity as a condition of financial support.[78]

AFRICAN AMERICAN FAMILIES IN DAYTON

As always, race played a part in the disaster response. Acknowledgment of this African American mother and her children is unusual and application of charitable principles to African American families is particularly unclear, as Dayton's African American community is largely invisible in period articles, reports, and surviving photographs of the flood— irrespective of their social or economic status. Dayton in the 1910s was generally seen as an exemplar of the progressive movement, with widespread development of social agencies.[79] But compared to northern Ohio, southwestern Ohio enforced more stringent social constraints that limited African American lives. Constituting only 5% of Dayton's 10,000 residents,[80] African American Daytonians faced barriers to shopping at stores, as well as receiving service in restaurants, drugstores, and saloons, and were assigned a separate upper gallery at theaters. Public schools were segregated, and African Americans were no longer hired as teachers. Access to full participation in employment was limited, especially after the late 1880s; at that point, African Americans were excluded from union membership, which controlled hiring for the skilled trades.[81]

African Americans interviewed in Dayton in 1912 by the African American academic Frank U. Quillin reported stronger prejudice each year following the Civil War, with greater prejudice directed toward those newly arrived from the south.[82] Most residential areas in Dayton were closed to African Americans by threat of violence, and they were restricted to less desirable locations of the city[83]—that is, those at higher risk during flood. On the streets nearest to the flooded Great Miami River were inexpensive apartments and bungalows; more affluent African Americans resided farther away from the river and major streets in relatively expensive, single-family homes.[84] It is likely that African American mortality and loss of property in 1913 were higher compared to those of the White population due to the residential proximity to the river system, but uncertain statistics about flood casualties prevent a clear conclusion.

MITIGATION OF FUTURE FLOODS

On May 2, 1913, just 32 days after the disaster's onset, the Dayton Citizens' Relief Committee called Dayton's civic leaders to a meeting at a local theater to form the Dayton Flood Prevention and Finance Committee. The public thought was that Dayton "was a ruined city."[85] Every man likely understood that his city would not survive without a plan to prevent future disasters, yet most were surprised by John H. Patterson's and Adam Schantz's demand to raise two million dollars that evening from the audience. Theater doors were locked to prevent premature departure; funds were secured and committed to forming the Miami Conservancy District, with fundraising completed by late May. Ernest Bicknell was present that evening: "Mr. Patterson took charge of the meeting and ran it virtually single handed. I was fortunate to be present that evening and witnessed a demonstration of moral and mental power which made an ineffaceable picture in my memory."[86] Subscription cards for the Flood Prevention Fund were labeled: "For the Love of Dayton: As a Testimonial of My Devotion and Patriotism."[87] By mid-1915, the district had overcome legal challenges, and in mid-1918, construction began on retarding basins and channel improvements that would prevent future flooding. In April 1922, heavy rainfall overflowed streams and rivers, yet the flood control works held[88]—and continue to do so into the 21st century.

WHEN SHOULD THE NURSES DEPART?

Dayton residents, who were initially reluctant and fearful, resisted the Red Cross nurses' planned departure 1 month after the flood. With some Red Cross agents also departing, Bicknell chose to interpret these changes as positive because it was important to remove a "public, visible sign of relief distribution which is always abnormal and demoralizing."[89] Furthermore, it became a "standing temptation and inducement to dependence."[90] Families needed a new start, and the end of the initial, post-disaster supports "cleared the slate" to permit this process to begin.[91]

The extremely active, temporary Red Cross administrative offices established in Columbus were closed on August 29, 1913, with Bicknell continuing communications through correspondence. Red Cross special agents also returned home; local flood relief committees or permanent local social service agencies directed continued aid, as residents sought assistance even 5 months post-flood. Local health services successfully handled localized outbreaks of typhoid fever that occurred through the summer of 1913.[92] Not only did home repair and reconstruction continue, but some residents found that they had underestimated repair costs and required increased support.[93] The closing of relief stations still allowed for continued assistance to individual families with additional funding for repair, food, or clothing;[94] yet, the gradual reduction of support from outsiders was an essential step during recovery: "If we wait for those who are receiving aid, voluntarily to announce that they have enough, we'll never get done. They must be carried forward to independence in spite of themselves."[95] These steps reflected the "true test" of the "efficiency of the Red Cross responders."[96]

RED CROSS NURSES IN FLOOD RESPONSE

The number of nurses who responded to the Ohio floods varied from 228 to 238 to 268 Red Cross nurses.[97] (Bicknell put the number at 268.[98]) Mary Gladwin summed up the nurses' excitement in being able to respond in this way: "We rejoice over the broadening of women's lives and the increased opportunities for service which are coming to us. We look forward eagerly to a more active participation in civic and national affairs."[99]

Gladwin also found the response to Dayton "notable," because "with it came an official recognition of the value of the nurse in teaching the principles of hygiene and sanitation to the people and in prevention of disease."[100] Gladwin's belief in local and state Red Cross committees took on a "different light" when she valued the teaching and preparation they offered for emergencies, such as the Dayton flood, where the nurses' public health interventions likely averted an epidemic. She realized that preparation for future disasters should begin with increasing Red Cross nurse enrollment, but that each chapter also should prepare nurses in disaster response and relief, including "careful studies" of its application.[101]

What made the nursing role forged by these Red Cross nurses possible? Southwestern Ohio had a long history of women's participation in disaster response. Beginning at least by 1884 in Cincinnati, women provided material relief during floods, even to delivering extensive amounts of food directly to those in need, by way of small boats through floodwaters.[102] Only 5 years earlier, during the 1907 Ohio River flood, women's agencies had delivered 5,800 baskets of food, as well as clothing and coal.[103]

The Red Cross nurses also selected interventions that were consistent with traditional nursing roles, such as working in hospitals or dispensaries, or assuming conventional charitable roles like delivering food. In 1913, Red Cross nurses used these familiar roles in creative ways to achieve innovative outcomes.

CONCLUSION

The overwhelming suddenness of disaster has led modern societies to plan a sufficient response before the disaster event occurs. But, which approach is best? And which approaches must or must not be used? As an expression of charity for the least fortunate, for which everyone is vulnerable, disaster response reveals both societal expectations and social anxieties. Who can be saved? Should the rescuer be risked on behalf of the rescued? Can charity be offered today, but still encourage those helped to later regain independent self-support? Are there types of charity that do lead to pauperization? And, to what and to whom should public and private donations be directed?

When those active in disaster response return to their own homes and communities, and as they resume previous roles and responsibilities, they begin to reflect on their experiences to try to comprehend all they have seen, felt, and done. As the "severest test yet given to the Red Cross Nursing Service, the way in which it was met was regarded as a triumphant proof that organization was now in perfect running order."[104] Jane Delano realized that all of the planning, and all of the risks of the Red Cross nurse innovation, had paid off when she returned to her Washington office and met a Red Cross worker on the stairs, who asked: "How goes the nursing service?" Delano could only manage to answer, "It Works! It Works!"[105]

NOTES

1. Mary Gladwin, "The Red Cross in Dayton," *The American Journal of Nursing* 13, no. 9 (June 1913): 684–685; Mary E. Gladwin, "The Red Cross Nurse in Dayton," *The American Red Cross Magazine,* 8 no. 3 (July, 1913): 40–41; see also Lavinia Dock et al., *History of American Red Cross Nursing* (New York, NY: The Macmillan Company, 1922), 134

2. Earnest Bicknell, "The Flood of 1913," *American Red Cross Magazine* 8, no. 3 (July, 1913): 15–28.

3. Byron Deacon, *Disasters and the American Red Cross in Disaster Relief* (New York: Russell Sage Foundation, 1918), 69. See also: "Since the San Francisco Fire No Such Serious Calamity Had Occurred in the United States Until the Great Ohio Floods of 1913," The American National Red Cross. (1914). *Ninth Annual Report of the American National Red Cross* [for 1913]. House of Representatives, 63rd Congress, 2nd session, USGPO, Document No. 1028, Washington DC, p. 20.

4. A. H. Horton and H. J. Jackson, *The Ohio Valley Flood of March-April 1913 [U.S. Geologic Survey, Water Supply Paper 334]* (Washington, DC: GPO) (quoted p. 13).

5. Elli Bambakidis, *1913: Preserving the Memories of Dayton's Great Flood: Proceedings of the Symposium, October 22, 2002* (Dayton, OH: Dayton Metro Library, 2004), xiii. See also: "It Rained 3 Trillion Gallons," *Dayton Daily News*, March 26, 1972. Dayton Metro Library, archives, Dayton Collection, MS 016, series II, subseries 5: Box 5, folder 1, Newspapers, 1913–1983.

6. *Dayton: Being a Story of the Great Flood as Seen From the Delco Factory* (Detroit, MI: The Franklin Press, April 1913).

7. James H. Rodabaugh, "The 1913 Flood," *Museum Echoes* 32, no. 3 (March 1959): 19–22 (quote p. 21).

8. Deacon, *Disasters and the American Red Cross*, 70. Many observers commented on, and many photographs of the devastation in Dayton show, the wrecks and remnants of pianos or pianolas (player pianos), a focus of family life, household entertainment, and a contemporary symbol of family prestige.

9. Foster Rhea Dulles, *The American Red Cross: A History* (New York, NY: Harper Brothers Publishers, 1950), 110.

10. Deacon, *Disasters and the American Red Cross*, 102. Survivors took safety where they could: "One great tree with spreading boughs was so thickly populated with women and children in various colored clothing, that it looked like some great Christmas tree hung with huge dolls." *Dayton: Being a Story of the Great Flood*, 5.

11. Earnest Bicknell, *Pioneering With the Red Cross: Recollections of an Old Red Crosser* (New York, NY: The MacMillan Company, 1935), 17.

12. Dayton Citizens Relief Commission, *Report of the Special Board of Consulting Engineers to the Dayton Flood Relief Committee* (Dayton, OH: Flood Relief Committee, March 26, 1914). Dayton Metro Library, Archives, Dayton Collection, MS 016, series II, subseries 3, Box 1, folder 2 [pamphlets]: 11.

13. ANRC, *Ninth Annual Report*, 19.

14. Bicknell, *Pioneering With the Red Cross*, 226.

15. Dulles, *The American Red Cross*, 107.

16. ANRC, *Ninth Annual Report*, 19.

17. Marian Moser Jones, *The American Red Cross From Clara Barton to the New Deal* (Baltimore, MD: Johns Hopkins University Press, 2013), 112–115.

18. Dulles, *The American Red Cross*, 107.

19. Ibid. Charity Organization Societies (COS) were established in many cities, especially larger ones, during the late 19th and early 20th centuries to

coordinate charitable efforts in their communities. Local United Funds or United Way organizations in the 20th to the 21st centuries have shifted their purpose somewhat, but are direct descendants of the COS movement.

20. ANRC, *Seventh Annual Report of the American National Red Cross [for 1911]*. House of Representatives, 62nd Congress, 2nd session, USGPO, Document No. 661 (Washington, DC, 1912), 37; See also: *Eighth Annual Report NARC*, 22.

21. ANRC, *Partners in Service: American Red Cross and the Black Nurses Association*, accessed October 29, 2014, http://www.redcross.org/news/article/Partners-in-Service-American-Red-Cross-and-National-Black-Nurses-Association.

22. ANRC, *Seventh Annual Report* (1912), 35–36.

23. Ibid., 36–37.

24. ANRC, *Eighth Annual Report of the American National Red Cross [for 1912]*. House of Representatives, 63rd Congress, 1st session, USGPO, Document No. 49, Washington, DC, 1913, 2.

25. ANRC, *Ninth Annual Report of the American National Red Cross [for 1913]*. House of Representatives, 63rd Congress, 2nd session, USGPO, Document No. 1028, Washington, DC, 1914.

26. Ibid., 31.

27. Ibid.

28. Portia B. Kernodle, *The Red Cross Nurse in Action, 1882–1948* (New York, NY: Harper & Brothers Publishers, 1949), 55.

29. Deacon, *Disasters and the American Red Cross*, 73.

30. Ibid.

31. Ibid., 74.

32. Ibid., 78.

33. Ibid., 75.

34. ANRC (1913), 10. Four nurses were from Kansas City, and nine nurses arrived from New Orleans.

35. Deacon, *Disasters and the American Red Cross*, 164–167.

36. George W. Cullum and Wirt Robinson, Ed., "Biographical Register of the Officers and Graduates of the U.S. Military Academy at West Point, New York," *Supplement, VI-A [1910–1920]* (Saginaw, MI: Seeman and Peters, printers, 1923), 1889 (p. 535 quote).

37. Bicknell, *Pioneering With the Red Cross*, 222; "His domination, to some, seemed a sort of social dictatorship and his rule was not without dissenters."

38. Mary Greenwood, "The Work of the Cincinnati Local Red Cross Nursing Service Committee," *American Journal of Nursing* 13, no. 11 (August 1913), 831–837 (quoted p. 831).

39. Annie Laws, "Cincinnati Red Cross Chapter Active in Flood Relief," *American Red Cross Magazine* 8, no. 3 (July 1913): 70–76 (quoted pp. 70–71).

40. Dulles, *The American Red Cross*, 112–113; Laws, "Cincinnati Red Cross," 70–76.

41. "Cincinnati Men and Girls Aided Flood Relief Work: Male Students Went With Special Trains, While Gentle Sex Packed Food and Clothing at Home," *New York Times*, April 6, 1913, 1.

42. Letter to "Dear Friend" on the letterhead of the Ohio Woman Suffrage Association (April 17, 1913), written by Harriet Taylor Upton, the Ohio Memory Collection, a Collaboration Between the Ohio History Collection and the State Library of Ohio, accessed October 29, 2014, http://www .ohiomemory.org/cdm/ref/collection/p267401coll36/id/16502.

43. ANRC, *Ninth Annual Report*, 32.

44. Greenwood, "Work of the Cincinnati," 834.

45. Ibid.

46. ANRC, *Ninth Annual Report*, 31. One of the Red Cross nurses from Detroit brought her camera when she responded to the flood; the photograph album of her experiences in Dayton was donated by a descendent to Dayton History, the official historical organization for Dayton, and surrounding Montgomery County, Ohio.

47. "Special Train Arrives From Washington With Red Cross Supplies and Nurses," *Cincinnati Enquirer*, Sunday, March 30, 1913. Dayton Metro Library, Archives, Dayton Collection. MS 016, Series II, Box 2, folder 2; see also: Delano, "Red Cross Nursing Service" (1913), 131; and Dalano, "The Red Cross," 596.

48. Mary Gladwin, *The Red Cross and Jane Arminda Delano* (Philadelphia, PA, and London: W. B. Saunders Company, 1931), 59.

49. Ibid.

50. Greenwood, "Work of the Cincinnati," 836.

51. ANRC, *Ninth Annual Report*, 32.

52. Mark Bernstein, *Miami Valley Hospital: A Centennial History* (Dayton, OH: Miami Valley Hospital Society, 1990), 33–35. This hospital was originally known as the Protestant Deaconess Hospital; Crandall arrived to find the seven deaconesses "nearing exhaustion from overwork," p. 33; Crandall

was a major force behind implementation of the visiting nurse service of the Metropolitan Life Insurance Company, Ella Phillips Crandall, "A New Extension of Visiting Nursing," *American Journal of Nursing* 10, no. 4 (January 1910): 236–239. Crandall's deep understanding and family connections in Dayton included her father's service on the "city's health board" in the 1890s, Bernstein, p. 33. As superintendent of the Visiting Nurse Association of Cincinnati, Abbie Roberts's departure in response to the Dayton flood strained the remaining nurses at the agency; their work, and that of Roberts, was recognized in the Annual Report of the Secretary: "It is the secretary's privilege also to pay a public tribute to the magnificent work which was done by Miss Roberts, Miss Boddy, and all of their assistants, during the trying days of the flood; it was given to some of them to go out of the city and help in perhaps a more apparent way, but each and all who remained at home did her full share in doing extra work if not actual flood relief work, in order that others might remain out of the city. Trustees were more than satisfied at the way in which things move during her absence." Annual Report of the Secretary, *Fourth Annual Report*, The Visiting Nurse Association of Cincinnati, November 1, 1912, to October 1, 1913.

53. Mary E. Gladwin, "The Red Cross Nurse in Dayton," *The American Journal of Nursing*, 13, no. 9 (June, 1913): 683–686. See also: Mary E. Gladwin, "The Red Cross Nurses in Ohio," *The Public Health Nursing Quarterly* 5, no. 3 (July 1913): 106–114. Gladwin departed Akron, Ohio, on Friday afternoon, March 27, leaving behind the same storm's local impact and flooding as it passed through northern Ohio (p. 106). Her group of Red Cross nurses met a man returning from Dayton, "who assured us that there were thousands of nurses in Dayton with nothing to do except to attend balls at the National Cash Register factory," Mary E. Gladwin, "The Red Cross Nurses in Ohio," *The Public Health Nursing Quarterly*, 5, no. 3 (July, 1913):106–114.

54. Miami Valley Hospital Society of Dayton, Ohio, *Twenty-Fourth Annual Report for the Year Ending December 31, 1913* (1914). The Miami Valley Hospital reported that 1913 was its busiest year, with a 40% increase in admissions. "While this increased work was to a certain extent due to the catastrophe of March 25, following which many patients were admitted because of unfavorable conditions in their homes, to a greater extent we believe it represents a normal, healthy growth, due to an increasing demand for hospital service" (p. 20).

55. Deacon, *Disasters and the American Red Cross*, 76.

56. Ibid.

57. E. F. McCampbell, "Special Report on the Flood of March 1913," *Monthly Bulletin, Ohio State Board of Health* 3, no. 5 (May 1913): 103.

58. Deacon, *Disasters and the American Red Cross*, 77.

59. McCampbell, "Special Report," (1913): 399.

60. Gladwin, *The American Journal of Nursing*, June 1913, 684; Lavinia Dock, Sarah Pickett, et al., *History of American Red Cross Nursing* (New York, NY: The Macmillan Company, 1922), 134.

61. McCampbell, "Special Report" (1913): 303.

62. Dulles, *The American Red Cross*, 112–113.

63. Gladwin, "The Red Cross Nurses in Ohio," Mary E. Gladwin, "The Red Cross Nurses in Ohio," *The Public Health Nursing Quarterly*, 5, no. 3 (July, 1913):106–114. (1913): 111; George H. Wood, *Report of General George H. Wood on the Dayton Flood of 1913. Part One: March 25th to March 31st, 1913. Part Two: April 1st to May 6th, 1913*, http://www.daytonhistorybooks.com/page/page/1537473.htm

64. Deacon, *Disasters and the American Red Cross*, 217.

65. Ibid., 83–85.

66. Ibid., 89.

67. Ibid., 83–85 and 89.

68. Ibid., 89–91.

69. Ibid., 90–91.

70. Mabel Boardman, *Under the Red Cross Flag at Home and Abroad* (Philadelphia, PA, and London: J. B. Lippincott Company, 1915), 154. See also: Deacon, *Disasters and the American Red Cross*, 74.

71. Deacon, *Disasters and the American Red Cross*, 175.

72. ANRC, *Ninth Annual Report*, 18.

73. Deacon, *Disasters and the American Red Cross*, 217–219. From: Appendix B: General Policies and Regulations Governing a System of Disbursement and Accounting for the Ohio Flood Relief Commission Funds and the Funds of the American Red Cross to Be Expended in Ohio.

74. Ibid., 218.

75. Jones, *The American Red Cross*, 149–154.

76. Deacon, *Disasters and the American Red Cross*,102–103.

77. Ibid., 193.

78. Jones, *The American Red Cross*, 149–154.

79. Una M. Cadegan, "Where History Comes From: The Dayton Flood and Why We Remember," in Bambakidis, *1913: Preserving the Memories*, 3–7 (quoted p. 5).

80. Frank Quillin, *The Color Line in Ohio: A History of Race Prejudice in a Typical Northern State* (Ann Arbor, MI: George Wahr, 1913), 134.

81. Ibid., 138–139.

82. Ibid., 134.

83. Ibid.

84. David A. Gerber, *Black Ohio and the Color Line: 1860–1915* (Urbana, IL: University of Illinois Press, 1976), 291.

85. Margaret Meenan, "Mother, New Dad Saved: Men Swam With Children to Safety," *Dayton Daily News* (March 27, 1962), 14. Dayton Metro Library, Archives, Dayton Collection, MS 016, series II, subseries 5: Box 5, folder 1, Newspapers, 1913–1983.

86. Bicknell, *Pioneering With the Red Cross*, 223.

87. C. Bock, *History of the Miami Flood Control Project* (Dayton, OH: The Miami Conservancy District, 1918), 21.

88. "Lest We Forget," March 25, 1947. Observance of the 34th Anniversary of the 1913 Flood and the Work of the Conservancy District. Dayton Metro Library, Archives, Dayton Collection, MS 016, series II, subseries 3, Box 3, folder 1, 1–3. See also: Dayton Citizens Relief Commission, 2–4.

89. ANRC, *Ninth Annual Report*, 21.

90. American National Red Cross. (1914). *Ninth Annual Report of the American National Red Cross* [for 1913]. House of Representatives, 63rd Congress, 2nd session, USGPO, Document No. 1028, Washington DC.

91. ANRC, *Ninth Annual Report*, 21.

92. Ibid., 18.

93. Ibid.

94. Boardman, p. 167.

95. Ibid., p. 168.

96. Ibid., p. 167.

97. Deacon, *Disasters and the American Red Cross*, 77.

98. Bicknell, *Pioneering With the Red Cross*, 215.

99. Mary E. Gladwin, "Lessons From the Flood Relief Work," *American Journal of Nursing* 13, no. 11 (August 1913), 830.

100. Ibid.

101. Ibid., 830–831.

102. Third District Society of Associated Charities of Cincinnati, *Fifth Annual Report* (Cincinnati, OH: Carnahan and Company, Printers, 1884), 4–5. In the period February 7–15, 1884, the "ladies" of the Society distributed "14,260 loaves of bread, 1890 pounds of coffee, 55 barrels of meat, 22 barrels of beans, 22 barrels of rice, and quantities of flour, potatoes, onions, crackers, etc." (p. 5). During the 1884 flood, other district committees also provided assistance, particularly of food. A similar response occurred to the 1907 flood. See also: *Report of the Cincinnati Flood Relief Committee, January and March, CE 1907* (Cincinnati, OH: Joseph Birning Printing Company, Power Building, Cincinnati, OH).

103. Cincinnati Flood Relief Committee Report. Although the main committee consisted only of men, an all-female committee, whose honorary chairman was male, provided shelter and relief supplies in the Cumminsville district. Mrs. E. D. Sefton, chairman, took encouragement from women's relief roles during the 1884 flood. She believed "The main thing is to distribute the relief in the right direction, so that the worthy ones get it." The women's work was coordinated with that of the nursing sisters serving Cincinnati's Good Samaritan Hospital, who offered nursing and medical assistance, supplies, and use of their facilities.

104. Dock et al., *History*, 134–135.

105. Ernest P. Bicknell, *Pioneering With the Red Cross: Recollections of an Old Red Crosser* (New York: The MacMillan Company, 1935).

CHAPTER 4

The Alaskan Influenza Epidemic, 1918 to 1919

Maria Gilson DeValpine and Arlene W. Keeling

The influenza epidemic reached Alaska through the regular channels of transportation and affected practically all of the coast of Alaska.... Those most affected were the natives.... We have at one place alone 90 orphans...I have authorized the sending of relief expeditions for the gathering up of these orphans...I have authorized the purchase of provisions for the indigent natives because they are not allowed to travel and trap...as a matter of fact, most of them are dead. I have authorized $107,000. The territory had a small fund of $5,000 for the control of epidemics but that was gone in no time at all. If it were merely for the relief of the white population, I should not come to Congress for one cent...but when it comes to what we consider wards of the Nation, who are not taxpayers and who, in other parts of the U.S. are attended to by the government, I consider that our small treasury should not be diminished by the sum necessary.... We cannot handle it ourselves; it has gone beyond our control.[1]

In January 1919, Alaskan Governor Thomas Riggs, Jr., appealed to the House Congressional Committee on Appropriations to help the northernmost territory of the United States respond to a deadly influenza epidemic.[2] After outlining the situation in the aforesaid statement, Riggs went on to ask the federal government to appropriate $200,000 to help Alaska, noting that the territory's entire medical relief fund was already budgeted to maintain its five hospitals and the few physicians and nurses there.

What ensued was a lengthy debate on the role of local versus federal government and their respective responsibilities during a major epidemic. The subcommittee chairman argued that it was "a matter the Red Cross should take up," because the Red Cross had raised $102,000,000 in the last drive and "did not exactly know what they would do with it."[3] In the end, after Riggs had argued successfully that the Native Alaskans were "our own American people, who belong to us," and that the Indian Health Services had been granting funds to support *other* native populations, the subcommittee agreed to appropriate $100,000 for the Alaskan territory.[4]

Riggs needed the federal government's help. A deadly flu had been devastating towns and villages throughout the territory since October 20, 1918, when the steamship *Victoria* docked at Nome, a small town on the coast of the Seward Peninsula. With winter closing in, it was the last time in autumn that the *Victoria* would sail to Nome. The ship carried not only passengers from Seattle but also the mail—to be distributed by dogsled to the native villages and in the remote area.[5] Unbeknownst to anyone, the ship also brought a mutated and highly contagious influenza A virus—one that had been wreaking havoc across the United States since early September. Called the "Spanish flu," the deadly virus had struck Boston, New York, and Philadelphia in rapid succession and then, following the railroad lines, spread south and west across the country, exploding in Seattle during the fourth week of September.[6]

The 1918 flu was also called "the purple death" because its victims often succumbed to a fulminating acute respiratory distress syndrome; their faces turned purple and blood poured from their noses and mouths. Later referred to as the "single most fatal event in human history," the 1918 virus killed an estimated 50 million people worldwide, most of whom were healthy young adults, aged 20 to 30 years.[7] Indigenous and colonized peoples suffered inordinately in the pandemic, and in Alaska, an estimated 5,000 natives died, compared to only 500 White people. This disproportionate effect of the epidemic on Native Alaskans was the result of the complex interplay of environmental factors, subsistence living conditions, and native cultural beliefs—leaving a situation that was beyond control for the organizations arriving too late on the scene. Preventive measures, including travel restrictions and quarantine, were marginally effective in the setting of this highly contagious, rapidly transmitted virus. Ventilation, food, and fluids—and in Alaska, warmth—were key to survival at a time when nursing care was the only available treatment.

This chapter traces the influenza epidemic in coastal Alaska and describes a case study of contentious public–private relationships in Bristol Bay, a place so remote that the influenza did not reach until 1919. It is a story of collaboration and conflict. Collaboration among territorial or protectorate governments, private enterprise, the Red Cross, and the U.S. Public Health Service (USPHS) was key to mitigating the disaster in these immunologically naive, underresourced, and often disenfranchised populations. Yet, not all groups cooperated.[8] This chapter also identifies conflict among the organizations.

THE EPIDEMIC

Early in the fall of 1918, having been warned of the seriousness of the epidemic from health officials in Seattle, Washington, Alaska's Governor Thomas Riggs stationed U.S. marshals at all Alaskan ports, trail heads, and the mouths of rivers. His goal was to ensure that travelers did not bring the disease into any of the territory's remote communities. He also imposed a marine quarantine of 14 days on any ship and its crew entering Alaskan ports.[9] So, when the *Victoria* docked in Nome after being at sea for 9 days, members of her crew were quarantined in a hospital for an additional 5 days. In addition, postal workers in Nome took additional precautions by fumigating the mail before it was delivered by dogsled to the outlying communities.[10]

Despite the precautions, on October 29, a man who had been working in the hospital during the quarantine period became ill. Meanwhile, the mailman, traveling by dogsled to the remote villages, spread the deadly influenza to Native Alaskans along the way. By the end of the year, 35% to 40% of the Native Alaskan populations in villages from Nome to Shishmaref (on the northern tip of the Bering Strait) were dead.[11] Meanwhile, Shishmaref—having been effectively quarantined—escaped the epidemic altogether.

Map of Alaska.

Other coastal towns did not escape the epidemic, however. The flu reached the southeastern Alaskan city of Ketchikan in October of 1918, arriving midmonth on ships from Seattle and Vancouver. Almost one third of the community succumbed, although only 16 would die from the illness.[12] On October 22, with the report of six cases in Ketchikan, the city council closed all public places. Four days later, after the onset of "two dozen more cases," city leaders set up a temporary hospital in the basement of the Methodist Church.[13] Within weeks, the epidemic spread all along the Alaskan coasts, attacking Juneau, Anchorage, Homer, Cordova, Kodiak, and small settlements on the Aleutian Islands.

On November 7, with many dead and the risk increasing, Governor Riggs issued a special directive to all Alaskan natives, urging them to stay at home and avoid public gatherings. It was an order in direct contrast to the natives' traditional value of community. As a result, many ignored it, continuing to gather in public places. Others—fearful of hospitals, or too sick to move from their homes and too sick to make a fire—froze to death. Some, too weak to tend their traps or hunt for food, died of starvation. Entire communities were laid waste, and when the adults died, children were orphaned. Meanwhile, their parents' bodies were left to freeze or be ravaged by sled dogs that had turned feral.

A COLLABORATIVE RESPONSE

Throughout the United States, the need for collaboration between the states and the federal government—as well as among established public and private organizations—had been evident immediately after the epidemic overwhelmed Boston in early September. Thousands of people had succumbed to the flu, hospitals were overcrowded, and nurses were in short supply because many of them were serving in Europe for World War I. On September 14, 1918, the USPHS had first asked the American Red Cross for nurses to help control the spread of the epidemic. By September 24, the director of nursing, Clara Noyes, had issued a telegram from American Red Cross headquarters, asking the local chapters across the country to organize "home defense: nurses to meet the present epidemic."[14] Three days later, Noyes sent another message, directing the local chapters to organize within their divisions "one or more mobile units of ten to fifteen nursing personnel to be sent to other localities if necessary."[15]

Communications had been effective: Across the country, local Red Cross volunteers, including many society women, were making

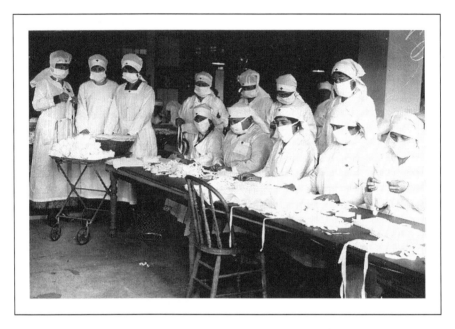

Boston Red Cross volunteers assemble masks at Camp Devens, Massachusetts.
Courtesy of the National Archives.

the masks mandated by the USPHS, while Red Cross home defense nurses—baby nurses, school nurses, tuberculosis nurses, and visiting and public health nurses—were responding to the needs of the communities. By the time a call reached Seattle asking for volunteers to help in Alaska, local Red Cross nurses were ready to join the effort. Members of the Alaskan Red Cross, organized in 1910, were also ready.[16]

In December 1918, 10 physicians and 10 nurses, carrying medical supplies furnished by the Northwest Division of the Red Cross, left Seattle for a relief expedition to Alaska. They traveled under the command of Dr. Emil Kurlish, captain of the USPHS.[17] The expedition members spent a month in Alaska, returning in late December or early January in time for Dr. Kurlish to record their activities in his January 18, 1919, report, which also documented the involvement of the Alaskan Red Cross chapters. He mentioned that they were "most active throughout the epidemic," not only in cooperating with Kurlish's expeditions but in "rendering needed assistance on their own account."[18]

Meanwhile, Governor Riggs sent relief parties into the Seward Peninsula. As he noted in a later report to Congress, he had been sending "supplies and medicines up five to six hundred miles by dog team" to outlying native villages. He had also been collecting orphans, 90 of whom he brought back to Nome.[19]

By January 1919, however, winter had set in and the next relief expeditions could not travel until spring. During that time, Alaskans were left to battle the epidemic on their own. In one case, when no nurses could be found, a local schoolteacher volunteered to work in the temporary hospital in Ketchikan, at Brevig Mission. As there were hundreds of orphans, the church was used as an orphanage. Meanwhile, hundreds of Native Alaskans died, their bodies frozen in place in their *barabaras*, the small structures of peat sod and mud in which whole families lived.

QUARANTINE EFFORTS FOR "INDIAN FLU" IN BRISTOL BAY

Due to its extremely remote geography, Bristol Bay, a salmon-fishing bay in southwest Alaska, missed the fall 1918 wave of the influenza pandemic entirely. The commissioner of health had taken extensive precautions to prevent the spread of influenza, requiring permits for travel between villages, closing schools, and prohibiting all public gatherings. In December 1918, Linus Hiram French, the acting assistant commissioner of health in the region, had sent a series of orders to surrounding villages and territories, further limiting travel.[20] To the teachers of the Bureau of Education, Linus French's directions were clear:

> I think it would be a good plan for you to post a notice on each of the trails going into Togiak about a mile from the village—like this: "All persons are forbidden to enter or leave this village, or to remove this notice. 'By Order of the Board of Health.'"[21]

Quarantine would prove to be effective; it did more to stop the spread of the deadly virus than anything else. The USPHS sent formal quarantine notices to all the villages in Bristol Bay and the Alaskan Territory, along with recommendations for treatment of the flu.[22] In addition to forbidding entrance to the villages, health officials closed schools and banned church services.

After several months, when the "Indian Flu" did not arrive in Bristol Bay, officials relaxed the ban on public gatherings and reopened the schools, although they still required individuals to obtain permits for travel.[23] The church services ban was revoked on the request of Fred Madsen of Naknek, who wrote to Dr. French that there was "no sign of anything like the flue [sic]" and asked if the natives could "have Church on Easter as they have been after me right along to have church."[24] Since Russian Orthodox was the main religion of the Native Alaskans in the region, churches reopened in time for the spring celebrations of Orthodox Easter. According to one woman, Father Hodavisky sailed from Unalaska to hold services at the newly reopened Orthodox Church in the Nushagak. Virtually all the adult natives in Nushagak Bay attended the Easter services and the influenza epidemic began immediately afterward. Because the flu was already raging in Unalaska, it was believed that Father Hodavisky brought the disease with him.[25] By mid-May 1919, hundreds of Native Alaskans were dead, dying, or orphaned from the flu in every village in Bristol Bay.[26] Later, in his 1920 report to Congress, Governor Riggs estimated that virtually all of the 800 to 1,000 native adults in Nushagak Bay perished during the summer of 1919, leaving 238 orphans.[27]

HELP ARRIVES

In late April 1919, the *Unalga*, a Coast Guard revenue cutter, arrived in Unalaska on its annual cruise of Alaskan Northern Waters. The ship was staffed with Navy nurses and physicians and provisioned to feed and care for any Native Alaskans afflicted with the flu.[28] In a terse diary entry, Navy Lieutenant E. A. Coffin noted what happened when they arrived: "*Unalga* feeding and nursing the entire town and burying the dead."[29] Later, more help arrived aboard the revenue cutters, *Bear, Marblehead*, and *Vicksburg*. These ships came in May and June, bringing Red Cross, USPHS, and more Navy nurses and doctors, as well as additional food and supplies.[30]

Meanwhile, the situation in Bristol Bay was dire. On May 19, 1919, the Alaska Packers' Association (APA) steamer *Nushagak* arrived at

Clark's Point, immediately followed by the *Star of Iceland*. Their help was needed. According to the APA Nushagak Station cannery medical officer, "the influenza had been epidemic throughout the Nushagak district for about a week"; "practically all of the residents, both white and natives," were ill and a "considerable number" had died already. "Medical supplies, food and fuel were scarce."[31] Other APA medical officers wrote that "the few natives not sick were sitting listlessly around in the cold dirty huts…only waiting resignedly to get sick, as is their custom when epidemics are raging." Whites were also suffering and dying.[32]

The disease had spread across Nushagak and Bristol Bay by the time the APA arrived. The peak of the epidemic can be seen in the daily mortality toll collected by the Kvichak Station cannery superintendent J. C. Bell and his medical officer, Isaac B. Wilson, at the village of Koggiung.[33]

Mother and child, 1905.
Courtesy of the Library of Congress.

The epidemic arrived at Kvichak Bay on May 22, 1919.[34] Three days later, Mr. Swift of the Libby, McNeill & Libby Cannery wrote to Dr. French: "I understand the Cutter *Unalga* has two Doctors on Board and would suggest that you wire to the Captain for help and that quickly or the Natives will all be dead."[35] The cutter *Unalga*, however, remained in Unalaska until mid-June, failing to answer this and several other calls for help from Bristol Bay.

Other villages were also left on their own. Nushagak Station Medical Officer E. B. Robinson found Ekuk village, a "small place in a deplorable condition," and left food and supplies "in care of Mrs. Hansen, herself formerly a trained nurse" to care for the remaining Natives."[36] Mrs. Hansen, a graduate of Providence Hospital Nursing School in Seattle, then worked as an unpaid nurse in Ekuk.[37] She had earlier traveled to Bristol Bay with her husband, a cannery supervisor at the Libby, McNeill & Libby Cannery.

THE ORPHANS

Locating the orphans of natives who had died of influenza before the children starved from lack of attention was imperative. Fred Blonde, an APA winter watchman who lost his wife to influenza, was assigned with APA nurse Edward Smith to care for the orphans found by Captain Olaf Hemming in late May. According to their report: "Most pitiful was the condition of the poor starved and filthy children...covered in reeking vermin...crying, huddled about their dead [parents]." They set up hospital tents with orphanage facilities, and remodeled existing buildings to accommodate the orphans.[38]

At the same time, the APA was caring for orphans from native villages surrounding the cannery facilities, Kanakanak Hospital received orphans from around the bay.[39] Dr. French and nurses Mary Conley and Rhoda Ray provided care for the orphans at the hospital. Meanwhile, with the close of the fishing season in late August, cannery officials brought their orphans to Kanakanak as well, subsequently closing up the canneries and returning to Seattle and San Francisco for the winter. The Kanakanak orphans—the remnants of three Native Alaskan and American Indian tribes in Bristol Bay—would eventually repopulate the region, overcoming ancient tribal conflicts as they grew to adulthood.

THE AFTERMATH

In addition to the appropriations allotted specifically to Governor Riggs, Congress provided other funds to the USPHS to send nurses and physicians to Alaska to help with the relief effort. The USPHS planned to send medical help in conjunction with the Coast Guard's annual survey of the Alaska coast.[40] In 1919, the American Red Cross authorized and paid for 12 nurses to join the annual expedition. These nurses accompanied Drs. McGillycuddy, Woodruff, and Fielder on the Coast Guard revenue cutters to Alaska. On June 3, 12 nurses and five doctors left San Francisco, and sailed on the *Marblehead* to Bremerton, Washington, where they "obtained sweaters and woolen socks for the nurses." After a voyage in "continuous storms," the party landed at Unalaska (in the Aleutian Islands) on June 16, 1919, after the height of the flu epidemic had ravaged that area. The doctors and nurses divided into small groups, transferred to several different cutters, and visited coastal villages, going "hut to hut" to assess the situation.[41] What they discovered was gruesome. According to the Red Cross report, the "most deplorable conditions were found"—"heaps of dead bodies on the shelves and floors of the huts"—the majority of cases "too far decomposed to be handled" and therefore "dragged out and buried."[42]

Red Cross Unit 3, comprised of Drs. Fielder and Woodruff and nurses Nichols and McCue, went to Naknek on the eastern side of the Bristol Bay, where they found "the epidemic over...very few adult natives" and 15 homeless orphans. There a "four-room house had been turned into an orphanage under the supervision of one of the employees of the Packing Company...while a small well-equipped hospital under the command of the Company Surgeon" provided care for the sick.[43] After visiting several other small villages, and finding more orphans, the relief parties returned to the ship on June 29 after 13 days of travel.

COLLABORATION, CONFLICT,
AND COMMUNICATION PROBLEMS

During the influenza response, three major organizations were involved in the rescue of the natives in Bristol Bay: the Coast Guard (including the Red Cross staff), the Bureau of Education Territorial Hospital, and the APA (representing the largest share of the salmon industry in Bristol Bay). Each organization had different expectations of its role in the rescue, and relationships among the organizations were quite difficult at times. In his annual report to the Department of Commerce, Warden Shirley Baker of the Bureau of Fisheries spoke of the Coast Guard and the Red Cross efforts as "the saddest repudiation of a benevolent intent,"[44] due to the substantial costs, late arrival, and limited rescue efforts on the part of those parties. Indeed, the arrival of the Coast Guard cutters *Unalga*, *Marblehead*, and *Vicksburg* in Bristol Bay near the end of the epidemic in that region presented the first of many problems for the rescue effort.

The relationships among the APA canneries, the Territorial Bureau of Education Hospital, the Coast Guard, and the Red Cross were difficult, and the problems were many. Some problems were caused by response team members coming down with the flu; other problems were due to ineffective or delayed responses. At Kanakanak Hospital in Dillingham, Dr. French and nurses Ray and Conley were ill with the flu and thus were unable to provide any assistance. They also were emotionally exhausted, having "had more sickness and deaths" than they could handle. Dr. French requested assistance from the Coast Guard revenue cutter *Unalga*, telling the APA, "have no help here available to send....We have the same conditions at Nushagak with probably fifty deaths. I will wire immediately for assistance from outside." Meanwhile, the APA superintendent at Kvichak Station had already wired the Coast Guard, asking Captain Dodge of the *Unalga* for help and "received no reply."[45]

Communication and response in the extremely large Alaskan territory were also problematic. On June 3, 1919, the Seward Red Cross contacted the superintendent of the APA Naknek Station asking for details of the epidemic and offering assistance. By this time, the APA had already made arrangements to care for the orphans at the hospitals set up in native villages around the canneries. Thus, the APA wired back that "children at Naknek were being well cared for" and assistance was not requested. Although help was needed nearby in the village of Ugashik, the APA superintendent did not request assistance from the Red Cross in Seward. He assumed that he could get help quicker from the Coast Guard cutter, the *Unalga*, anchored in the nearby Bristol Bay rather than wait for the Red Cross to send assistance by sea (a 1,100-mile voyage) or by land, which required a 300-mile portage across Lake Iliamna. Because time was of the essence, he turned to the *Unalga* for help. He wired the *Unalga* requesting assistance for the Ugashik village, writing: "can you assist at this station? We can handle situation here at Naknek at present." He later reported: "no answer was ever received to this message."[46] The Red Cross, however, sent nurses by the land route later in June to assist in the Ugashik village.

On June 23, 1919, the Kvichak APA Station Superintendent J. C. Bell received a report of 20 unburied bodies and the possibility of orphans at Lake Iliamna, a 4-day, 82-mile journey upriver from Bristol Bay. The Coast Guard cutters, *Unalga*, *Marblehead*, and *Vicksburg*, had arrived 4 days earlier into the bay region with Navy and Red Cross nurses and doctors. Because the APA did not have low draft vessels suitable for river travel, the APA superintendent requested the Coast Guard to make the journey up the river. Lieutenant Fielder and Dr. Woodruff took a boat and provisions, but returned after 30 hours, noting that no bodies had been found. Bell requested confirmation of the situation from U.S. Territorial Commissioner Neilsen and personnel from the Libby, McNeill & Libby Cannery, who replied: "at Herman's Trading Station there was one woman in tent between the bank and village. Lying under a raincoat were a man and a boy and many lying on the bank. Also there were four or five bodies six or seven miles above Reindeer Station."[47] The report of the local agencies contradicted that of the Coast Guard.

By late June, the Coast Guard's unresponsiveness and the APA's lack of authority strained the collaboration of the agencies to the breaking point. Dissent over the handling of the dead bodies upriver brought the matter to a head, and Superintendent Bell "in presence of ... witnesses," informed them that "without authority I assumed the quarantining and policing of the district," took "responsibility of care of the sick, burial of the dead, cleaning, clothing" and supported the orphans, "feeding the entire village and other work of similar nature." He then "requested that as the *Marblehead* expedition represented the United States Government, the entire proposition would be turned over to it, that the Alaska Packers' Association's employees would be taken away from the village and from the Isolation Hospital, the food patrol stopped and from then on the entire relief to be handled by the Government." Angrily, he told the Coast Guard staff that "they were not serious in their intentions to carry out the relief work." In response, Lieutenant Fielder assured Superintendent Bell that "if he could personally visit his ship and consult with the Commander" that they would promptly institute measures to take this situation off his hands.[48]

Despite these promises, the APA did not hear from the Coast Guard again. The revenue cutters set sail in late June, leaving Bristol Bay and returning to Unalaska in the Aleutian Islands. Subsequently, APA Superintendent Bell learned that Lieutenant Fielder, eager to have the Coast Guard leave the area, sent the following telegram to the *Marblehead*: "Conditions on the Kvichak River satisfactory. Natives dead and buried. No children. Conditions warrant our return to ship." In a scathing letter on July 5, 1919, Bell reported to the APA headquarters in San Francisco, "We have not been able to fathom whether conditions were satisfactory to them or to the natives who are dead and buried. At any rate that is the last we have heard of them. *And as usual the job is up to the Alaska Packers Association*" (emphasis original).[49]

Later, when Governor Riggs requested the APA to estimate the cost of its rescue efforts so that Congress could reimburse the expenses, the APA refused to do so. As a result, the company was never reimbursed.[50] The APA did, however, bring 50 tons of provisions from San Francisco at the beginning of the fishing season, distributed food and supplies to the natives, and reprovisioned in mid-season to further supplement the rescue.[51]

THE ISSUE OF RACISM

Despite offers of assistance and treatment for the natives, racism was widespread among the rescue groups. APA medical officers consistently described the natives as "indolent," and immunologically inferior, claiming that if they had had "one drop of White blood," it would have been sufficient to ward off disease.[52] Others described the natives as "resigned to their fate according to their custom." Despite these overt racist comments, the APA's attitudes did not seem to affect their care for the natives. Indeed, the APA and the hospital staff expended superhuman efforts to save the Native Alaskans in Bristol Bay. U.S. Commissioner Neilsen, who had lived in the region for many years and spoke the native language, negotiated the quarantine, and arranged care for the orphans and burial of the dead. In other cases, prejudice *did* affect care. For example, in one instance, the Coast Guard revenue cutter nurses refused to care for the starving and maggot-infested native children, claiming that they were "too dirty." Worse, according to one report, some of the physicians and nurses from the revenue cutters were "looking around the village for souvenirs and furs," returning to the cutter "without having done any relief work at all."[53] In another instance, Lieutenant Coffin of the *Unalga* documented the long-standing mistreatment of the natives by his ship's commander, who "collected everything he liked" of souvenirs and furs from them. According to Coffin, "the people were afraid of him and felt they had to let him have the things he selected."[54]

COLLABORATION BETWEEN THE ALASKAN RED CROSS AND THE BUREAU OF INDIAN AFFAIRS NURSES

There were several nurses working in the region who collaborated well and it may be instructive to examine the context of that situation to understand why. Not uncommonly, nurses hired for the season by the salmon canneries went to work at Territorial Bureau of Education Hospitals in coastal Alaska (later the Bureau of Indian Affairs [BIA]). Nurses working at the hospitals frequently moved between facilities in Bethel, Kanakanak, Kotzebue, Nome, and Juneau.[55] Among these were several nurses who were all alumnae of the Providence Hospital Nursing School.

Edna Morris and Catherine Miller, 1917 graduates of Providence, worked for the Alaska Chapter of the Red Cross. Their paths crossed with their former classmates during the epidemics, first in the village of Ekuk and then at the Kanakanak Hospital in Dillingham. Later, writing about her service, Catherine Miller recorded that she and Edna Morris traveled via ship across the Cook Inlet, and then by dogsled, foot, and fishing boat across the Alaska Peninsula, where they were surprised to find their classmate, Christine Hanson, working at the Libby, McNeill & Libby cannery, where her husband was the cannery supervisor. "She told us that the Indian village had suffered severely and that she, with the assistance of a couple of cannery hands, had devoted all their efforts to nursing those sick with influenza…all proper means and materials were lacking to them; and their treatment of patients consisted mainly in the use of mustard plasters." The Red Cross nurses proceeded to Dillingham and found "two other graduates of Providence, Miss Rhoda Ray and Miss Mayme Connelly, both employed in the hospital under the supervision of Dr. French."[56]

Each of these nurses had one or more shared contexts with the others: working for the same organization, graduating from the same nursing school, and finding themselves in the same underresourced geographic area. In addition, all of the nurses were Westerners and residents of Washington state. These established relationships with their shared contexts, as well as professional and cultural similarities, may have made these nurses' collaboration during the disaster a more natural response than that experienced by the public and private organizations involved.

Working together, the nurses managed the entire hospital without janitorial, kitchen, or laundry staff. As Catherine Miller described it: The Red Cross nurses "took charge of the patients in the hospital and Miss Ray and Miss Connelly took charge of the orphans." Cooperation and plain hard work were essential. According to Miller's account: "we girls met this emergency by devoting two days of each week to the wash tub. This was really no small matter—to launder the clothing of fifty or more children besides all of the hospital linen."[57] In late August, when the epidemic was over and they were assured there would be no recurrence, the Red Cross nurses left, taking nurse Conley with them.[58]

CONCLUSION

The lack of access to medical and nursing care in the isolated, remote regions of the Alaskan territory, a dependence on subsistence living, the freezing temperatures, the Native Alaskan culture of community, and the severity and virulence of the disease were all part of an interdependent cascade of factors that resulted in devastation to the native population in the 1918 and 1919 influenza pandemic in Alaska.[59] The epidemic also gave rise to what Drabek and McEntire call "emergent phenomena"—in this case, interorganizational collaboration to meet the demands of the epidemic.[60] The response to the epidemic came from various groups: health officials; local, territorial, and federal governments; the military; private shipping lines and cannery facilities; and Red Cross volunteers, physicians, and nurses. They would have worked well together if they had created a network of organizations prior to the occurrence of the epidemic and had relied on patterns of communication previously established and tested by groups in the lower 48 states.

The epidemic in Bristol Bay had its own set of unusual circumstances. The onset of the flu in the Bay region took them completely by surprise. The quarantine had been relaxed in the belief that the epidemic was over. In addition, religious celebrations in the region that required a priest from a flu-infested area firmly established the fact that the natives had essentially a single source that exposed them to the flu virus, which spread around Bristol Bay in less than 2 weeks. The timely arrival of the fully provisioned APA meant that, although the disease was still rampant, starvation could be ameliorated and orphans identified and cared for. In contrast, the Coast Guard—although provisioned and directed to intervene—destroyed any potential collaboration and caused interagency conflict through staff misbehavior, lackluster efforts, poor accountability, and its delayed arrival (well after the peak of the epidemic).

Given the speed with which the flu spread through the villages in Bristol Bay, there is no evidence that improved interagency collaboration would have mitigated the deaths in the bay region. Yet, the frustration of those involved was acute. With the tiny territorial hospital over-whelmed and the Coast Guard arriving too late and too uninterested to do much good, the efforts from the private sector—the canning indus-try—can be applauded. Indeed, the APA channeled all its resources from salmon operations to the rescue efforts, giving over virtually all of its facilities, provisions, and staff to the rescue of the natives. Clearly, the small number of hospitals throughout the territory, with only eight physicians and 11 nurses, could not handle the epidemic alone, and the local governments could not afford the cost of the response without help from private entities and the federal government. The challenge was to rapidly mount the response effort, ensure the collaboration of all parties, and do so in a harsh geographic and unique cultural setting with few resources.

NOTES

1. Thomas Riggs, "Influenza in Alaska and Puerto Rico," in *Hearings Before the Subcommittee of House Committee on Appropriations, 65th Congress* (Washington, DC: Government Printing Services, 1919), 3–18 (quoted pp. 3–4). See also Excerpts Hearings on Alaska Influenza Devastation, "Grassroots Science," accessed May 11, 2009, http://ykalaska.wordpress. com/2007/01/03excerpts-hearings-on-alaska-influenza-devastation.

2. Thomas Riggs, "Influenza in Alaska and Puerto Rico," *Hearings Before the Subcommittee of House Committee on Appropriations, 65th Congress* (Washington, DC: Government Printing Services, 1919), 3–6.

3. Ibid., 6.

4. Ibid.

5. Matt Ganley, "The Dispersal of the 1918 Influenza Virus on the Seward Peninsula in Alaska: An Ethno Historic Reconstruction," *International Journal of Circumpolar Health* 96 (1998): 247–251. See also, "Influenza Hits Alaska People," *Seattle Chronicle* 113, no. 116 (November 8, 1918): 9.

6. Alfred W. Crosby, *Americas' Forgotten Pandemic: The Influenza of 1918.* 2nd ed. (Boston, MA: Cambridge University Press, 2003), 92–94. Although much has been written about the 1918 influenza pandemic, the story of the medical and nursing response in Alaska, and local government and private enterprise's attempt to mitigate risk to the people of Alaska, has received only minimal

attention. In fact, most of the Alaskan story came to light only after 1997 when scientists John Hultin and Jeffrey Taubenberger exhumed the remains of Native Alaskans buried deep in the permafrost beneath Brevig Mission, a small village just north of Nome. Using tissue from Native Alaskans who had died in the epidemic, the scientists identified the 1918 influenza strain as H1N1—a virulent strain of flu responsible for what the natives called—"The Big Sickness." See also, Arlene W. Keeling, " 'Alert to the Necessities of the Emergency': U.S. Nursing During the 1918 Influenza Pandemic," *Public Health Reports* 3, no. 125 (2010 Supplement): 105–112.

7.   Jeffrey Taubenberger, "The Once and Future Pandemic," *Public Health Reports* 3, no. 125 (2010 Supplement): 16–26.

8.   Crosby, *Americas' Forgotten Pandemic*, 238–263.

9.   "Alaska," *The Great Pandemic*, pp. 1–2, accessed January 21, 2013, http://www.flu.gov/pandemic/history/1918/your_state/pacific/alaska/index.html.

10.   Ganley, "The Dispersal of the 1918 Influenza Virus," 248.

11.   Ibid., 249. In Nome, 160 of 200 Native Alaskans died from flu by November 25; by the end of the epidemic, more than 1,000 people died in Nome, 90% of whom were natives. At Cape Wooley, most of the adult residents of the village died within 6 days of the first case. In Mary's Igloo, 68 of 127 villagers died in November alone. That month, in Brevig Mission, 72 of the 120 natives died in less than 10 days. Wales, the largest native community, lost 172 of its 325 residents.

12.   Dave Kiffer, "When 'the Great Influenza' Shut Down Ketchikan," *Stories in the News* 11 (November 26, 2008): 1–6, accessed September 28, 2010, http://www.sitnews.us/Kiffer/Influenza/112608_1918.html.

13.   Ibid., 3.

14.   "The Influenza Epidemic," *NARA College Park*, Box 689, epidemic, 803.11 (1918): 1–3 (quoted p. 1).

15.   Ibid., 2.

16.   Shirley Baker to the Commissioner of Fisheries, November 26, 1919. *Records of the U.S. Fish and Wildlife Service*, RG 22, National Archives at Anchorage, AK: 2. Red Cross nurses from Seward would later collaborate with hospital nurses, the native people, and Nurse Hanson at Ekuk village in Bristol Bay in 1919. Warden Baker of the Department of Fisheries, in his report to the Department of Commerce, extolled the nurses' virtues in the rescue effort:

In addition to Misses Conley and Ray [Bureau of Education Territorial School Service nurses], who did strikingly effective service and exhibited a devotion to duty of a very high order, and which would have won them medals if performed by them in the service of their country on the field of battle, Miss Edna Morris and Miss Katherine Miller [Alaska Chapter, American Red Cross], sent to Bristol Bay by the Bureau of Education and the Territorial Government, also rendered service worthy of special mention and high praise.

17. "Alaska Handled Flu With Efficiency and Dispatch," *Report of the Northwest Division of the ARC*, Box 689, CP-NARA, 803.11 epidemic flu. His report contained the barest of facts: The U.S. Forestry Service "carried a doctor, a nurse and supplies to Prince of Wales Island where they were badly needed." He also noted that Juneau, Cordova, and Kodiak had also been affected. Of these, "Kodiak suffered greatly from influenza with 47 deaths out of 450 cases."

18. Ibid.

19. Thomas Riggs, "Influenza in Alaska" (1919).

20. L. Hiram French to Thomas G. Riggs, December 18, 1918, private collection of Dr. David Black.

21. Ibid.

22. Frank W. Lamb, assistant surgeon, Public Health Service, "Instructions Treating and Preventing Spread of Influenza and Pneumonia," 1918, *Records of the Bureau of Indian Affairs*, RG 75, National Archives at Anchorage, AK.

23. L. Hiram French to Walter Craig, January 18, 1919, private collection.

24. Fred Madsen to L. Hiram French, March 6, 1919, private collection.

25. John Branson and Tim Troll, Eds., *Our Story: Readings From Southwest Alaska* (Anchorage: Alaska Natural History Association), 129. Treatments included calomel, mustard plasters, and castor oil.

26. Alaska Packers' Association, *Report on 1919 Influenza Epidemic* (San Francisco, CA: APA, October 1919).

27. Thomas Riggs, Jr., *Report of the Governor of Alaska* (Juneau, AK: Territory of Alaska, Office of the Governor, September 26, 1919), 409.

28. 1920 Coast Guard Report Cruise of Northern Waters (1919).

29. E. A. Coffin, "Diary and Notes," Alaska Historical Society (1919), 2.

30. Ibid., 3.

31. Ibid., 35.

32. Ibid., 21. According to their reports: "Mrs. Fred Blonde, Jr., age 23" and "Mrs. Mike Nergusen, age 42" both died at Clark's Point early in the epidemic.

33. Ibid., 35.

34. Ibid., 33.

35. H. F. Swift to Dr. L. H. French, May 25, 1919, private collection.

36. Alaska Packers' Association (October, 1919), 28.

37. Christine Hansen. *Seattle Post Intelligencer* (June 1981). Sisters of Providence Archives, Seattle, Washington. See also, The Golden Sheaf, *Providence Hospital, 1877–1927*, Sisters of Providence Archives, Seattle, Washington; Bureau of Indian Affairs, *Nurses 1918 Through 1955*, Alaska Nurses Association, 17–23, University of Alaska, Anchorage, Alaska; Branson and Troll, Eds., *Our Story*, 132; Katherine Miller, "Combating the 'Flu' at Bristol Bay," *The Link* (Seattle WA: Alumni Association of Providence Hospital School of Nursing, 1921): 62–64; Shirley Baker to the Commissioner of Fisheries, November 26, 1919, *Records of the U.S. Fish and Wildlife Service*, RG 22, National Archives at Anchorage, AK; and Thomas G. Riggs, *1918–1919 Diary*, September 1919, *Papers of Governor Thomas Riggs*, Historical Collections, Alaska State Library, Juneau, Alaska. A number of Providence Hospital Nursing School graduates, working for the Bureau of Education Territorial Hospital and the Seward Red Cross, figured prominently in the rescue efforts in Bristol Bay. Down river from Ekuk, the June 4th discovery of three sick children and two dead adult natives drifting in a "funeral boat" off Naknek lent great urgency to the already devastating situation.

38. Alaska Packers' Association, *Report on 1919 Influenza Epidemic*, 21.

39. Formerly Kanakanak School and now Kanakanak Orphanage.

40. U.S. Senate, *Influenza in Alaska Hearings Before the Committee on Appropriations, United States Senate Sixty-Fifth Congress Third Session on S.J. Resolution 199, A Joint Resolution for Relief in Alaska* (Washington, DC: Government Printing Office, 1919), 3.

41. Julia McGillycuddy, *Blood on the Moon: Valentine McGillycuddy and the Sioux* (Lincoln, NE: University of Nebraska Press, 1941), 285. Dr. McGillycuddy later sailed from Unalaska on the *Unalga* with four nurses, and landed at Cape Constantine. The group then journeyed up the Wood River in Nushagak Bay on the "Attoo," a low-draft boat suitable for navigating the salmon-spawning rivers. Their mission was to survey the villages in the region.

42. ARC Report, "Alaska, Flu" (July 1919). 803.11 Epidemic, Flu. College Park NARA.

43. Unit 3 Report, ARC. CP-NARA. 803.11, Epidemic Influenza, Box 689, Alaska.

44. Shirley Baker to the Commissioner of Fisheries, *Records of the U.S. Fish and Wildlife Service*, 1.

45. Alaska Packers' Association, *Report on 1919 Influenza Epidemic*, 36.

46. Ibid., 36.

47. Ibid., 38.

48. Ibid., 39.

49. Ibid., 41.

50. Alaska Packers' Association, *Service: The True Measurement of Any Institution Lies in the Service It Renders* (San Francisco, CA: Alaska Packers' Association, 1922).

51. Alaska Packers' Association, *Report on the 1919 Influenza Epidemic*.

52. Ibid.

53. Shirley Baker to the Commissioner of Fisheries, *Records of the U.S. Fish and Wildlife Service*, 2.

54. E. A. Coffin, *Diary, 1919–1924, MS 4–37-17*, Historical Collections, Alaska State Library, Juneau, Alaska, p. 9.

55. In fact, the two Kanakanak Hospital nurses—Rhoda Ray and Mary Conley—can be found on BIA employment lists at different hospitals in Alaska during their brief careers in the north, as can Mrs. Hanson, the nurse from Ekuk Village who received provisions from the APA for the natives in the area. Christine Hanson and her husband are also found on the BIA employment lists in 1919 immediately after the flu epidemic when they replaced Nurses Ray and Conley. *BIA Nurses 1918 Through 1955*, Alaska Nurses' Association, 17–23, University of Alaska, Anchorage, Alaska.

56. Miller, "Combating the 'Flu' at Bristol Bay," 64.

57. Ibid., 65.

58. Governor Riggs met Miss Morris and Miss Conley in Valdez on their journey home to Seattle and noted in his diary, "there were also two of the nurses who were at Nushagak during the flu epidemic. Miss Morris and Miss Conley. They had a hard time with all the poor little orphans." Riggs, *Papers of Governor Thomas Riggs*. Mary Conley left Alaska, returning to Providence in Seattle where she became the head nurse in charge of maternity services. She returned to Territorial service at hospitals in Juneau, Akiak, and Metlakatla in 1920 and 1921. She became briefly famous for a 700-mile dogsled trip she undertook to meet Karl Thiele, the Territorial secretary. She married Secretary Thiele in Juneau, and died in childbirth in 1923. James Wickersham, May 17, 1923, to February 27, 1925. MS 107 6 35. July 17, 1923.

59. Louise Comfort, "Risk, Security and Disaster Management," *Annual Review Political Science* 8 (2005): 335–356 (quoted p. 338).

60. Thomas Drabek and David McEntire, "'Emergent Phenomena and Multiorganizational Coordination in Disasters' Lessons From the Research Literature," *International Journal of Mass Emergencies and Disasters* 20, no. 2 (August 2002): 198.

CHAPTER 5

The Bombing Blitz of London and Manchester, England, 1940 to 1944

Jane Brooks

> *I was washing a patient, and then there was an almighty bang and the next thing I know I was blown underneath the bed. I stood up and there was debris flying everywhere . . . and I thought, "what will sister say when she comes on duty in the morning," you know, that was my first thought. . . . And I turned round and looked up the ward, and the end of the ward where these six beds were, was just a gaping great hole.*[1]

A 19-year-old student nurse, Jean Bowes, was working the night-shift on June 1, 1944, when a bomb exploded in her ward in a London hospital. The damage was extensive, and although this was a terrible event, miraculously, only six patients and one nurse were killed. Cleaning up the ward by herself was out of the question. In fact, everyone in the hospital mobilized to help. A number of outside organizations also participated in providing relief: The American Red Cross delivered clothes and gave Bowes a fruitcake, while the Lord Mayor's Disaster Fund supplied each of the nurses with £12.[2] Bowes herself was sent home for just 2 weeks to recuperate and then returned to duty.[3] Although this incident of bombing occurred during

Map of Great Britain.

the V1,[4] "doodlebug" bombings of 1944 and not the earlier bombings of Britain that are known as the Blitz, it illustrates some key issues explored in this chapter. Very young and junior nurses assumed positions of great responsibility, but without the authority they needed. A number of voluntary organizations supported those affected by the disaster. Without their collaboration and cooperation, reconstruction efforts would have been significantly hampered. However, the participation of some of these organizations met with controversy. In particular, leaders of professional nursing organizations were unhappy with the use of nontrained nurses within the Air Raid Precautions (ARP) teams.

This chapter explores the effects of the Blitz and the later V1 and V2 bombings on nurses in Britain, and most especially the nurses in the north of England. This chapter considers the nurses' work with victims of bombing, the lives under Blitz conditions, and the wider requirements of nurses as vital war workers. Many of the stories are from nurses who either nursed during the Blitz of 1940 to 1941 or were young girls during that time and later nursed in the V1 and V2 bombings of 1944 to early 1945. The particular focus on the north of the country is purposeful because much has been written about the effects of the Blitz and later bombings on London, often to the detriment of narratives of the rest of the country.[5] Given the importance of cities in the north of England as strategic sites of industry, this does seem like a gross oversight; however, this London centrism in relation to the Blitz is not a recent phenomenon. Tom Harrisson, founder and director of the Mass Observation Project,[6] maintained that even at that time, London was seen as the crucial focus. Winston Churchill himself considered the country's capital city "the only one that mattered much."[7]

GENDER BIAS IN BRITAIN'S CIVIL DEFENSE

According to Gabriel Moshenska, Britain's civil defense was one of the most advanced in the world when war broke out in September 1939,[8] but like many organizations of the time, it was a gendered environment.[9] In the preparation years before the war, the British held to the belief that men would undertake most of the ARP work, not just its organization. In the gender-segregated era between the two world wars, it was understood that women would work as nurses and canteen workers, or may tragically be victims themselves, but they would not serve within the machine of war.

During the war, however, the theoretical division of these gendered roles was difficult to maintain in practice.[10] Once Britain entered the war in 1939, men of working age were enlisted into military service. Thus, ARP work, like much of the war work in Britain, became the work of women and young girls or old men unfit for war, although even then, it was the men, most of whom were in reserved occupations,[11] who were considered to be in charge.[12]

The ARP wardens' job was to ensure that ARPs were followed and to support the local people after a raid. The mostly male authorities chose men to be employed as wardens and assigned women to first aid parties or to work as clerks for the fire service. One memorandum on the ARP in Manchester declared: "Each sector should arrange, amongst its own Wardens, a First Aid Party. This is a job for which the Senior Warden could make the best use of all the ladies in his sectors."[13] *The Air Raid Precautions Handbook No. 10* stated: "although the medical officer of health is primarily responsible for all medical services, it may be desirable for the local authority to appoint an officer under him to be in charge of its first aid parties."[14] Thus, it is clear that from the beginning of the ARP regulations it was the men who were in charge of all aspects of organization.[15]

Between Britain's declaration of war on Germany on September 3, 1939, and May 1940, Britain experienced what is known as the "Phoney War," a period of indecision on both sides.[16] One thing, however, that was clearly decided during this time was the evacuation of civilians. The evacuation of children in World War II was one of the greatest mass evacuations of civilians ever. Between September 1 and 3, 1939, more than one million children were evacuated from their city homes to rural areas in Britain. Some of these children stayed away for the duration of the war; however, when the anticipated bombs did not come that autumn, many returned home.[17]

However, even this plan that directly affected women and their children was also influenced by traditional gender roles. The order to leave came from the male authority; the repercussions of the order were left to women and children. The evacuation of families from Folkestone on the southeast coast of England was, according to Joan Pinder, undertaken by the police who went to people's homes to ask if they had families or friends elsewhere with whom they could stay.[18] However, once the children were evacuated, it rested on women and girls to find accommodations for them. For example, Eileen Rashleigh, a Brownie in the late 1930s, remembered being required to go around homes in her town asking if anyone would "take" one of the 3,000 evacuated children who arrived in her town in September 1939.[19]

Edith Harris also shared another example of women having to deal with the practical implications after having taken instructions from men. Edith was about 17 years old and was working at a children's home when war was declared on September 3, 1939. She was returning from a walk with more than 20 children when she heard the first air-raid siren. A man shouted to her to "take cover," but Harris recalled, "What could I do? There was just me and twenty-four children."[20] During the Phoney War, the ARP strategies that had been implemented even before the onset of hostilities and which were to affect the lives of all Britons started to appear futile.[21] The Civil Nursing Reserve (CNR) that had been organized in 1938 as an "essential component of the wartime emergency services" (to provide first-aid posts with registered nurses) started to disband. Many of the women—only about a quarter of whom were ever registered nurses—"were bored by the lack of work and sought alternative employment."[22] But soon enough, boredom would no longer be a problem as the war with Germany intensified.

THE BOMBING BLITZ

The Phoney War ended for the civilian population on September 7, 1940, when the German Luftwaffe attacked London, beginning what was soon to be called the "Blitz." The air raids continued until May 11, 1941. On September 5, 1940, the *Daily Express* front page announced, "Shouting at the top of his voice in the Berlin sports palace last night, Hitler threatened to raze the cities of Britain by indiscriminate night bombings. An hour later, London's searchlights and guns came into action and the capital had its most spectacular night raid yet. At one time, the south-eastern sky was filled with bursting shells from the London barrage."[23] The broadsheet newspapers, although less dramatic in their reporting, were equally keen to promote the spirit of the British public: "In spite of the terrible violence of the German attacks and their wanton destruction of life and property, confidence remains strong here that they will not break down Britain's defense or her resolution."[24] *The Times* was also keen to illustrate the cowardice of the Germans, "In one part of the S.E [southeast] coast yesterday, people saw the coming and going of several hundred German aeroplanes, but the going was entirely different, for they went back as stragglers."[25] Despite the horror that these headlines depict, the awe of beholding the burning sky enticed some members of the public to leave the relative safety of their shelters and homes to watch the "display." Irene Van de Vord watched from the hill near her home in Morden and was thrilled to witness London ablaze, "all the London sky, all red...flames."[26]

View of smoke rising from the London docks along the River Thames in London after an air raid during the Blitz, September 7, 1940.

NATIONAL ARCHIVES AND RECORDS ADMINISTRATION

As the capital city, London was subject to the most persistent bombing raids, especially the East End docklands, but other cities in England also suffered attacks. Coventry in the Midlands of England was bombed on November 14, 1940. The reasons were clear: The town produced critical components for the war machine, including radio sets and parachutes. Moreover, it was the base for the Dunlop tire factory that produced tires for aircraft, barrage balloons, and rubber for anti-gas clothing during the war.[27] By the end of the raid, Coventry's 600-year-old cathedral was in ruins, bombs blocked every railway line, and stations were so badly hit that they had to be closed.[28] In one night, 568 people were killed and 1,256 injured—many critically.[29] The bombs started to fall on Liverpool in the north west of the country on December 20 and 21, 1940. As the major Atlantic port, Liverpool suffered a constant stream of raids between those dates and May 1941, by which time 1,900 people had been killed.[30] The city of Manchester, also in the north of England and a center of industry since the Industrial Revolution in the 19th century, was bombed on Sunday and Monday, December 22 and 23, respectively, just two nights before Christmas 1940.[31] Salford, a city in its own right from 1926, but that is geographically joined to Manchester, was bombed in June 1941. This event is singled out and is discussed in more detail later as 14 nurses were killed that night.[32] The raids on the Manchester and Salford conurbation were far more disparate than those on Liverpool, the twin cities experiencing what Beaven and Thoms have described as "knock-out drops," mostly in the city centers, public utilities, and civic buildings.[33] The ramifications for the civilian populations were therefore wide ranging, preventing travel and recreation, and thus seriously undermining the steadfastness of the community. For many, what was to become known as the "Blitz spirit" was tested to its extreme.

At the end of the Blitz in May 1941, 43,000 British civilians were dead and a further 71,000 seriously injured, although this was a far cry from the 1 to 2.8 million that had been estimated in 1939.[34] By May 1941, Hitler turned his attention to the East and Russia, giving the British public a well-earned rest from repeated air-raid attacks. Subsequently, after the invasion of occupied Europe that commenced with the D-Day landings in Normandy on June 6, 1944, Hitler's attention once again turned to the British Isles. The V1 (doodlebugs) and V2 bombings began on June 13, 1944. Because they were pilotless rockets, the distance that they could cover was limited, and only the capital and the southeast of England were affected. The last civilian casualty was killed in Kent on March 27, 1945, and the final German bomb to land in Britain was on March 28, 1945.[35] The British public's nightmare was over. Before that, however, there was much work for the country's nurses, ARP workers, and voluntary organizations to do to support civilians through the bombing campaigns.

THE NURSING RESPONSE

Discussing how she felt at the time of one raid, nurse Sarah Collins reported, "I don't remember being frightened, I remember being working [sic]."[36] Other British nurses involved with the devastation would agree. Angus Calder recalled: "As heavy bombing of London began in the later summer, the word 'Blitz' became 'almost overnight a British colloquialism for an air raid.'" But from the beginning it suggested more than that. It was instantaneously and spontaneously "mythologized" and the "Blitz spirit" prevailed.[37] Most nurses—like much of the civilian population—struggled with the realities of the situation and accepted the conditions as part of being at war; getting on with life in as normal a way as possible was vital to the nation's resolve.[38] There were long working hours and compulsory war work for young and old alike. Jean Edwards, 16 and a half years old in 1941, was recruited to a cottage hospital as a "student nurse." She recalled that it was very hard work. She was totally unprepared; she received no training at all and was required to work in whichever ward or department to which she was sent. She was, she said, "virtually a slave... I look back in horror."[39] Nevertheless, the opportunity to assist in the operating theater was met with excitement on her part; thus, her participation in this war work did not seem so dreadful, because she liked the drama, "you know when you're young, it's dramatic...and I thought here am I,

I didn't do anything, except tend to swabs and things like that, but I thought, hmm, 'am doing quite an important job.' "[40] Clearly being part of the war effort was important to even the youngest of workers.

SHELTER LIFE AND SHELTER DEATH: COOPERATION FOR THE GREATER GOOD

In the preface to his pamphlet on ARP, John Burdon Sanderson (JBS) Haldane, the Marxist geneticist and intellectual, stated:

> This book is intended for the ordinary citizen, the sort of man and woman who is going to be killed if Britain is raided from the air. I believe that you readers can enormously reduce your own risk of being killed and the risk of your children being killed, if you demand the necessary protective measures.[41]

As early as the 1930s, British authorities had organized air-raid precautions throughout the country and designed a system of shelters to keep people from harm. No attempt was made to assure that the shelters were comfortable as authorities wanted the people to continue working for the war effort rather than spend all their time in the shelters. Neither did the authorities want the shelters to be large enough so as to provide "breeding grounds for mass hysteria, even subversion."[42] Thus, a series of aboveground shelters was designed for people to build either in their gardens (the "Anderson Shelter") or in their houses (the "Morrison Shelter"). However, the shelters' efficacy was questionable. Elsie Davies and Elizabeth Bowring were both nurses during the V1 and V2 bombing campaigns, but were still children during the Blitz. Davies, who lived in Manchester, recalled having an Anderson Shelter. Although she was never harmed, she recalled that she and her family would be up all night[43] because the corrugated metal shelter provided no protection from the noise. In reality, according to a pamphlet on air-raid protection, such shelters did "not even pretend to be proof against a direct hit or near hit."[44] Elizabeth

Bowring, whose family lived in the south of England, described the air-raid shelter in her parents' home: "we had a dug out in the garden, but it was so cold and you had snails climbing up the walls and you had to sit on a bench in a hole in the ground." The family then decided to sleep in the cupboard under the stairs, but Bowring's father did not approve and said to her mother, "we must observe the proprieties!" Her mother was seemingly far more pragmatic and replied: "for heaven's sake Charles, there's a war on."[45] Such stories illustrate a number of crucial aspects of British life during the bombing campaigns; at first, the need for humor, and second, the need to reassess the attitudes of Victorian parents and those in authority. The bombing campaigns were an unprecedented period in British history and needed an unprecedented response from the public. Edgar Jones et al.'s study into psychiatric illness during the bombing campaigns conclude that "morale fluctuated, but never broke."[46] Given that Bowring was later still only a student nurse when sent to care for the soldiers returning from the D-Day landings, she would need a sense of humor, plenty of spirit, and an open mind in order to cope.

Despite the availability of private shelters, much of the population in London eventually took to the underground train stations; elsewhere, they took to public shelters made available under official buildings. The largest shelter in Manchester was a subterranean canal, in which thousands of people would congregate during a raid. These tunnels were dark and damp with "vast chasmic [sic] chambers," not a pleasant place to be.[47] According to the British Broadcasting Corporation (BBC) website, there is still a notice from the Second World War on the wall stating that gambling and insobriety would not be accepted[48] and concerns about sexual morality and illicit relationships in the dark of the shelters were never far away.[49] For nurses and other hospital staff, underground shelters were created under the hospitals themselves. Mary Hyde recalled that the summer of 1940 in Manchester was peaceful and then, in the autumn, the bombing started.[50] She remembered the first bomb that fell at the end of the year 1940 and landed in the ballroom of the old Nurses' Home of Manchester Royal Infirmary. Fortunately, no one was killed as they had all been either on duty or in the shelters below the hospital.

Nurses view a bombed room at Manchester Royal Infirmary.

Cooperation with authorities and the ARP regulations was key to survival, and although it caused physical stress, there was also an element of patriotic spirit and resiliency to the disaster conditions. Hyde recalled: "we got used to going down to the shelters eventually, but it was terribly cold when we first went down because we were sleeping on the stone floor. It was awful, you know, you were all stiff in the morning...but it was quite jolly."[51] Reflecting on this 70 years later, it is difficult to see how sleeping on a cold damp floor in a basement could possibly be "jolly." Nevertheless, this idea of camaraderie when under fire is a frequent narrative of the Blitz and later bombing campaigns, as the writings in the following two autobiographies illustrate. Janet Wilks, an army nurse based in the south of England, wrote, "Most of us being young and more than a little crazy, we were irrepressible, and found a lot of fun in every situation; the sight of grotesque figures waddling down the paths to the shelters, bundled up to the eyebrows; stumbling sometimes into each other; dropping things and cursing volubly. We settled ourselves as though it were a party."[52] Wilks also remembered the "engaging, good-looking" medical officer who would join them in the shelter; clearly the allure of the opposite sex was present even in the hospital shelters.[53] Eve Williams, a voluntary aid detachment nurse in Portsmouth on the south coast of England, wrote: "The raid seemed to give us a spirit of unity. We were drawn together more."[54]

The notion that the nation "pulled together" was important to maintain order, a fighting spirit, and the all-important collaboration among the various air-raid services. On January 7, 1941, *The Manchester Guardian* reported a conversation between the regional commissioner for the fire brigade, Sir Harry Haig, and the lord mayor before the Manchester Blitz. When asked by Haig what he thought would be the response of Manchester to a raid, the lord mayor replied, "their reaction would be precisely the same as any other city. As a matter of fact, I think we can claim that the reaction was even more courageous."[55] A month previously, after the bomb had hit the Nurses' Home of the Manchester Royal Infirmary, a report in *The Manchester Guardian* of the incident maintained that, "one hundred and twelve nurses were in the shelter in bed in the bunks," and that, despite being covered in dirt and suffering from shock, they "maintained perfect order."[56] It is clear that the press had a responsibility to claim the fighting spirit of the nation, whether or not the nation felt that spirit. Given the conditions in the shelters, it is not hard to believe that this camaraderie may have sometimes been wanting.

In some shelters, there were literally hundreds of people crowded night after night, trying to sleep on the cold floor. The overcrowding in the London underground system was of great concern to the government and public health officials and demands that there be a nurse and a doctor present in the larger ones were frequent; nevertheless, this rarely occurred. In a pamphlet, *Song in the Shelter*, produced by Bernard Henry of the Communist Party, Henry described his progress through the public shelters in London, singing opera and

Southeast London shelter.
Courtesy of the Library of Congress.

organizing singing competitions. In it he offered a stark description of the conditions:

> Even regular medical inspection, let alone first aid posts, were entirely, so far as I could find out, lacking in most of the public shelters. Children are living in these surroundings, sleeping close to closet buckets which sometimes overflow, lying on damp benches against wet walls, perhaps attacked by rats.[57]

For some, the horror was even worse than rats and human excrement. Not all the shelters were able to protect the public from death or horrendous injury.

SHELTER LIFE AND SHELTER DEATH: DEATH UNDERGROUND

According to Penny Starns, many in London viewed the underground stations as natural shelters, but tragically, they were not always safe. Bank Station was hit in the autumn of 1940; the explosion burned victims until they were unrecognizable. Dame Kathleen Raven, then a nurse at St. Bartholomew's Hospital, said: "I have never seen such burns in my life—black charred bodies, still alive."[58] On October 14, 1940, a bomb hit Balham High Street in South London at an intersection of underground railway tunnels. It killed 68 of the 600 people sleeping in the tunnels.[59] Elsewhere in Britain, there were similar shelter tragedies, all of which affected the public's morale. One such shelter was below the Wilkinson's lemonade factory in North Shields, near Newcastle Upon Tyne, in the northeast of England. On May 3, 1941, a bomb destroyed it, killing 105 people who were sheltering there.[60] Unfortunately, there is no information anywhere as to the involvement of nurses in either of these two disasters. The ARP workers in Newcastle worked hard to free the injured survivors of the Wilkinson factory bomb, and those alive were then sent to Tynemouth Jubilee Hospital and Preston Hospital in North Shields.

Although there is a list of the injured, sadly, there is no mention of the care they received or by whom, but the information that is available illustrates the power of community spirit. What is perhaps rather interesting about this story is that the air-raid warden was a Mrs. Lee, and her husband, a first-aider, turning the gender issue firmly on its head.[61]

In 1939, *The Manchester Guardian* reported that the shelters, which had been prepared under the Manchester Royal Infirmary, were "gas-proof and with some protection against high explosive (not against direct hits)... they have strong concrete ceilings, which, it is hoped, will bear the weight of collapsing buildings."[62] Given that a year later none of the nurses was harmed in the explosion, it appears that their summation was correct. Tragically, not all hospital shelters were so safe. On June 2, 1941, Salford Royal Infirmary, a hospital about 3 miles away from the Manchester Royal Infirmary, received a direct hit. Seventeen nurses were in the basement shelter, and only three survived as the walls collapsed on them.[63] A resident surgical officer of the hospital and the assistant staff officer in charge of first-aid parties were awarded George Medals, and a member of the ARP rescue services was awarded the British Empire Medal for trying to extricate the nurses.[64] A hurried letter from Mr. H. B. Shelswell, the general superintendent of the hospital, to Major Pilkington, chairman of the hospital, clearly describes the collaboration among the various members of the hospital staff and the volunteers:

> Thirteen nurses, including one Sister, have lost their lives and three nurses have been injured—none seriously. Their home is almost completely wrecked and there are still some bodies buried under the debris. Most of the nurses were juniors....
>
> I need hardly say that the staff, and particularly the R.S.O. and Mr. Lunt, a resident student, acted with great bravery and physical endurance. Matron has seen most of the relatives and has tried to get in touch with all.... Everything possible has been done and there has been no lack of willing helpers. I shall of course not think of going away for a holiday for the present.[65]

SHATTERED GLASS AND BROKEN BODIES

Student nurse Joan Carr was only 18 years old and training at the Jewish hospital in North Manchester in 1940, although she was not herself Jewish. On the night of the bombings just before Christmas, she had gone to visit a friend in the southern part of Manchester called Rusholme. "The bombing started at six o'clock at night and we had to go into the air raid shelter and we were sitting there all night. Set off to come home on the bus as far as I could get and then I had to walk the rest of the way through Manchester all a blaze with bombed buildings...and finally got to Elizabeth Street to find the nurses' home had been bombed."[66] Carr admitted that she was probably in shock, because she just turned around and tried to get a bus back to her parents' home on the outskirts of the city. She did not tell anyone that she was going. When she arrived home, her father contacted the hospital to let them know that his daughter was alright. She later returned to work to find that the whole hospital had been evacuated to Crumpsall General Hospital in North Manchester.

As the bombings continued, many of the participants agreed that they became lackadaisical about going into the shelters. Given that her bedroom had been on the top floor of the now-destroyed nurses' home, Carr had been lucky to escape death, having lost only her possessions in the raid. She admitted that many people did not always stay in the shelters when a raid was overhead, and that, frequently, she and her nursing colleagues had gone back to their rooms in order to have a good night's sleep.

Unfortunately, not everyone escaped unscathed with this increasingly careless attitude about remaining in the shelters. In fact, many died or suffered serious injuries, and others experienced the loss of family members. Sister Elizabeth Morris recalled one mother being brought into the London Hospital, Whitechapel, after a V2 raid in 1945:

> She was badly injured, but the girl [her daughter] they couldn't find and they found her dead body three weeks later on top of a wardrobe in another street...and this poor lady, she couldn't go to the funeral, so we sat her by the window

130

so she could see the funeral pass by and all she could say was, "she dyed her hair the night before and she said 'I'm not going to look at it until I wake up mum,' and she never woke up."[67]

Like other young nurses, Rosemary Stevens, who cared for trauma victims in London, learned a great deal in a short time about the care of the injured.[68] As one witness recalled:

> In 1940 at the height of the Blitz on London, one night our house received a direct hit and was totally destroyed. My parents and I were unhurt, but my sister, aged seventeen was critically injured and evacuated to Botleys Park War Hospital at Chertsey [Surrey]. The next day I went with my parents to the hospital. The chaotic scenes I saw there I can recall graphically to this day—wards crammed with beds, beds up the middle of the wards and out in the corridors. People covered in dust and blood, groaning and crying and in their midst, working desperately yet calmly were nurses from St. Thomas' [Hospital] trying to comfort patients and restore some sort of order. Sadly my sister did not survive.[69]

Margaret Thomas recalled the first bombing raid on London that occurred soon after she began her training. They were, she said, all moved down to the ground floor in the nurses' home so that they would not be affected by the broken glass, which always accompanied a raid.[70] This was probably a wise decision given another nurse's experience. When Alice Vaughan was working as a nursing assistant in Birmingham, a woman came into their hospital with broken glass in her arm following a raid. Vaughan stated that they were unable to remove it all.[71] Jean Edwards recalled the V1 and V2 bombs when she was working at the London Hospital, Whitechapel, in the East End, when again many of the injuries came from broken glass. Her recollections of the aftermath of one flying bomb included the help she received from the matron of the hospital, "who [usually] went around like the Queen Mother, with her sleeves rolled up, everyone was just having to help."[72] However, her most stark memory was the direct hit on a block of flats in which 124 residents were killed and only 49 survived. When victims of air raids were brought in dead, it was often the nurses who were required to lay out the bodies. Joyce Stephens was a newly qualified nurse in London during the V1 and V2 bombings. She recalled a young girl aged 14 years being brought in dead after a raid. The girl had slipped on a step and broken her neck in her home trying to evacuate her grandfather when the sirens sounded.[73]

EMERGENT BEHAVIOR: ARPs, NURSES, AND VOLUNTARY WORKERS

Although many of the nurses working on the home front during World War II worked in hospitals, there were also many nurses who worked in the community setting and, therefore, were engaged in caring for victims of bombing raids or were employed within ARP units. On January 10, 1941, *The Manchester Guardian* reported that a nurse, Ivy Marsh, who was a member of a mobile ARP unit, "rescued a wounded police officer from beneath wreckage and attended his wounds as bombs were crashing about her."[74] In another instance, Ms. Ethel May Peacock, a maternity nurse from Salford and a member of St. Olave's District Nursing Association, "stayed with a woman in a block of flats, which had been set on fire by bombs and brought her baby safely into the world." For this, Peacock was made a Member of the British Empire (MBE).[75] Unfortunately, it was not always possible to help. Joan Cremieu-Javal remembered her work with the River Emergency Service on the Thames in London. The heat and flames from the bomb were so intense that the captain of the boat could not sail: "It's too hot, can't take the boat. I am not being responsible for it any longer, I am turning back."[76] Sometimes, even the most brave had to admit defeat.

One aspect of the nurses' war work was "fire watching duty" as part of compulsory ARP work. On September 14, 1942, the "Fire Prevention (Business Premises) (No. 3) Order, which included women in the fire watching service, came into force."[77] Sadie Abraham joined the CNR after conscription of women in 1941.[78] However, prior to this, she undertook fire-watching duties every Sunday night: "After the church service,

I'd come home and then go back down at about 9 o'clock and climb up to the top of the roof and be ready to throw incendiary bombs off the roof or dump them in the sand."[79] According to the exemption rules, "Whole-time nurses and midwives" were exempt,[80] but this does not appear to have applied to nurses in training. Both Lucy Sherbourne and Betty Crisp recalled undertaking fire-watching duty at nighttime after a day on the wards. Even though the nation's hospitals had a supply of possible fire-watching labor, too often the job fell to the student nurses. Sherbourne remembered the many raids on London in 1944, "long hours on duty and then every third night I'd have to fire watch..., we had one or two rather nasty experiences," after which she was sent with colleagues and some very sick patients to a hospital in Knaresborough, North Yorkshire.[81] Betty Crisp recalled the fire-watching duty from the pathology laboratory with a stirrup pump in hand, again after being on duty as a nurse.[82] To make matters worse, gender inequalities of the era meant that women engaged in crucial civil defense work were not paid at the same rates as their male colleagues.[83] However, as nurses, they never failed to accept their duties willingly, despite the obvious detriments to their health and pockets.

Although many of the nurses discussed their war work, none discussed engaging in many of the teaching activities that were so vital in preparing untrained personnel in emergency nursing and first-aid work. It is possible that this is because most of the participants were young student nurses during the war years and not registered nurses with experience. Even probationer nurses participated in the wider preparation for air raids. Sherbourne regaled the excitement of going out with the ambulances following an air raid: "it was frightening, but there was always a lovely feeling of camaraderie, you had somebody with you."[84] Emily Soper was proud to have been allocated to the blood transfusion unit in her training hospital:

> To be prepared just in case we got casualties. We had a sister and a staff nurse come from what was called a Civil Defence Unit...so when the siren went, we had to report to our little quarter, that we had allotted to us. So we had to be ready, but, fortunately again, we were not required to use our blood

transfusion expertise on any casualties, but we were dele-
gated to help our own doctors.[85]

Teamwork was critical, and collaboration among hospital staff, ARP
workers, the fire service, and the police meant that lives were saved,
which may otherwise have perished. After a hospital was bombed in
September 1940 and two women's wards were damaged, *The Manchester
Guardian* praised the nurses, doctors, and ARP workers for working for
"hours in the light of torches to save as many as possible. Fifteen women
were recovered from the wreckage alive by 4 a.m." The report continued, "Sister Gantry, of the maternity Wards, clad only in her nightdress,
crawled in and out of the wreckage giving injections of morphia to the
women."[86] Following the raids on the capital, industrial nurse Marjorie
Eileen Perkins was awarded the George Medal alongside Dr. Malcolm
Manson and Grace Rattenbury of the Women's Voluntary Service, several
police officers, and ARP workers. Perkins had supported the workers in
her area, helped them and others to a shelter, and then continued to care
for casualties despite, at one point, being rendered unconscious.[87]

Following the devastating raid on Salford Royal Infirmary on June
2, 1941, which killed 14 nurses, members of the CNR and Women's
Voluntary Service were praised for their hard work.[88] Nonetheless, the
use of nontrained nurses often caused discord because under the original pay scales, an inexperienced nurse employed by the CNR could
earn more than an experienced ward sister who could not.[89] Moreover,
the organizations for trained nurses were suspicious of any organization that employed untrained nurses instead of trained ones and, thus,
diluted the value of a 3-year hospital training. However, despite this
apparent animosity from the professional organizations, there is little to
suggest that the feeling prevailed on the wards and in other arenas where
registered nurses and their unqualified colleagues worked together, nor
that assistant nurses did not do valuable war work. Auxiliary nurse
Denise Forster of the Belfast Civil Defense Ambulance Service was "buried when the ambulance depot was demolished by a bomb." Forster
then, allegedly, "extricated herself with difficulty, and then set to work
to release others who had been trapped at the same time."[90] According
to another assistant nurse, Walker, the only difference in the work that

she was expected to do and the work of the registered nurses was that the registered nurses gave injections.[91] It does seem as if those who were employed as probationer nurses at the time were learners in name only; therefore, it was probably nonsensical to differentiate the work that they could do with that of the assistant volunteer nurses. One probationer nurse maintained that during the Blitz she had no lectures at all.[92] Another nurse, June Huntly, recalled that their "lectures went a bit awry, because we seemed to be on duty [more] than off duty."[93] In yet another instance, Lucy Sherbourne remembered returning to the Hammersmith Hospital in London after several months of evacuation in the north of England. No effort was made to offer the students support or lectures, even though they were in the last 6 months of training.[94]

Clearly, in both the Blitz and the V1 and V2 bombings, the boundaries of work between registered nurses and aides blurred. Irene Van de Vord recalled that assistant nurses catheterized patients, depending, of course, on permission from the ward sister.[95] Eileen Rashleigh was a girl guide, about 13 years of age, when she volunteered at her local hospital and cared for burned pilots who were nursed naked in saline baths, 24 hours a day.[96] Sadie Abraham, who joined the CNR, was given 10 days' training, after which she was sent to work on the wards and was expected to administer medications and do wound dressings. She recalled: "we were just flung in at the deep end really and you just had to learn as you went along and get on with it. It was wartime and we were needed.... It was a testing time."[97] As Jean Bowes maintained, since there was a war on, "there was so much demand on all the services,"[98] everyone just had to contribute. Elizabeth Bowring stated, "you weren't scared, you just got on with it."[99] Yet another young nurse recalled: "British people maintained their spirit, they really did...and never doubted that we would win the war."[100] Indeed, the "Blitz spirit" prevailed.

"BRITAIN CAN TAKE IT": THE IMPACT OF BEING A NATION UNDER FIRE

Elizabeth Bowring maintained that, "one of the good things that I thought about the war was when in 1940 they started chucking bombs all over the place, I was able to give up my piano lessons. I hated my piano lessons and when they started dropping bombs, my mother said, 'well perhaps you'd better not go.'"[101] Bowring's somewhat humorous take on life in embattled Britain reflects a prevailing attitude that is discussed within much of the literature of a country, which carried on as far as normal. Rosemary Sanders stated, "you went on as far as possible with your normal life; there was hardly time to do anything else."[102] This was illustrated in the actions of the nurses during raids when instead of going down into the shelters, they stayed in the wards with their patients. However, in other respects, people did alter their daily lives considerably. It is clear that for many young women their rather sheltered lives were changed dramatically by the bombing. As one nurse noted: "everyone was taking risks." Thus, although girls had been protected and there perhaps remained a rhetoric that they still were, it was actually just not possible to do so. Discussing the reality of young girls who supervised the antiaircraft (Ack-Ack) units, Mary Purvis remarked: "you're not going to worry when they go out at night in Cambridge are you?"[103]

There were also more practical repercussions to the war and the bombing campaigns. After her father left home on active service, Eileen Rashleigh and her mother moved to the apartment above their paper shop, because her father did not want them walking through the streets at 5 a.m.[104] Moreover, following female conscription in 1941, many young women who never wanted to be nurses were forced into it. Jean Bowes recalled the particularly tragic death of one such young Welsh student nurse, who had already tried to leave her training hospital, because she disliked nursing so much, but was sent back by her parents. She was killed by a bomb that decimated the ward.[105] Jean Bowes still spoke with tremendous sadness about this young girl and admitted how deeply it affected her: "But what had struck me at the time, was that this girl had come into nursing and she didn't want to do it... it was horrendous."[106]

CONCLUSION

The bombing of Britain and the war on the home front had a significant impact not only on individual nurses, but also on the nursing profession as a whole, especially in regard to its relations with the wider community at war. The stories of the nurses illustrate the crisis in which much of the country was immersed. They also provide evidence of cooperation and collaboration—a willingness, even among the youngest and least interested—to engage in nursing work. However, this engagement in nursing work by untrained women and often children was not without its detractors. Certainly, as historian Penny Starns has discussed elsewhere, the dilution of the profession by women with limited or no nurse training was seen as an impairment to its professional status.[107] Nevertheless, this engagement with other organizations and untrained women also had an important and positive effect on the profession, for it enabled nurses to establish their skills, as trainers, as organizers, and as expert practitioners. The nurses were able to demonstrate that they were agents in the preservation of order and life and capable of brave and effective work with people from all other walks of life.

NOTES

1. Jean Bowes (pseudonym), an oral history interview by Jane Brooks on October 19, 2011, in Bournemouth, United Kingdom. Bowes started nurse training on October 7, 1943, in London

2. Given that a qualified nurse's salary at this time may be only about £100 per annum, this was not an inconsiderable sum for a first-year student.

3. Jean Bowes, an oral history interview on October 19, 2011. It was only later that the trauma of the deaths was to affect Bowes and she left nursing completely for several years.

4. The V1 bombs or "doodlebugs," as they were called, were pilotless bombs, first launched in June 1944. They could travel up to 149 miles. A droning engine could be heard and then the engine cut out and the bomb fell. The first V2 hit London in September 1944; they took only 5 minutes from launch in Germany or Holland to arrive in London and could not be heard. Accessed May 21, 2014, www.westendatwar.org.uk/page_id_152_path_0p28p.aspx.

5. For example, Juliet Gardiner's celebratory, but otherwise informative, book on the Blitz focuses on nearly all of her history in London and devotes fewer than six pages to the Liverpool and Manchester Blitz combined. Juliet Gardiner, *The Blitz: The British Under Attack* (London: Harper Press, 2011).

6. The Mass Observation Unit's archive webpages describe it as follows: "The Archive results from the work of the social research organisation, Mass Observation. This organisation was founded in 1937 by a group of people, who aimed to create an 'anthropology of ourselves.' They recruited a team of observers and a panel of volunteer writers to study the everyday lives of ordinary people in Britain. This original work continued until the early 1950s," accessed May 20, 2014, http://www.massobs.org.uk/a_brief_history.htm.

7. Tom Harrisson, *Living Through the Blitz* (London: Penguin, 1976), 32.

8. Gabriel Moshenka, "Government Gas Vans and School Gas Chambers: Preparedness and Paranoia in Britain, 1936–1941," *Medicine, Conflict and Survival* 26, no. 3 (2010): 224.

9. Lucy Noakes, " 'Serve to Save': Gender, Citizenship and Civil Defence in Britain, 1937–41," *Journal of Contemporary History* 47, no. 4 (2012): 735.

10. Anonymous, *Air Raid Precautions, Handbook No. 10, The Training and Work of First Aid Parties* (London: HMSO, 1939): 3. MOSI Archives, Manchester, A1986.456/1/3/9.

11. The Schedule of Reserved Occupations exempted certain key workers from conscription into the armed forces. These included medical practitioners and police officers.

12. Noakes, " 'Serve to Save'," 735.

13. Anonymous, "Ref: Memo. A.R.P. /L.1. Senior Wardens: Sector Plan and Warden List," Museum of Science and Industry (MOSI) Archives, Manchester, A1986.456/1/1/11.

14. Anonymous, *Air Raid Precautions*, 6. MOSI Archives, Manchester, A1986.456/1/3/9.

15. Harrisson, *Living Through the Blitz*, 35.

16. Brian Bond, "The Calm Before the Storm: Britain and the 'Phoney War,' 1939–40," *Royal United Services Institute for Defence Studies* 135, no. 1 (February 1990): 61–67.

17. James S. M. Rusby and Fiona Tasker, "Long-Term Effects of the British Evacuation of Children During World War 2 on Their Adult Mental Health," *Aging Mental Health* 13, no. 3 (May 2009): 391–404.

18. Joan Pinder, a telephone oral history interview by Jane Brooks on January 6, 2014. Pinder started nurse training in 1942 at the Royal Bath Hospital.

19. Eileen Rashleigh, a telephone oral history interview by Jane Brooks on October 15, 2013. Eileen was a patrol leader in the Girl Guides in 1940 and was a volunteer at her local hospital where airmen who were badly burned were treated. She was only 11 years old when she started this work.

20. Edith Harris (pseudonym), an oral history interview by Jane Brooks in Bournemouth on October 20, 2011. Edith started working in a children's home prior to the commencement of the war and then started nurse training in 1940 in the southeast of England.

21. Noakes, " 'Serve to Save'," 735.

22. Penny Starns, *Nurses at War: Women on the Frontline, 1939–45* (Stroud: Sutton Publishing, 2000), 8. See also, Susan McGann, Anne Crowther, and Rona Dougall, *A History of the Royal College of Nursing, 1916–90: A Voice for Nurses* (Manchester: Manchester University Press, 2009), 104.

23. Anonymous, "Hitler Screams Threat: Big Raid Beaten," *Daily Express*, September 5, 1940, 1.

24. Anonymous, "Unshaken Britain: 'Blows That Cannot Be Decisive,'" *The Times*, September 10, 1940, 4.

25. Anonymous, "Enemy Repulsed Three Times: Alert Fighters. Air Battles in Kent, Surrey and Essex," *The Times*, September 2, 1940, 4.

26. Irene Van de Vord, a telephone oral history interview by Jane Brooks on December 5, 2013. Mrs. Van de Vord was "called up" in 1941, but was a conscientious objector. However, she was willing to work as a nurse and worked in a hospital in Guildford in Surrey.

27. Gardiner, *The Blitz*, 140.

28. Ibid., 147.

29. Ibid., 148.

30. B. Beaven and D. Thoms, "The Blitz and Civilian Morale in Three Northern Cities, 1940–1942," *Northern History* 32, no. 1 (January 1996): 196.

31. Harrisson, *Living Through the Blitz*; Gardiner, *The Blitz*, 139 and 201–203.

32. Walter Merrill, "Report of the Air Raid Damage Inflicted, 2nd June 1941," Salford Royal Infirmary Blitz, G/HSR/DS1; Anonymous, "Funeral of Nurses Killed in Raid: Five Buried in Communal Grave," *Salford City Reporter*, Friday, June 13, 1941. Archives and Local History, Manchester Central Library.

33. Beaven and Thoms, "The Blitz," 199.

34. Brett Holman, " 'Bomb Back, and Bomb Hard': Debating Reprisals During the Blitz," *Australian Journal of Politics and History* 58, no. 3 (2012): 398. See also p. 402.

35. Martin Gilbert, *The Second World War: A Complete History* (London: Phoenix Books, 2009), 653.

36. Sarah Collins, an oral history interview by Jane Brooks on October 18, 2011. Collins started nurse training in 1936 in London.

37. Angus Calder, *The Myth of the Blitz* (London: Random House, 1991), 171.

38. Irene Van de Vord's comments on the notion of "getting on with it" are particularly salient given that she was a conscientious objector: "you just got on with life in those days, you know... well you worried about the people who you knew, but you didn't, I don't remember thinking about the war from a political point of view."

39. Jean Edwards, a telephone oral history interview by Jane Brooks on November 6, 2013. Edwards started nurse training in June 1943 at the London Hospital, Whitechapel.

40. Ibid.

41. J. B. S. Haldane, *A.R.P.: Air Raid Precautions* (London: Hesperides Press [Kindle Version, 2013; originally published in 1938 in London by Victor Gollancz, founder of the Left Book Club in 1936, which was dedicated to halting the spread of fascism and promoting socialism). Retrieved from http://www.abebooks.co.uk/books/publishing-pioneer-yellow-typography/victor-gollancz.shtml.

42. Harrisson, *Living Through the Blitz*, 37.

43. Elsie Davies, an oral history interview by Jane Brooks in Manchester. Davies started children's nurse training in 1942 at Booth Hall Children's Hospital and her general nurse training in 1945 at Park Hospital, both in Manchester.

44. Communist Party of Great Britain, *Mass Murder or Planned Protection?* (London: Communist Party of Great Britain, 1940), 4, CP/ORG/MISC/11/01: Labour History Archive Study Centre: People's History Museum, Manchester.

45. Elizabeth Bowring, an oral history interview by Jane Brooks on July 31, 2012, in Shropshire. Bowring started nurse training in September 1941 at Redhill Hospital in Surrey.

46. Edgar Jones, Robin Woolven, Bill Durodie, and Simon Wessely, "Civilian Morale During the Second World War: Responses to Air Raids Re-examined," *Social History of Medicine* 17, no. 3 (2004): 478.

47. "The New Manchester Walks: In Step With the City." Accessed July 22, 2014, http://www.newmanchesterwalks.com/walks-tours/underground-other-unusual-things/underground-manchester.

48. British Broadcasting Corporation (BBC), "Underground Manchester." Accessed July 22, 2014, http://www.bbc.co.uk/insideout/content/articles/2009/01/16/north_west_s15_w2_underground_manc_video_feature.shtml. Unfortunately, it is not possible to substantiate this claim as the tunnels are closed to the public at present.

49. Calder, *The Myth of the Blitz*, 2744.

50. Mary Hyde, an oral history interview by Jane Brooks on September 11, 2013, in Manchester. Hyde started nurse training on April 1, 1940, at the Manchester Royal Infirmary.

51. Ibid.

52. Janet Wilkes, *Carbolic and Leeches* (Ilfracombe: Arthur Stockwell Ltd., 1991), 99.

53. Ibid., 100.

54. Eve Williams, *Ladies Without Lamps* (London: Thomas Harmsworth Publishing, 1983), 11. The voluntary aid detachment (VAD) nurses were voluntary, untrained women who undertook nursing work during both world wars. Much has been written about them in recent years. One of the most famous autobiographies of a VAD is Vera Brittain, *A Testament of Youth* (London: Weidenfeld and Nicolson; Reissue edition, 2009). Brittain was a VAD nurse during the First World War.

55. Anonymous, "A City of Firefighters: Regional Commissioner's Call to Manchester," *The Manchester Guardian*, January 7, 1941, 6.

56. Anonymous, "Nurses' Escape: Bomb Bursts in Home Close to Shelter. Manchester Raid," *The Manchester Guardian*, December 10, 1940, 7. Hyde did recall that they were indeed provided with beds at some point, but it is not clear if they were, in fact, in bunks at the time of this air raid or sleeping on the floor.

57. Bernard Henry, *Song in the Shelter* (London: Bernard T. Henry, 1941), 17. I have not been able to locate any further information about the author.

58. Starns, *Nurses at War*, 20–21. Dame Kathleen Raven was later matron of Leeds General Infirmary, a member of the General Nursing Council and on the Council of the Royal College of Nursing, and chief nursing officer at the Department of Health. McGann, Crowther, and Dougall, *A History of the Royal College of Nursing*, 223; John Marshall, "Obituary: Dame Kathleen Raven: A Consummate Civil Servant Who Fought for Nurses and Patients," *The Guardian*, Friday, April 23, 1999. Accessed May 27, 2014, http://www.theguardian.com/news/1999/apr/23/guardianobituaries.

59. Gardiner, *The Blitz*, 94.

60. Craig Armstrong, "A Northern Community at War, 1939–1945: 'Tyneside Can Take It'," *Northern History* XLIV, no. 1 (March 2007): 133–152.

61. Peter Bolger and Peter Hepplewhite, "Air Raid Disaster 1941: Wilkinson's Lemonade Factory," http://northshields173.org.

62. Anonymous, "Precautions at the Infirmary: No Intermission of Active Preparations," *The Manchester Guardian*, January 14, 1939, 13.

63. Anonymous, "Nurse Victims of Air Raid: Last Body Recovered," *The Manchester Guardian*, June 5, 1941, 3.

64. Anonymous, "Salford Doctor With G.M.: Awards for Brave Rescue Work When Nurses' Home Was Bombed," *The Manchester Guardian*, September 6, 1941, 8.

65. H. B. Shelswell, "Dear Major Pilkington" (June 2, 1941), Salford Royal Infirmary Blitz. G/HSR/DS1.

66. Joan Carr, an oral history interview by Jane Brooks on November 22, 2013, in Lancashire. Carr started nurse training in 1940 at the Jewish Hospital in Manchester.

67. Sister Elizabeth Morris, a telephone oral history interview by Jane Brooks on October 8, 2013. Morris started nurse training in 1944 at the London Hospital, Whitechapel.

68. Rosemary Sanders (pseudonym), an oral history interview by Jane Brooks on October 18, 2011, in Bournemouth. Sanders started nurse training in 1940 at West Middlesex Hospital in London. It is worth noting that Sanders maintained that you could not always tell the difference between those who had been in an accident and those who had been bombed.

69. Jo Dunstone, personal correspondence to Jane Brooks on April 24, 2012. Dunstone later trained as a nurse at St. George's Hospital in London. She maintained in her letter that although she had always wanted to be a nurse, the death of her sister acted as a further catalyst to the decision.

70. Margaret Thomas, a telephone oral history interview by Jane Brooks on February 17, 2014. Thomas trained in Hackney, London, beginning June 1940.

71. Alice Vaughan (pseudonym), a telephone oral history interview by Jane Brooks on October 11, 2013. Vaughan undertook Red Cross training and worked as an assistant nurse in two Birmingham hospitals.

72. Edwards, an oral history interview by Jane Brooks on November 6, 2013.

73. Joyce Stephens, a telephone oral history interview by Jane Brooks on November 28, 2013. Stephens started nurse training in 1939 at St. James' Hospital, Balham, in South London.

74. Anonymous, "Nurse Rescues Policeman in Raid," *The Manchester Guardian*, January 10, 1941, 10. Marsh was presented with a gold watch by the chief constable to mark her "signal [sic] gallantry and courage."

75. Anonymous, "Gallantry in Air Raids: A Very Brave Nurse Wins M.B.E.," *The Manchester Guardian*, September 27, 1941, 7.

76. Barbara Mortimer, *Sisters: Memories From the Courageous Nurses of World War Two* (London: Hutchinson, 2012), 101.

77. Labour Research Department, *Fire Watching for Men and Women: Worker's Pocket Book Series* (London: Labour Research Department, 1942), 2, CP/ORG/MISC/11/01: Labour History Archive Study Centre: People's History Museum, Manchester.

78. Penny Summerfield, *Reconstructing Women's Wartime Lives* (Manchester: Manchester University Press, 1998), 45.

79. Sadie Abraham, telephone oral history interview by Jane Brooks on September 3, 2013. Abraham joined the Civil Nursing Reserve in 1942 and was given 10 days' training in Chichester on the southeast coast of England before commencing ward nursing work. She would have been only about 18 years old.

80. Labour Research Department, *Fire Watching for Men and Women*, 12.

81. Lucy Sherbourne, a telephone oral history interview by Jane Brooks on October 29, 2013. Sherbourne started nurse training in October 1943 in London.

82. Betty Crisp, a telephone oral history interview by Jane Brooks on January 13, 2014. Crisp started nurse training in September 1940 at the Royal Devon and Exeter Hospital in the southwest of England.

83. Anonymous, "Women in the New Britain," *The Town Crier*, March 15, 1941. Labour History Archive Study Centre: People's History Museum, Manchester. It should be noted that women earned less than their male counterparts in most industries during the war, even when they were engaged in "men's work." For a full discussion of the pay differentials see, Summerfield, *Reconstructing Women's Wartime Lives*, 126–132.

84. Sherbourne, a telephone oral history interview on October 29, 2013.

85. Emily Soper, a telephone oral history interview by Jane Brooks on September 6, 2013. Soper started nurse training in 1938 in Glasgow. On qualifying, Soper joined the Queen Alexandra's Imperial Military Nursing Service and was posted to Normandy after the D-Day landings.

86. Anonymous, "Hospital Patients and Nurses Killed by Bomb: Thursday Night Raids: North West Again," *The Manchester Guardian*, September 7, 1940, 4.

87. Anonymous, "More Awards for Gallantry in Civil Defence: Medical Officer's Work in Tunnel Wreck. Two Women George Medallists: A Coventry Nurse's Courage," *The Manchester Guardian*, February 8, 1941, 9.

88. Entwhistle, *Salford Royal Infirmary, 1827–1977*, 74.

89. McGann, Crowther, and Dougall, *A History of the Royal College of Nursing*, 105.

90. Anonymous, "Medal for Nurse: Bravery in Belfast Raid After Being Buried," *The Manchester Guardian*, November 1, 1941, 5.

91. Walker, a telephone oral history interview on November 26, 2013.

92. Debbie Palmer, *Who Cared for the Carers? A History of the Occupational Health of Nurses, 1880–1948* (Manchester: Manchester University Press, 2014), 143.

93. June Huntly (pseudonym), an oral history interview by Jane Brooks on October 19, 2011, in Bournemouth. Huntly started nurse training in 1943 at the West London Hospital in Hammersmith.

94. Sherbourne, a telephone oral history interview on October 29, 2013.

95. Van de Vord, a telephone oral history interview on December 5, 2013.

96. Rashleigh, a telephone oral history interview on October 15, 2013.

97. Abraham, a telephone oral history interview on September 3, 2013.

98. Bowes, an oral history interview on October 19, 2011.

99. Bowring, an oral history interview on July 31, 2012.

100. Abraham, a telephone oral history interview on September 3, 2013.

101. Bowring, an oral history interview on July 31, 2012.

102. Sanders, an oral history interview on October 18, 2011.

103. Mary Purvis (pseudonym), an oral history interview by Jane Brooks on December 12, 2012. Purvis started nurse training in 1944 at Addenbrookes' Hospital.

104. Rashleigh, a telephone oral history interview on October 15, 2013.

105. Bowes, an oral history interview on October 19, 2011.

106. Ibid.

107. Starns, *Nurses at War*, 35.

CHAPTER 6

The Bombing of Pearl Harbor, Hawaii, December 7, 1941

Gwyneth Rhiannon Milbrath

All of these people were bleeding and covered with the dust where the building and the floors in the barracks caved in. One man, with his leg terribly mangled, had a tourniquet made by one of the medics. There was another guy who came up to me and said, "Oh, nurse, come to my first Sergeant. I think he's dying." I went over, and he was already dead. I said, "It's too late." Of course, there was complete chaos ... [the patients were] coming in with limbs off, practically dead from having hemorrhaged. There were just all kinds of wounds and blood and dust from the building that exploded on them. Some had machine gun and bomb fragment wounds. They were just butchered.... We just had to line them up.[1]

Recalling the morning of December 7, 1941, when the Japanese bombed Pearl Harbor, Hawaii, Monica Conter, RN, described her experience in these words. She was working at Hickam Field Hospital, separated only by a fence from the harbor where 21 U.S. military ships were devastated within a few hours.[2] The attack in the early morning hours of a beautiful Sunday took the U.S. military by surprise; the

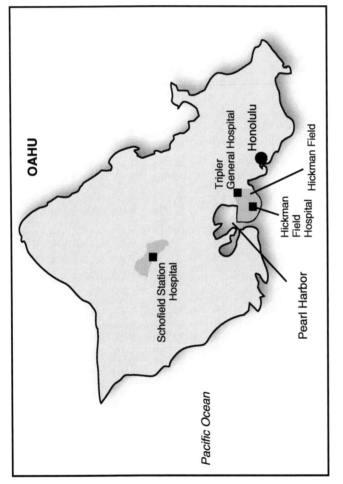

Oahu in the Hawaiian Islands.

OAHU

Pacific Ocean

Schofield Station
Hospital

Tripler
General Hospital

Honolulu

Hickman
Field
Hospital

Hickman Field

Pearl Harbor

nurses, as well as physicians and other hospital personnel, were unprepared for the onslaught of critically injured men.

Much has been written about the military events of December 7, 1941; however, little has been documented about the nurses' work and experiences in Pearl Harbor. This chapter describes the role and experiences of the nurses serving at Hickam Field Hospital on December 7, 1941, and the days immediately following, highlighting the care they provided and the resilience they displayed. Primary sources included transcripts of oral interviews and correspondence of two Army Nurse Corps (ANC) nurses, located in the U.S. Army Medical Department Center of History and Heritage, San Antonio, Texas.

THE UNITED STATES PREPARES FOR WAR

Decades earlier, during World War I, the number of nurses in the ANC grew from 403 nurses on active duty to 21,480.[3] Following the war, however, this number dramatically decreased. By December 1941, prior to the United States' entrance into the war, fewer than 1,000 nurses were on active duty.[4] The few military nurses who were stationed on bases in the United States in the years just prior to December 1941 kept busy by treating communicable diseases and orthopedic injuries from sport or training exercises.[5] As the war in Europe intensified, more young women became part of the ANC; however, numbers were not yet high enough to meet the potential demands of a large war. So, on December 7, 1941, there were only 82 Army nurses stationed in Hawaii serving at three Army medical facilities: Tripler General Hospital, Schofield Hospital, and Hickam Field Hospital.[6] Six nurses were stationed at the newly opened, small, Hickam Field station hospital, located on one of the two primary Army air bases in the Pacific.[7]

The conflict between the United States and Japan started in the 1930s when the Empire of Japan began a campaign to conquer China. After struggling with an independent conquest, Japan joined the Axis Alliance in 1940 and swiftly occupied all of Indochina within the next year. Due to American economic interests in East Asia, the Americans began sending financial aid to China and stopped exporting raw materials, including oil, to Japan. With Japan now cut off from oil supplies, Japanese military leaders planned to conquer Southeast Asia to find new sources. One obstacle, however, was the U.S. Pacific fleet stationed in Pearl Harbor, Hawaii. In the spring of 1941, Japan began to train and prepare for a strike against the United States of America.[8]

PREPARED FOR WAR?

Monica Conter (Benning), RN, and Mary Kathleen Coberly (Finn), RN, both nurses in the U.S. ANC, started their Army careers at Walter Reed Hospital in Washington, DC.[9] While in Washington, Lt. Conter was chosen to be pictured in the "Uncle Sam Needs Nurses" campaign and was featured in posters and movies.[10] In a 1982 interview, she recalled her role as the official model for the ANC during the 1930s and 1940s: "My picture appeared all over the country when the first reserve nurse was called into active duty. I got to meet all of these famous people at a

Become a Nurse: War propaganda poster used to encourage young women to become a military nurse, featuring Monica Conter Benning.
Courtesy of the American Nurses Association.

lawn party at the White House. It was very exciting.... [But at the time] I was dying to get overseas, and I kept bugging them about when I was going to get to Hawaii, the Island."[11] Lieutenant Coberly had originally requested foreign duty in the Philippines, but was asked to go to Hawaii when another nurse was unable to go. Coberly and Conter traveled together on the *USS Mariposa* from San Francisco to Hawaii with a large group of Army personnel.[12]

The military (both Army and Navy) nurses stationed in Hawaii were primarily working at the Navy Hospital at Pearl Harbor, Tripler General Hospital, Schofield Hospital, Hickam Field Hospital, or aboard the hospital ship *USS Solace*.[13] Arriving in Hawaii on July 11, 1941, Coberly and Conter were eventually transferred from Tripler Hospital to the brand new, 30-bed Hickam Field Hospital when it was opened on November

Hickam Hospital at Hickam Field, Oahu, U.S. territory of Hawaii,
as seen from the base tower, 1941.

Courtesy of the U.S. Army via Hawaii Aviation Preservation Society.

149

17, 1941.[14] Hickam Hospital was located only three blocks away from the flight line (the area where the aircraft are parked and serviced) and next to the headquarters building. It stood three stories high and was constructed with reinforced concrete.[15] The ground floor was primarily home to administrative offices, the second floor housed the operating theater and clinic, and the third floor consisted of patient wards.[16] The hospital also had screened porches around most of the perimeter to allow the tropical Hawaiian breezes to flow through the building.[17]

The Hawaiian Air Force, part of the U.S. Army, was headquartered at Hickam Field and was made up of 7,460 officers and enlisted men who were stationed at one of the three bases: Hickam Field, Wheeler Field, and Bellows Field. Hickam Field was the newest airbase that was completed and officially activated on September 1, 1938. Hickam Field, the principal Army airfield in Hawaii, was the only Air Force station large enough to land the B-17 bombers.[18] This heavy bomber aircraft (also known as the Flying Fortress) became part of the Army Air Corps fleet in 1935 and was the first four-engine heavy bomber developed for the U.S. Army Air Corps.[19]

Although Coberly and Conter enjoyed working at Hickam, they also thoroughly enjoyed the time spent off duty. All registered nurses in the ANC were considered officers and therefore were able to mingle with other officers. In fact, on December 6, 1941, both nurses had dates at the Pearl Harbor Officer's Club.[20] Monica Conter and her date decided to walk to the harbor shortly after arriving at the club. She remembered, "It was the most beautiful sight I've ever seen. All the battleships and the lights with the reflection on the water. We were just overwhelmed. I'll just never forget it."[21] Mary Kathleen Coberly opted to stay at the Officers' Club and dance, recalling her dance partner said, "And you know, this is so beautiful. They talk about the Japanese but [they] could never get in here."[22]

The morning of December 7, 1941, Lieutenant Conter reported for duty at Hickam Field Hospital. Her job that day was to care for the dozen or so patients recovering from minor illness—among them, patients with cellulitis and pneumonia. She and fellow Army nurse Irene Boyd were the only two nurses on duty early that morning. Coberly and Chief Nurse Annie Fox had the day off; Sally Entrikin, RN, was scheduled to arrive at 8:00 a.m., and an additional nurse was just heading back to her quarters to sleep after working through the night.[23] No one expected what would happen next.

THE ATTACK

At 6:00 a.m. on the morning of December 7, 1941, six Japanese carriers stationed 200 miles north of Oahu launched the first wave of 181 planes set to destroy Pearl Harbor.[24] Although there had been some early reports of abnormal air traffic on the morning of December 7, the warning signs had gone unheeded. As a result, the U.S. military forces at Pearl Harbor were completely surprised and unprepared for the Japanese aerial attack. The Japanese flew low over the harbor, guns blazing, a few minutes before 8:00 a.m. that Sunday morning.[25] They attacked the military strongholds in Oahu, dropping half-ton bombs and raining down machine gun fire. Both Hickam Field and Wheeler Army Field were priority targets. Wheeler Airbase, located in the mountains of Oahu, was attacked on the first strike; the second strike was focused on Hickam Field—the site of the Army Air Headquarters and Hickam Field Hospital.[26] During and immediately following the two waves of the Japanese aerial attack, hundreds of wounded and dying soldiers were rushed to first-aid stations, mobile hospitals, ship sick bays, and medical dispensaries.

Kathleen Coberly and fellow ANC nurse Sarah (Sally) Entrikin were in their quarters a couple of blocks from the hospital when the bombing began. Both watched the attack from their bedroom window, facing Pearl Harbor. Entrikin later recalled that she "could see the planes and the smoke and the rising sun on the sides of the planes. And it was a frightening thing. The phone rang...and [her date for the previous evening] said, 'Honey, we're at war.' And all the phones went dead."[27] Coberly, frightened and numb from the shock of what she had just witnessed, quickly threw on her uniform just before one of the Army officers arrived to take her and Entrikin to Hickam Hospital.[28]

Meanwhile, Monica Conter and fellow ANC nurse Irene Boyd were already on duty at the hospital. Conter remembered hearing a plane overhead losing altitude and feared it might crash. According to her, she "ran out on the porch overlooking the [airfield]...about that time, all broke loose...I saw the rising sun on these planes that were flying low."[29] After confirming the attack with her commanding officer, Conter began to evacuate the patients from the third floor to the first floor where they believed they would be safer. While others were relocating patients using the elevator, the electricity went out; all of the clocks stopped at 7:55 a.m.[30]

EMERGENT BEHAVIOR: TRIAGE

As the casualties started arriving approximately 10 minutes after the start of the raid, Conter was downstairs on the main level trying to triage the seemingly endless influx of the critically wounded.[31] "All of these patients were coming in, and we were putting them all out on the porch. There were some who were killed, and we were putting them out in the back yard behind the hospital. They were just beginning to stack up and the noise was terrible. I can't tell you how terrible the noise was."[32]

Without warning, a terrifyingly loud 500-pound bomb exploded on the front lawn of Hickam Hospital, about 60 or 70 feet from the building.[33] Kathleen Coberly had been working in the second-floor operating theater when the bomb almost hit the hospital. As she later recalled:

> All at once there was this terrible noise and the building shook and the windows were shattered there in the operating room. And it seemed like the whole building was going to tumble down.... We heard the plane and then another noise and the hospital shook again. Finally when we got outside to look around there was a crater, a huge crater on one side of the hospital and then another crater on the other.[34]

In the midst of the confusion, the patient on the operating table died from his injuries.[35] The wounded continued to line up inside and outside of the hospital, and the medical staff was quickly overwhelmed. The nurses prioritized pain relief and control of bleeding for the hundreds of patients lined up on the porch. Army pilot Lieutenant Philip Sprawls watched Lieutenant Conter work that day. "They laid victims on the porch floor for first aid. Many died, even while she was extracting the hypo needle [tetanus or morphine]! The blood actually ran on the floor. She showed me where it came up over the soles of her shoes."[36]

"TAKE THEM TO TRIPLER!"

The aerial assault on Pearl Harbor was the first time in U.S. history that Army nurses had been on the front line of battle; in the past, they were always in hospitals at least 10 miles away from the battle-field.[37] The small team of doctors and nurses equipped to care for about 30 patients at a time was soon overwhelmed by the number of casualties dropped on the hospital's doorstep. The team refocused its efforts, and converted Hickam Hospital into an evacuation hospital, transferring all critical cases to Tripler General Hospital or the civilian Queen's Hospital in Honolulu. Ambulatory patients were kept at Hickam, and the rest were divided among other hospitals farther inland. ANC nurse Lieutenant Sally Entrikin observed the overwhelming scene firsthand:

> Inside the hospital, doctors, staff, and volunteers were over-whelmed by the ferocity of the attack and the number of wounded flooding the facility.…There were only six of us nurses, and we couldn't possibly begin to take care of all the wounded and dying men. The decision was made to treat patients with first-aid-type care and send them to Tripler General Hospital in ambulances. Soon there weren't enough ambulances so the local people drove patients in their cars.[38]

The scene in front of the hospital was no better than that within the hospital. The wounded and those carrying the wounded were swarm-ing around the front lawn, and the driveway was full of trucks and ambulances. There was no more room at the hospital, and one of the nurses and a doctor came out shouting, "Don't unload any more, we are full…. Take them to Tripler! Take them to Tripler!" As the trucks and ambulances started pulling away, one vehicle did not move. "The red-headed young driver had his head in his arms resting on the steering wheel…his face looked like raw hamburger…one look and the doctor ordered two nearby men to pull the driver in with the wounded he had brought in the ambulance."[39] Hickam Hospital became a revolving door for many of the injured soldiers as the nurses and doctors quickly triaged, bandaged, and medicated the injured, and then arranged transportation to a larger facility.

As patients continued to stream into the hospital on chairs, doors, or anything else rescuers could use to transport the wounded, additional volunteers arrived to assist the Hickam nurses. Officers' wives who had some civilian nursing experience arrived at the hospital and were set to make bandages, alongside other patients and volunteers.[40] Even with the help of the volunteers, the medical team did not have enough supplies to keep up with the demand. Hickam Hospital did not have a stockpile of military or medical supplies, and the doctors had some initial difficulties persuading personnel at Fort Shafter, where Tripler Hospital is located, to transfer what they needed. Coberly remembered overhearing one of the doctors requesting supplies:[41]

> I heard one of our doctors calling Fort Shafter asking for ambulances, gas masks, helmets, supplies, everything. And then he listened. And there was this burst of profanity and then a plea for help. He said, "Please. We are at war. The Japanese are bombing the hell [sic] out of us down here. We're sending patients to Tripler. Now we need ambulances. We need help; we need gas masks and helmets. This is not a false alarm. We're not just having maneuvers...this is the real thing." And in no time at all the ambulances came...supplies arrived....Help arrived from Tripler, in short order, they were [also] needed at [Tripler] hospital.[42]

During the bombing, all patients were kept on the hospital's first floor. With each exploding bomb in the harbor and the gunfire raining down on the air base, nurses and patients alike would drop to the floor to protect themselves.[43] The noxious fumes from the explosions filled the air inside the hospital, and a number of people yelled "Gas! Gas!" adding to the panic and confusion.[44] They feared that gases from the bombs might also be lethal, and used moist towels as makeshift gas masks until actual gas masks and helmets were distributed later that day. After one of these close calls, Lieutenant Conter turned to Kathleen Coberly and asked, "Do you suppose they know back in Apalachicola, Florida where I'm from [,] that we're at war?" [Kathleen responded], "Monica, the whole world knows we're at war."[45]

NURSE LEADERSHIP

First Lieutenant Annie Fox, chief nurse at Hickam Field, displayed calm and fearless leadership during this time of chaos and destruction. Later, on October 26, 1944, she was awarded the Bronze Star in recognition of her heroic actions during the Pearl Harbor bombing at Hickam Field Hospital.[46] The citation reads:

> For heroic and meritorious service in military operations against the enemy during the attack on Hickam Field by Japanese forces on 7 December 1941. During the attack Lieutenant Fox, in an exemplary manner, performed her duties as Head Nurse.... In addition, she administered anesthesia to patients during the heaviest part of the bombardment, assisted in dressing the wounded, taught civilian volunteer nurses to make and wrap dressings, and worked ceaselessly with coolness and efficiency, and her fine example of calmness, courage, and leadership was of great benefit to the morale of all with whom she came in contact. The loyalty and devotion to duty displayed by Lieutenant Fox on this occasion reflected great credit upon her and the military service.[47]

Under the leadership of Lieutenant Fox, the Hickam Field nurses were able to triage and provide emergency care and first aid to more than 500 mildly injured to mortally wounded soldiers during and immediately after the air raid. Despite the gruesome event in which she saw traumatic injuries and piles of dead sailors, Conter focused on providing the best care she could to as many men as possible. In a letter home on December 17, 1941, Monica described her overall reflections about that day. "During my whole career, I have never had such personal

155

satisfaction with my work as I did that day. All—everybody—put forth and with success."[48]

NURSING AND FIRST-AID CARE AT HICKAM FIELD

A first-aid textbook written in 1943, shortly after the bombing of Pearl Harbor, detailed the type of care wounded soldiers would have received. About 60% of the casualties sustained in the Pearl Harbor attacks were the result of severe burns sustained from the flaming battleships and oil burning on the surface of the water in the harbor.[49] At Hickam Field, however, the primary mechanism of injury was not the burning fuel. Rather, injuries occurred due to the blast and debris from the exploding bombs, or from structures collapsing.

Destruction at Hickam Field, Oahu, Hawaii, December 7, 1941.
Courtesy of U.S. Army Medical Department, Office of Medical History.

The majority of injuries seen by the medical staff from the aerial bombardment consisted of multiple fractures, hemorrhage, and extensively torn muscles, with many of those injured going into shock.[50] The rapid detonation of the half-ton bombs caused the steel jacket to be blown into small, sharp fragments at a high enough velocity and rotational force to

156

carry them more than 1,500 yards. The combination of the forward and rotational momentum caused severe damage to the human tissue and bone with little external evidence of injury, with an estimated one third of those wounded suffering mortal injuries. Those standing upright during the blast were most likely to be injured, with wounds to the legs being most common. The recommended treatment was to splint any fractures or suspected torn muscles, provide warm blankets, sedate with morphine, and allow the patient to rest. Those incurring more serious injuries involving the abdomen or chest would receive surgical treatment immediately to manage any organ damage or internal bleeding.[51]

During World War II, physicians were just beginning to understand blast injuries, which were understood to be caused by the enormous pressure increase from the bomb detonation of those located close to the site of impact. Many dead bodies found near the detonation site appeared to have no external injuries; however, the body had micro-hemorrhages in the brain, lungs, adrenal glands, and other organs containing air space. Those who survived appeared relatively healthy except for acting dazed or confused, and had no hallmark changes in their blood pressure or pulse indicative of shock and severe injury. Unfortunately, those sustaining blast injuries routinely died once they were given general anesthesia. Thus, it was advised to treat all soldiers located near the blast zone as having the potential for a blast injury. Treatment included close observation and administration of warm oral fluids and cortical extract.[52]

Wound care at this time heavily emphasized the need to protect the wound from bacteria and to control any bleeding. Direct pressure was applied for 2 to 3 minutes to control bleeding before bandaging. For most wounds, nurses would apply a pressure dressing using a dry, sterile dressing or a freshly ironed handkerchief or towel.[53] If a pressure dressing was inadequate to control the bleeding, the nurse applied a tourniquet to either the patient's upper arm or thigh with enough pressure to compress the artery against the bone. She then loosened the tourniquet every 30 minutes and reassessed the wound for any bleeding. If the bleeding had decreased, she would apply direct pressure to the wound and then apply a pressure dressing, thus allowing the restoration of blood flow to and from the injured extremity. Nurses did not irrigate wounds due to the risk of rebleeding; rather, they sprinkled 3 to 10 g of sulfadiazine into the wound, covered it with a dressing, and prepared the patient for transport to the hospital or to await surgery if needed.[54]

Those providing wound care were especially concerned about tetanus and other infections occurring because sterility was not always possible inside the war zone. All soldiers received a tetanus immunization prior to entering the combat zone, and those with injuries from shrapnel, bullets, or other metals were given a booster vaccine. Other advances in wound care included packing and dressing wounds instead of closing them with sutures. This allowed the sterile packing material to absorb infectious drainage from the wound and decreased the incidence of wounds colonized with anaerobic bacteria, including the often fatal gas gangrene. There were no reported deaths due to tetanus in Pearl Harbor; however, there were 15 cases of gas gangrene, all from wounds prematurely closed with sutures. The addition of sulfa drugs to wound care drastically decreased mortality rates from infection in World War II compared to World War I. Every soldier carried a packet of sulfa drugs and was instructed to take it orally as soon as he was wounded. In the hospitals, nurses not only applied sulfa directly to any open wounds, they also administered oral sulfa therapy both pre- and postoperatively.[55]

Unfortunately, the Hickam nurses worked under less than ideal circumstances. There was no electricity and no sterilization abilities for the needles they were using for injections.[56] The soldiers' cries for water went unanswered because the water supply was reportedly poisoned.[57] The nurses resorted to wiping the needle and the site with alcohol prior to administering a morphine injection. To document the care they gave each patient, the Hickam nurses attempted to tag patients with basic identifying information, as well as whether they had received a morphine or tetanus injection. Initially, the nurses were able to tag patients, but stopped when the second Japanese raid decimated the Hickam Field barracks and brought in even more soldiers with even worse injuries.[58]

The nurses worked tirelessly relieving the pain of the injured and dying soldiers by giving pain medication injections, using whatever supplies were available, and prioritizing treatment above cleanliness and sterility.[59] As Conter recalled:

> In the meantime, we were giving morphine. They had some sterile water from somewhere, and they gave us 10cc syringes. We would fill those…and go down that porch giving shots…trying to stop the hemorrhaging and the pain…we would give it just as fast as we could….We told them not to let anyone give them another shot….It was a thing to do in an emergency, which is an understatement. Just going down the porch giving those 10 shots with a 10cc syringe….We went in to fill up and came back out where we left off and gave more…that's how I reacted and everybody else was doing it. That was the only thing we knew to do in the middle of all of this. We hoped we were saving their lives, keeping them from pain, and maybe stopping some of the hemorrhaging.[60]

After controlling any bleeding, the nurses gave high priority to preventing, recognizing, and treating shock. The medical knowledge at the time understood shock as the failure of the peripheral vascular system to provide adequate circulation caused by the loss of one to two quarts of blood and resulting in pallor, mental status change, gasping respirations, increased heart rate, and a profound drop in blood pressure. Nurses worked at preventing their patients from going into shock by controlling any bleeding, immobilizing fractures to prevent further bleeding from movement, warming the body with blankets, giving warm oral fluids, and controlling the patient's pain. Pain was understood to worsen shock; therefore, the nurses administered morphine not only to relieve pain but also to improve a soldier's chances of survival. They gave the morphine intramuscularly in doses of a quarter to half grain, or 15 to 30 mg. If a soldier was showing early signs of shock, the nurse would position his legs above his head and give oral fluids immediately unless the patient needed an emergent operation. Solutions with 3% to 5% glucose or 0.9% sodium chloride were given either subcutaneously or intravenously. IV fluids were preferred because glucose solutions provided some nourishment and aided in stimulating the kidneys to remove toxins from the body. However, soldiers with massive bleeding saw only temporary improvement from IV fluid administration because the solution would quickly leave the peripheral vascular system. For soldiers suffering from severe shock, blood products, including fresh whole blood or blood plasma, were key in preventing mortality resulting from shock and massive hemorrhage. The technology of "banking" blood products was newly introduced during this period, allowing blood and plasma to be safely stored up to 8 days prior to administration.[61]

Crush injuries and compound fractures plagued those injured at Hickam Field. Crush injuries were treated by immediately compressing the affected tissue with an elastic bandage with approximately 40 to 60 mmHg of pressure. The pressure bandage compressed the tissue enough to decrease swelling, but allowed blood to flow to the injured tissue, thus preventing gangrene.[62] Compound fractures were best treated in the operating theater; however, first-aid care involved splinting the affected bone, reducing the fracture if possible, applying sulfonamide powder into the wound, and covering it with a dressing. Under normal circumstances, compound fractures were a high priority for surgery; however, due to the large number of critical cases at Hickam Field, most orthopedic repairs had to wait for 24 to 72 hours. Despite this delay in treatment, no cases of gas gangrene or deaths from other infection occurred. This accomplishment was a substantial improvement in medical and surgical treatment compared to World War I.[63]

RESILIENCE AND RECOVERY

Four days after the attack, Monica Conter wrote a brief note to her parents on the mainland, informing them of the fact that she had survived the bombing and was coping with the "new normal" of 12-hour shifts and trauma care:

> December 11, 1941
> My dearest Daddy, Mother, and all,
> Was uninjured in the air raid. Am feeling fine—doing 12 hour duty. Do not worry—Everything under control. Hope you

received my OKAY telegram I sent on Monday. Will have lots to tell you someday. Love to the sweetest parents in the world—your loving daughter, Monica.[64]

The new normal included changes to the nurses' practice. The medical operations at Hickam Hospital moved from the first-floor clinics to the third floor where the patient wards were located. The nurses had little time off. Conter remembered that the first night after the attack, she went to her room only briefly—to change her uniform—and then returned to work that night. Due to fears of an invasion or another attack, the nurses had to work by flashlights that were dimmed by blue cellophane, and no one was allowed to light a cigarette. Everyone was on edge—both within Hickam Hospital and those on guard that night at the air base. Bombing continued throughout the night, and soldiers could not differentiate between the sounds of friendly and enemy aircraft. Each time they would hear gunfire, they feared the Japanese had returned. As a precaution, they would seek cover. Patients and staff ran down the third-floor stairs, clutching their gas masks and helmets, to the first floor where they believed they would be safer.[65] Eventually, the patients and hospital staff just stayed the night on the ground floor, sleeping against the walls. By Monday, some private rooms in radiology were made available for officers to sleep at the hospital. Conter remembered, "I just kept my uniform on and took my shoes off because we expected the [enemy] to come back any minute...my heart was pounding so hard that the bed was shaking."[66] Staff and patients were both apprehensive and fearful of more raids or a Japanese invasion.[67]

Although the nurses were terrified of being killed in another raid or taken as a prisoner in an invasion, they coped by using humor and talking about their experiences with others who had lived through the experience or by writing about it to family members back home. In a letter home to her parents on December 17, 1941, Conter reported that Kathleen Coberly requested to be baptized by the chaplain during the bombing. Conter also expressed fear that her family would assume the worst based on what they had heard from the media.[68] She attempted to send a telegram the day after the bombing to inform her family she was fine, and followed it up with several letters.[69] In one letter written

161

on December 22, after detailing her experience during the air raid, she concluded with, "I do appreciate purposed interest in my welfare. But tell everyone I couldn't have missed it for anything. You know I always loved activity and excitement. For once, I had *enough*."[70]

The nurses remained in the hospital around the clock for about 3 weeks after the attack, working together with the physicians to care for their patients. Cooperation and collaboration were essential to their work. Coberly remembered, "bandaging a patient and someone is holding things and holding the light and assisting me and finally I looked around and there he is, a doctor who had gone over on the same ship with us and he was on duty at Schofield [Hospital] and I said, 'Oh, I should be assisting you.' And he said, 'That's all right. You just go ahead. You're doing fine.' "[71] Professional boundary lines blurred as both doctors and nurses did their part.

Eventually, two relief nurses were sent to Hickam Hospital to allow for the other six nurses to rest. Lieutenant Coberly remembered only being able to go to quarters if she was escorted; she would bathe, pick up fresh clothing, and return to the hospital to work during the day and sleep in the x-ray room at night.[72] Lieutenant Conter confided in one of the Army pilots, Lieutenant Phillip Sprawls, that neither she nor any of the other nurses had rested in more than 30 hours.[73]

Within months of the attack, when most of the patients had stabilized, the U.S. armed forces mandated additional training for medical personnel in case of a second attack. Fearing the potential for chemical warfare similar to that used in World War I, the Army provided multiday training to doctors and nurses to help them recognize and treat gas casualties. Decontamination showers were set up at the rear of the hospital to bathe patients in the event of an exposure to harmful gases. Nurses also trained to recognize the different gases by their scent, as well as how to protect themselves from the noxious fumes.[74] In the event of an emergency, the hospitals had alert calls that would summon the staff to report to their duty station.[75]

As the days passed, life began to return to a new normalcy as the nurses, officers, and soldiers adapted to strict wartime rules and regulations. By December 17, the nurses were able to return to their quarters and resume 8-hour shifts. The new normal included censored mail, restrictions on drinking alcoholic beverages, and curfews. Conter recounted the new reality in a letter, describing to her family the inability to wear her new clothes, not being able to drink any alcohol, the military imposed curfew at 5:30 p.m., nightly blackouts, and the shortage of silk hose on the island.[76] On December 22, Conter reported "we are able to take a deep breath once again, but you should really see me hurry and get into my uniform, helmet, and gas mask when the air raid alarm is sounded. We take our helmets and masks with us everywhere we go."[77]

CONCLUSION: LOOKING BACK AND MOVING FORWARD

As illustrated in the early hours of December 7, 1941, the men and women living and serving in Pearl Harbor were not prepared for the massacre that ensued over a 2-hour period that morning. The casualties of the "day that would live in infamy" included 21 of 90 ships anchored in the harbor; 157 damaged and 188 destroyed aircraft; and 2,403 dead and 1,178 wounded Americans, including both civilian and military losses.[78] Hickam Field suffered the majority of the airfield casualties and property damage, with 139 casualties and 303 wounded, most likely due to the Japanese air strike on the barracks and the large amounts of concentrated bombing.[79] The heroic and collaborative actions of the medical corpsmen, physicians, and six nurses saved hundreds of lives and eased the suffering of those mortally wounded. The quick decision to evacuate patients to the larger Tripler General Hospital most likely saved hundreds of lives and allowed nurses to focus on pain management, triage, and bleeding control.

During World War II, more than 59,000 American nurses served in the ANC, bringing nurses closer to the front lines than they ever had been before. Starting in World War II, nurses cared for soldiers under fire in field hospitals, evacuation hospitals, hospital trains, hospital ships, and on medical transport planes. The skill and dedication of these nurses contributed to the extremely low post-injury mortality rate among American military forces in every theater of the war. Overall, fewer than 4% of the American soldiers who received medical care in the field or underwent evacuation died from wounds or disease.[80]

Hickam Field Air Force Base was designated as a National Historic Landmark in October 1980. The tattered, bullet-ridden American flag is on display in the Pacific Air Forces Headquarters, with the "bullet-scarred walls," which have been preserved as a reminder to never be caught unprepared.[81] December 7, 1941, changed the course of American and world history, as well as the lives of the nurses who cared for those fallen and wounded in battle.

NOTES

1. Interview of Monica Conter Benning, May 24, 1982; 2010.8.3, Box 8, Research Collection, U.S. Army Medical Department (AMEDD) Center of History and Heritage, Fort Sam Houston, Texas

2. Administrative History Section, Administrative Division, Bureau of Medicine and Surgery, *The United States Navy Medical Department at War, 1941–1945*, vol. 1, parts 1–2 (Washington, DC: The Bureau, 1946), 1–31, accessed February 20, 2014, http://www.history.navy.mil/faqs/faq66-5.htm.

3. Army Heritage Center Foundation, "Army Nurses of World War One: Service Beyond Expectations," accessed October, 2014, http://army-heritage.org/education-and-programs/educational-resources/soldier-stories/130-army-nurses-of-world-war-one-service-beyond-expectations.html.

4. Judith A. Bellafaire, "The Army Nurse Corps: A Commemoration of World War II Service," *US Army Center of Military History*, http://www.history.army.mil/books/wwii/72-14/72-14.HTM (last modified October 3, 2003).

5. Mary T. Sarnecky, *A History of the U.S. Army Nurse Corps* (Philadelphia, PA: University of Pennsylvania Press), 175, 177 (hereafter cited as Sarnecky, *Army Nurse Corps*); see also "Pearl Harbor Nurse Remembers Japanese Attack."

6. Bellafaire, "The Army Nurse Corps."

7. Sarnecky, *Army Nurse Corps*, 182.

8. Department of Defense, 50th Anniversary of World War II Commemorative Committee, *Pearl Harbor: 50th Anniversary Commemorative Chronicle*, "A Grateful Nation Remembers" 1941–1991 (Washington, DC: The Committee, 1991), http://www.history.navy.mil/faqs/faq66-1.htm.

9. Conter Benning, AMEDD (1982); see also Interview of Mary Kathleen Coberly Finn, May 24, 1982, 2010.8.3, Box 31, Research Collection, U.S.

Army Medical Department Center of History and Heritage, Fort Sam Houston, Texas.

10. Ed Unser, "Nurse at Pearl Harbor Recounts the Peril," *Gannett Satellite Information Network*, December 6, 2007, http://archive.news-press.com/article/20071206/NEWS01/312060001/Nurse-Pearl-Harbor-recounts-peril.

11. Conter Benning, AMEDD (1982).

12. Coberly Finn, AMEDD (1982).

13. Erica Warren, "Army Nurse Recalls Attack on Pearl Harbor," *San Diego Union-Tribune*, December 7, 2003, http://www.utsandiego.com/news/2003/Dec/07/army-nurse-recalls-attack-on-pearl-harbor/1/?#article-copy.

14. Coberly Finn, AMEDD (1982); see also Sarnecky, *Army Nurse Corps*, 175.

15. Alan Clark, "7 December 1941: The Air Force Story: Chapter V," *HyperWar Foundation*, accessed May 1, 2014, http://www.ibiblio.org/hyperwar/AAF/7Dec41/7Dec41–5.html.

16. Conter Benning, AMEDD (1982).

17. "The Air Force Story" (2014).

18. "Hickam Field/Hickam Air Force Base Chronology (1935–1985)," http://hawaii.gov/hawaiiaviation/hawaii-airfields-airports/oahu-pre-world-war-ii/hickam-field-air-force-base/Hickam%20AFB%20Chronology%201935–1985.pdf.

19. http://www.airforcemag.com/MagazineArchive/Pages/2006/October%202006/1006bomber.aspx.

20. Conter Benning, AMEDD (1982); see also Coberly Finn, AMEDD (1982).

21. Conter Benning, AMEDD (1982).

22. Coberly Finn, AMEDD (1982).

23. Conter Benning, AMEDD (1982); see also Coberly Finn, AMEDD (1982).

24. "A Grateful Nation Remembers" (1991).

25. Ibid.

26. "Pearl Harbor Raid, "7 December 1941—Attacks on Airfields and Aerial Combat," *Naval History and Heritage Command*, accessed May 1, 2014, http://www.history.navy.mil/photos/events/wwii-pac/pearlhbr/ph-air.htm.

27. Coberly Finn, AMEDD (1982).

28. Ibid.

29. Conter Benning, AMEDD (1982).

30. Ibid.

31. Ibid.

32. Ibid.

33. "The Air Force Story" (2014).

34. Coberly Finn, AMEDD (1982).

35. Ibid.

36. Hawaii Aviation, "Eye Witness Accounts of the Bombing of Hickam AFB," Phillip C. Sprawls, accessed May 1, 2014, http://hawaii.gov/hawaiiaviation/world-war-ii/december-7-1941/first-hand-accounts-of-the-bombing-of-hickam-afb.

37. "The Air Force Story" (2014).

38. Bombing of Hickam AFB.

39. William F. Rudder, Sr., "Bombing of Hickam AFB."

40. Conter Benning, AMEDD (1982).

41. Coberly Finn, AMEDD (1982).

42. Ibid.

43. Ibid.

44. "The Air Force Story" (2014).

45. Conter Benning, AMEDD (1982).

46. "Report of Decorations Board: Annie G. Fox, Bronze Star Medal," *National Archives and Records Administration*, October 26, 1944, http://www.archives.gov/exhibits/a_people_at_war/women_who_served/articles_women_who_served/annie_fox_bronze_star.html.

47. Ibid.

48. Conter Benning Letters, December 17, 1941. Research Collection, U.S. Army Medical Department Center of History and Heritage, Fort Sam Houston, Texas.

49. Bureau of Medicine and Surgery (1946).

50. Warren Cole and Lieutenant Colonel Charles Puestow, *First Aid: Surgical and Medical, 2nd edition* (London: Appleton-Century Company, 1943), 202.

51. Ibid., 200; see also p. 202.

52. Ibid., 203–204.

53. Ibid., 77; see also pp. 69–70, 108.

54. Ibid., *First Aid*, 114; see also pp. 69–70, 116.

55. Ibid., 77; see also pp. 187–188; see also p. 325.

56. Conter Benning, AMEDD (1982).

57. Sarnecky, *Army Nurse Corps*, 176.

58. Conter Benning, AMEDD (1982); see also Coberly Finn, AMEDD (1982); see also "Pearl Harbor Raid" (2014).

59. Conter Benning, AMEDD (1982).

60. Ibid.

61. Cole and Puestow, *First Aid*, 88–94; see also p. 121.

62. Ibid., 116.

63. Ibid., 188.

64. Conter Benning Letters (December 11, 1941).

65. Conter Benning, AMEDD (1982).

66. Ibid.

67. Coberly Finn, AMEDD (1982).

68. Conter Benning Letters (December 17, 1941).

69. Conter Benning Letters (December 11, 1941).

70. Conter Benning Letters (December 17, 1941).

71. Coberly Finn, AMEDD (1982).

72. Ibid.

73. Phillip C. Sprawls, "Bombing of Hickam AFB."

74. Conter Benning, AMEDD (1982).

75. Coberly Finn, AMEDD (1982).

76. Conter Benning Letters (December 17, 1941).

77. Conter Benning Letters (December 22, 1941).

78. Bureau of Medicine and Surgery (1946).

79. Hawaii Aviation, "Hickam Field," *Hickam AFB History Office*, accessed May 1, 2014, http://hawaii.gov/hawaiiaviation/hawaii-airfields-airports/oahu-pre-world-war-ii/hickam-field-air-force-base.

80. Bellafaire, "Army Nurse Corps."

81. "Hickam Field" (2014).

CHAPTER 7

The Nuclear Catastrophe in Hiroshima, Japan, August 1945

Ryoko Ohara, Madonna Grehan,
Sioban Nelson, and Trudy Rudge

"It was really hell. I cannot find the right words to express my emotions" about that day.[1]

Recorded in 2002, this harrowing scene of human misery and devastation is how 17-year-old Chieko Matsumoto, a Japanese Red Cross Society (JRCS) nursing student in her second year, described the immediate aftermath of a nuclear bomb attack that wreaked destruction on the city of Hiroshima on the morning of August 6, 1945. The use of atomic weapons in this way was the first of its kind in world history and a turning point in World War II (WWII). Within weeks, Japan surrendered to the Allied forces, ending hostilities in the Pacific. The bombing was a man-made disaster of such proportion that it is difficult to comprehend today.

In the chaos that ensued after the atomic bomb was dropped, tens of thousands of survivors of the initial blast poured into what remained of Hiroshima's hospitals. Among the health workers at the front line

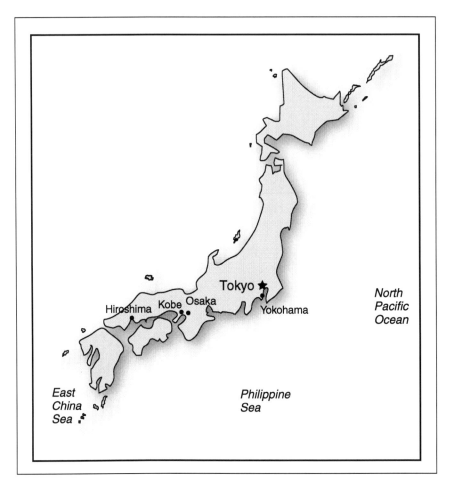

Map of Japan.

of this calamity were nurses, both students and graduates, prepared to a degree for such events but not for the devastation on this scale. This chapter unfolds the catastrophe, as it happened, beginning with the evening immediately before the bombing (August 5) through the first 24 hours afterward (August 6). The chapter combines extracts from the recollections of five nurses present at Hiroshima on that day with published accounts of the bombing.

170

Eyewitness testimonies of the atomic bombing are few.[2] A small number of Hiroshima's nurses recorded brief reminiscences of this time in their lives, but most of these sources were published for reunions of the nurses concerned, rather than for public consumption.[3] The five women whose evidence is presented in this chapter participated in an oral history project at Hiroshima.[4] Aged in their 70s and 80s at the time of the interview,[5] all were nurses of the JRCS and had worked at Hiroshima, either at the time of the bombing or as part of the relief teams sent there in the weeks afterward. One of the interviewees, by participating in this oral history project, talked about her experiences at Hiroshima for the first time. Reasons for the extended silence of these former nurses are complex,[6] but their motivations in discussing that event as part of this research are less complex. Each interviewee felt that what had occurred was important to be placed on the record, expressing hope that her testimony would illustrate the real and horrific impact of the bomb and expressing a desire that her evidence of the disaster would serve as a warning against the use of atomic weapons.[7]

In what follows here, the nurses' narratives offer chilling impressions of the immediate aftermath of this unprecedented nuclear disaster. Their observations underscore a scale of destruction that transcended any training that the staff had undertaken and any preparations in place for such emergencies, illustrating just how difficult it was to create any sense of order in the face of this level of ruin. Their memories of the bombing highlight the ethical dilemmas that young nurses faced in this virtual war zone. Without doubt, their stories are harrowing; yet they demonstrate remarkable examples of initiative, improvisation, cooperation, and fortitude in the face of extreme adversity. This chapter begins with a brief background on JRCS nurses and hospitals. The chapter discusses the relationship to the Japanese military junta and explains why Hiroshima's strategic location made it a target for a nuclear attack. The nurses' recollections of events from August 5 to 7, 1945, and their struggle to nurse in the face of insurmountable devastation are then presented.

NURSES AND HOSPITALS OF THE JRCS
UNDER JAPAN'S MILITARY RULE

Of the five interviewees whose recollections are presented in this chapter, three were students, aged 17 years and in their second year at the JRCS Nursing School, having completed more than 12 months of training. The other two nurses, ages 20 and 26 years, had graduated and were licensed [registered].[8] The JRCS introduced nurse training in 1890 to educate individuals and to prepare them for working in disasters.[9] In October 1891, when Japan experienced the Nobi earthquake, resulting in 7,000 fatalities, the JRCS responded by sending its nurses to assist the survivors of the disaster.[10]

The JRCS nurses became associated with military nursing during the First Sino-Japanese War (1894–1895). Over time, and despite the fact that the JRCS was a nongovernment organization, JRCS nurses were being identified with war relief work more than with disaster relief.[11] With schools of nursing all over the country, the JRCS came to be the most prominent and popular of all nurse-training schemes in Japan, producing large numbers of graduates by the 1940s.[12]

In 1896, the JRCS determined that applicants for training had to be 18 years or older and complete an examination at enrollment. A regulation called the "National Nurse Rule" was enacted in 1900, which set the training period at 3 years. In 1941, Japan faced shortages of nurses. The eligibility age for entry to the regular nursing course was lowered from 18 years to 17 years. In 1944, it was lowered again from 17 years to 16 years. At the same time, the age at which girls graduated from secondary school was lowered too, so that younger Japanese could be used as labor in the war effort.[13]

The JRCS had no difficulty in attracting trainees, even throughout the war, because being a JRCS nurse offered women an unusual and respected place in Japanese society. Right up to WWII, it was uncommon for a woman in Japan to have a visible social role and to work in paid employment. It was even less common for women to be involved in war work, a realm of society that distinctly belonged to men. There were other aspects that set the JRCS nurse apart from her country women. JRCS nurses wore appealing Western-style uniforms of dark blue, with laced-up boots, at a time when the vast majority of Japanese women wore the traditional costume kimono.[14] With the education of JRCS nurses imbued with sentiments of "loyalty and patriotism," they were portrayed as contributing to the imperial cause, helping "the soldier who devotes himself to his country." The status of JRCS nurses was so high that Japanese girls saw them as heroines.[15]

Japan's militarization in the years leading up to WWII extended to taking control of JRCS hospitals, JRCS nursing, and its nurses. Subsequently, the JRCS assumed responsibility for the education and training of all military nurses in Japan, broadening and strengthening support for the military effort while reinforcing the status of the JRCS nurse. By 1942, the military in Japan had complete control over the JRCS. In response to nursing shortages, nurses went wherever the military needed them. Entrance restrictions to JRCS training were eased under the military rule, which ensured a continuing source of labor for the military to staff its hospitals, several of which were in Hiroshima city.[16]

Having been proclaimed a main military city of Japan in 1871, Hiroshima's status as a strategic military base became more important during WWII. Located on Japan's west coast, with a large port and close to the Eurasian continent, soldiers and munitions could be transported quickly to war zones;[17] similarly, Hiroshima housed soldier casualties who returned via this location. Up to WWII, the Hiroshima Army Hospital was the city's only military facility, but its capacity was stretched during the war.[18] In the expansion of the army hospital system that followed,[19] the JRCS hospital was subsumed as a military facility and renamed, somewhat confusingly, the First Hiroshima Army JRCS Hospital. It housed soldiers with less serious injuries and illnesses.[20]

The JRCS Hospital had a large training school for nurses on-site. In April 1945, more than 400 students were enrolled there. JRCS nursing students who were in the second year, or above, were used as staff at the First Hiroshima Army JRCS Hospital, given the severe shortages of fully qualified nurses. The students worked under instructions from a small number of licensed nurses, some of whom were fully trained, and some of whom were equivalent to nurses' aides. Nevertheless, the students had substantial responsibility toward those under their care.[21] Nobuko

173

Hayashi, Chieko Matsumoto, and Terue Kobayashi, whose testimonies are featured in this chapter, were second-year students at this facility.

To prepare for the influx of more seriously ill and injured soldiers, the military constructed temporary satellite army hospitals known as "branch" hospitals. Licensed nurses who had completed their education staffed the branch army hospitals. This chapter includes testimonies from two licensed nurses: Shige Hirano, age 26 years, and Mieko Imamura, age 20 years, who were stationed at the Eba and Mitaki branches, respectively.

By mid-1942, in response to Japan's advance into the Pacific region, the Allied forces began work on a coordinated military strategy known as the Manhattan Project. Central in this plan was the use of nuclear weapons to attack Japanese territory. Allied authorities selected Hiroshima as a target for several reasons. In addition to targeting a military site, the Allies aimed to study the effects of the bombing. Hiroshima was an important military base with many military factories that had not been bombed before. With few mountains and a relatively flat landscape, the Allies expected Hiroshima's topographical features to facilitate their observation of the atomic bomb's effects.[22]

The implementation of the Manhattan Project gathered pace throughout 1944 with intensification of the American Armed Forces air raids on Japan, enabling the Allies to gather intelligence. In July 1945, 152 Boeing B-29 Superfortress airplanes bombed Kure, a port city to Hiroshima's southeast, resulting in around 2,000 deaths.[23] In the following weeks, greater numbers of B-29 bombers flew over Hiroshima. Air-raid sirens signaled impending attack but the planes flew by without incident,[24] leading the city's people to believe that the many Buddhist temples in the area protected the city. Rumors abounded that the Allies sought to preserve Hiroshima because it would provide strategic access in a future invasion of Japan.[25]

THE BOMBING

The day of the bombing, Monday, August 6, 1945, was a sunny day in Japan. During the preceding night (August 5), there was much aerial activity; precautionary air-raid sirens were sounded and escalated to air-raid sirens requiring evacuation to bomb shelters, but later these were cancelled.[26] In the morning, at 7:31 a.m., after no aerial activity had been seen for some hours, the precautionary warning was lifted. Hiroshima city's occupants emerged from shelters to go about their daily business. A little more than 40 minutes later, three airplanes flew over the city from the northeast. One was the B-29 bomber *Enola Gay*, carrying an atomic bomb code named *Little Boy*.[27] The other two aircraft were observation airplanes, one of which dropped three parachutes loaded with equipment to record the pressure of the impending atomic blast and to transmit a record of the event.[28] Although the three airplanes could be seen from the ground, for reasons that remain unexplained, no air-raid siren was sounded.

At 8:15 a.m., from an altitude of 8,500 m, the *Enola Gay* fired its atomic bomb on Hiroshima. *Little Boy* exploded at 570 m above ground, erupting as a fireball that reached more than 1,000,000°C at its core. The point at which this molten mass hit the ground is known as the "drop zone." At the center of the drop zone, the temperature of the earth's surface was more than 4,000°C. A blast and an accompanying shock wave that exceeded 400 m/sec followed the fireball. It incinerated everything within a 1-km radius: people, buildings, houses, trees, and even rocks. Estimates vary, but it is estimated that around 60,000 people died instantly.[29] In the hours that followed, shocked and injured survivors sought help at Hiroshima's hospitals. The First Hiroshima Army JRCS Hospital and the Eba and Mitaki Army Branch hospitals were within 4 km of the atomic bomb's drop zone.

Hayashi, Matsumoto, and Kobayashi, the 17-year-old nursing students, had completed 16 months of training and were on duty at the First Hiroshima Army JRCS Hospital on the morning of the bombing, caring for some of the 250 inpatient soldiers with less serious injuries.[30] Aside from the military patients, however, some treatment was provided to civilians as outpatients,[31] and there were small numbers of civilian inpatients in the pediatric and gynecology wards.[32] The precise number of people in the hospital on August 6 is not known,[33] but was estimated by one of this study's participants to be around 250.[34] The staff on duty included 27 physicians, 34 licensed nurses, 22 nursing students, 6 pharmacists, and a number of other workers including an x-ray technician, a clinical laboratory technologist, cooks, and office personnel.[35]

At 9 p.m. on August 5, student nurse Hayashi began her night shift with another student on an upper floor of the hospital in the surgical ward. Within 20 minutes of beginning work, Hayashi and her colleague had to respond to the first of many air-raid warnings and sirens that sounded that night. The first precautionary warning was issued at 9:20 p.m. and upgraded 7 minutes later to a full evacuation siren. Hayashi and her colleague transferred their patients to the bomb shelter in the hospital's basement.[36] After 2.5 hours, at 11:55 p.m., the evacuation siren was downgraded to a precautionary warning. It was upgraded 30 minutes later to an evacuation siren and then downgraded to a precautionary warning at 2:10 a.m. Finally, at 2:15 a.m., the warnings were cancelled. The first 5 hours of Hayashi's night shift, thus, were taken up with moving the patients via a stairwell from the upper floor of the hospital to the basement and returning them to the ward.[37]

The job of evacuating these men to and from the basement each time the air-raid alarm sounded was heavy work for the two young nurses.[38] But it was even more difficult for a solitary nurse. Hayashi's patients were officers with leg injuries, many of whom were overweight and unable to walk without assistance. Some of the soldiers refused to leave the ward even though evacuations were compulsory. If a soldier refused to evacuate, a nurse had to stay with him, leaving the other nurse to complete the other patients' transfers and placing the nurse in the ward in potential danger. In the last hour of Hayashi's shift, a precautionary warning sounded again. At 7:09 a.m., the two nurses readied themselves to repeat the evacuation, but the alert was cancelled at 7:31 a.m. Relieved and exhausted, Hayashi nevertheless was conscious that: "It was already eight o'clock and the day shift nurses were about to arrive. I had to hurry to finish before the changeover at 8:30 a.m." If she did not finish her work, then the day staff had to add that to their already heavy schedule.[39]

One of the night-shift nurses' tasks was to wash bandages, which had to be reused because supplies were perilously low. Tired and ready for sleep, Hayashi entered the pan room just after 8 a.m. to do this final job. As she stood at the sink, she felt the force of the atomic bomb blast:

> A violent blue flash and the blast shot through the room. The pan room was narrow, and the wall was full of shelves for storing pans, hot-water bottles, Balkan frames for fracture treatment and so on. All those things crashed down on top of me. Then I lost consciousness.[40]

Hayashi's fellow student nurses Matsumoto and Kobayashi had just started work on the day shift in the outpatients section. Matsumoto had prepared clinic rooms for the day's patients and was on her way downstairs to the basement where she was to tidy up the shelter after the evacuations overnight.[41] Matsumoto explained what happened when the bomb struck:

> I was walking near the windows, and then I was flung downstairs by the blast of the bomb. Intuitively, I thought that my hospital had been bombed, and that I would die. After that, I did not remember anything for a while.[42]

Student nurse Kobayashi had finished preparations for the day's consultations and was waiting for patients to arrive. Hearing the sound of an airplane, she put into place her emergency response training and headed to the locker room to retrieve an air defense hood, a protective covering made of padded cloth that is tied around the neck.[43] Kobayashi ran back to her post, arriving just as the bomb went off. She felt the "bomb blast and a strong flash at the same time. Then the medicine shelf collapsed and all the medicine bottles fell down on top of me and smashed. My uniform was dyed red with Mercurochrome."[44]

The force of the bombing blew Kobayashi off her feet and into the corridor. Lying there on the floor, she recalled her defense drill training. All of the staff practiced drills for evacuation regularly at the hospital.

They also practiced forming the "relief teams" aimed at dealing with the aftermath of the attack. First, the staff were to protect themselves and, second, they were to report to those in charge of the relief teams. Kobayashi explained how she followed the procedure:

> I closed both eyes, held my nose for a while and kept quiet. There were none of my friends with me, so I experienced the bombing alone. A few minutes passed, and then I heard people groaning. I opened my eyes and looked outside, but it was utterly dark,[45] even though it was daytime. I thought that we must have been bombed.[46]

Some time had passed when Kobayashi heard an announcement calling for the medical workers of the hospital to assemble. Conscious of her obligations to present for duty on a relief team, Kobayashi made her way out of the building. She noticed people everywhere, some with head injuries. Some groaned; others were not moving.

THE IMMEDIATE AFTERMATH

Already civilian survivors were running to the hospital entrance seeking help. At the emergency assembly point, the hospital's physicians, the pharmacist, and some senior nurses organized the others into relief teams.[47] Kobayashi explained her colleagues' response to seeing her alive: "'Are you all right?' they asked me, because I was dyed red [by the Mercurochrome], and I said 'I am all right.' Everybody was saying, 'are you all right?' or 'you are here,' and so on."[48] Immediately, the hospital staff sprang into action. A physician and some senior nurses divided all available and able staff. Patients who were unhurt joined them because so few hospital staff seemed to be available. People also gathered medical supplies. A clinical inspection engineer directed patients with minimal injuries to form three teams: a fire prevention and defense group, a nursing and relief support group, and a cooking group.[49]

Exterior of the Hiroshima Red Cross Hospital (during WWII, it was called the First Hiroshima Army JRCS Hospital), February 1946.

(JRCS, Japanese Red Cross Society; WWII, World War II).
Photographed by Masaru Kuroishi and reproduced with the permission of the Hiroshima Peace Memorial Museum.

Outside of the hospital, student nurse Matsumoto regained consciousness. It was completely dark, with what she described as "black rain" falling.[50] Matsumoto was confused. She wondered how she had come to be lying on the lawn outside the hospital, when the last thing she remembered was standing on a step inside the hospital building before the explosion.[51] Looking down at herself, she saw that she was not wearing her watch or shoes, and was without her bag. Drifting in and out of consciousness, Matsumoto was aware that the black rain had stopped and it was sunny. At this point, Matsumoto's first thought was that she should return to her station in the outpatients' section. She tried to stand up but found that: "I couldn't even move my legs. Then, I realised that there were many fragments of glass sticking out of them."[52] She could do nothing but remain where she was, exposed to the full heat of the sun.

Civilian survivors rushing to Hiroshima Red Cross Hospital,
August 6, 1945, at around 2 p.m.
Drawn by Yoshiko Ogawa, a 19-year-old working at the hospital, reproduced
with the permission of the Hiroshima Peace Memorial Museum.

In the hours after the bombing, people thronged to the First Hiroshima Army JRCS Hospital from all across the city. A modern, three-story building made of reinforced concrete, this hospital was only 1.6 km from the drop zone.[53] With much of the outer frame relatively intact, thousands of survivors took up resting places in the entrance foyer, in corridors, on steps, and in basements. They lay down on the hospital's lawn where student nurse Matsumoto also lay injured.[54]

Many of those seeking help died. Among the dead at the First Hiroshima Army JRCS Hospital were staff: 3 trained nurses and 22 nursing students who had been on duty.[55] No sooner than the corpses

Damage to the Hiroshima Red Cross Hospital, October 1945.

Photographed by Toshio Kawamoto, courtesy of Yoshio Kawamoto, and reproduced
with the permission of the Hiroshima Peace Memorial Museum.

were evacuated, others lay down in their place.[56] For student nurse
Matsumoto, memories of this brutal scene have stayed with her.

> People were crying out for water, or calling for their mother,
> just before death.... [Many] had lost their hair. Their clothes
> were either in rags or they were almost naked. Some of them
> had burnt skin hanging from their fingers, some of them had
> glass fragments embedded in their bodies....I was so horri-
> fied by people's bodies and by the extent of the damage.[57]

One man, a soldier, fell down next to Matsumoto on the grass. His
neck had been cut extensively, exposing his pharynx every time he
breathed. Although severely injured herself, Matsumoto's sense of her

responsibility as a nurse was strong. She thought: "I must save this soldier, but my mind was so confused. It was the first time that I had seen such a seriously wounded patient." She placed a towel on the soldier's wound, knowing that "It was not the correct treatment, but I didn't know what else to do." Despite her best attempts, the soldier died soon after. The severity of the situation began to dawn on Matsumoto and she felt intensely afraid. She lay on the lawn, unable to move anymore and unable to help those around her.[58]

Student nurse Hayashi had been lying unconscious for more than 2 hours in her upstairs ward. Emerging from that state around 11 a.m., Hayashi felt exceedingly hot and tried to understand what had happened. The wards seemed calm, quiet, and empty. She later learned that the surviving patients believed her to be dead and so left her where she fell. As Hayashi slowly came to her senses and saw the extent of the damage, she realized that the hospital had been attacked. Wandering to the other wards, she found the student nurse she had been on duty with when the bomb fell, and together they walked around the grounds of the hospital.[59]

THE DESTRUCTION OF THE STUDENT NURSES' DORMITORY

About 300 meters away from the main hospital building, the nursing students' living quarters, a two-story wooden dormitory, was reduced to rubble. The dormitory housed nurses sleeping after the night shift, as well as 80 nursing students suffering from dysentery.[60] All were buried under the debris of the collapsed building. A senior teacher of the school, head nurse Oshie Kinutani, who lived in the dormitory as an administrator, had managed to extricate herself from the crushed building and could hear her trapped students calling for help. She immediately headed to the hospital building for assistance, being met on the way by the hospital's secretary; he despatched around 25 army patients to begin the rescue effort,[61] and hospital staff and more patients joined them. Kinutani climbed into the rubble to pull out survivors. Later in the morning, a house fire near the hospital threatened to spread to the dormitory. Kinutani gathered more personnel to stop the fire's spread, directing one of the hospital cooks to supervise the firefighting.[62]

Memories of the Hiroshima Red Cross Hospital, August 6, 1945.
Artist: Tomiko Ikeshoji (Kubo); reproduced with the permission of the
Hiroshima Peace Memorial Museum.

Soldier patients searched for survivors lying under the crushed nurses' dormitory. Voices of "help me," "rescue me" were heard from inside of the building.

When student nurse Hayashi encountered the crushed dormitory, like others, she was in a state of shock, unable to fully comprehend what had occurred. Seeing her friends and colleagues trapped under the rubble, she joined in their rescue without hesitation. But as she pulled at the wreckage, it dawned on Hayashi that she had been on duty in the hospital and she was overcome with a sense of responsibility. She thought: "I am still working. I have not finished my handover to the day duty nurses." This student nurse hastily returned to her ward of soldiers where she found that several men were missing.[63]

This was a serious situation because, as the nurse-in-charge, she "had to assume all the responsibility during my service. I turned pale" at the idea of losing patients. Hayashi knew that if the military patients had absconded, she would be held responsible for their escape. Terrified, she ran all over the hospital searching for the missing soldiers, ignoring the devastation around her: "I didn't understand what had happened to us, because I could only think about my duty. When I found my patients, I took them to the basement shelter again." Once they were there, Hayashi left the hospital building to see what she could do elsewhere.[64]

Her colleague student nurse Matsumoto remained stunned and injured on the ground outside the hospital, surrounded by corpses and unable to move her legs for the shards of glass that had penetrated them. As evening fell, she became aware of shouting and yelling, and she "felt afraid, really and truly afraid, when I heard those shouting voices...I started to panic, because I could not move." The voices were of those fighting the raging dormitory fire. Later that evening, one of the many volunteers who had arrived at the hospital to help was able to move Matsumoto to safety. Her rescuer was a young university student who carried her on his back. As Matsumoto put it: "My friend saved my life. I could not find the words to express my gratitude for what he did."[65] For many of the nurses, however, survival was a small consolation because in the days after the bombing they learned of the deaths of their classmates.

By the afternoon of August 6, the fire that had threatened the nursing students' dormitory had spread.[66] Nurse Hayashi, despite a severe pain in her back, returned to the dormitory where many of her friends still lay trapped in the rubble, crying out for help. It was an impossible task to rescue them; there was no piped water and no fire engines to douse the flames. Even 60 years later, Hayashi's feelings of helplessness and distress at being unable to save her friends had not abated. "Many of the students died in that fire," she said. "Who could extinguish such a big fire with only buckets of water?"[67] For more than 8 hours, rescuers pulled approximately 150 nursing students from the wreckage. The fire continued to burn until late evening when a naval rescue party arrived and managed to extinguish it. They found three bodies in the ashes.[68]

THE WORK OF RELIEF TEAMS

Every week, all hospital personnel, including nursing students, were trained for such emergencies. Preparations for nighttime attacks also were in place. Every night, a team of senior staff stayed on duty, including the hospital administrator, a physician, a pharmacist, a nurse, and the head physician. The magnitude of the task that faced the hospital staff who survived the atomic bomb blast was overwhelming; but throughout August 6, able-bodied staff implemented the emergency response plans. Their preparations paid off, as relief teams were formed without instruction. There was a medical relief team, a firefighting unit, a toxic gas unit, an administrative unit to retrieve documentation, and a general affairs unit.[69] Civilians aided them.

Student nurse Kobayashi joined one of the civilian relief teams organized to carry injured people into the hospital wards. She wrote each patient's name on a piece of paper, attaching that to the individual as a means of identifying the critically ill and dying. The dead were carried outside to the hospital's lawn, in the hope that families would come to claim the bodies.[70] It was difficult work. Of the total deaths caused by the atomic bomb, it has been estimated that 70% occurred on the first day, the main causes being trauma and burns.[71] The bombing, the subsequent fires, the nurses' own injuries, and shock were not the only challenges faced at Hiroshima on August 6, 1945. With the city's electricity system totally destroyed, the hospital was in complete darkness. As night fell, survivors groaned with pain from burns and injuries, but there was no pain relief to offer them. The only comfort the nurses could provide was to stay by the patients and to talk to them "because they were very frightened." Kobayashi also felt afraid. At age 17, she had so little experience of death.[72]

After assisting at the nurses' dormitory fire, student nurse Hayashi, who had been on duty since the evening of August 5, returned to the basement to check on her soldier patients. Despite the influx of civilians, the soldiers remained Hayashi's responsibility and she needed to give the men water. The water pipes in the basement had been destroyed and hence Hayashi had to collect drinking water for the men from the floor above the basement refuge. In total darkness, Hayashi made her way along the corridors crowded with civilian survivors. She felt someone cling to her legs and a voice pleaded with her, "Give me water." She was torn between her obligations to the military patients and the hundreds of dehydrated civilians who called to her for help. Hayashi recalled this dilemma, saying, "I couldn't provide satisfactory amounts of drinking water for both the civilians and my patients ... [but I] had to get drinking water for my patients because I was in charge of them."[73]

In the first 24 hours after the bombing, the relief teams offered what help they could to survivors. In addition to hydration, providing nourishment to survivors was a priority. Late in the evening of August 6, volunteers from a neighboring city brought rice balls for survivors at the hospital to eat.[74] The hospital's secretary, who earlier had participated in the rescue of student nurses at the dormitory, also began preparing meals for the exhausted staff and the patients. The secretary mobilized a cooking team consisting of soldier patients and fashioned a stove so that rice gruel could be cooked on it, using cereals stored in the hospital. They served this meal with hard biscuits at 3 a.m., 18 hours after the bomb was dropped.

The first external relief unit arrived on the afternoon of August 7. It consisted of 10 nursing students and a doctor from the Yamaguchi JRCS Nursing School situated 50 km from the drop zone. This school had a personal connection with one of the First Hiroshima Army JRCS Hospital's physicians, Dr. Fumio Sigeto.[75] Sigeto was the principal of the Yamaguchi JRCS Nursing School up to late July 1945 and had been in Hiroshima only for 2 weeks.[76] The Yamaguchi JRCS Nursing School relief team left to help on August 6 but was the target of an air attack on the journey, resulting in their delayed arrival.[77] Student nurse Hayashi saw the team's arrival as just what was needed at the time:

> I didn't know exactly how many physicians had survived and without them the patients could not be treated. At that time, my in-patients were not being treated by the physicians, and

so we applied edible oil or Mercurochrome to the patients' burns. Then, [as] help arrived from various places...I was so relieved, because serious medical treatment had not yet been given to the patients.[78]

Hayashi was conscious that her soldier patients had not received any treatment, other than first aid, since early in the morning of August 6. Because the soldiers were her responsibility, she felt that she should be providing ongoing care for them. Some had new wounds that needed suturing; penetrating wounds needed to be explored by a surgeon to remove glass and other fragments before being sutured. Soldiers who were recovering from previous surgery needed their sutures removed, and so on. These procedures were what Hayashi considered to be "serious treatment" and nurses were not permitted to do them. With almost no resources available, and so few medical personnel, performing care other than basic first aid was beyond the reach of the JRCS nurses at Hiroshima.

Not far from the First Hiroshima Army JRCS Hospital were two of the army's branch hospitals. They also were close to the atomic bomb's drop zone. The recollections of two JRCS nurses stationed at these branch hospitals are presented next.

MITAKI AND EBA BRANCH HOSPITALS

The JRCS graduate Hirano was working at the Mitaki Branch of the Hiroshima Army Hospital on the day of the bombing. A temporary wooden building with a capacity for 1,100 beds, the Mitaki Branch had an internal medicine department; a surgical department; officers' wards; and departments of dermatology, urology, ophthalmology, otorhinolaryngology, and tuberculosis. According to official accounts, on the day of the bombing, there were 650 patients and 110 nurses at the hospital. Located 1.7 to 2.0 km from the atomic bomb's drop zone,[79] the building was almost entirely destroyed in the initial explosion, killing most of its inmates and leaving local people without access to a treatment center.[80]

Hiroshima Army Hospital at Mitaki, August 9, 1945.

Photographed by Yotsugi Kawahara and reproduced with the permission
of the Hiroshima Peace Memorial Museum.

Hirano trained at the JRCS Nursing School in Hiroshima. Because of shortages of nurses, the military sent her to work at the Mitaki Army Hospital as the hospital's head military nurse.[81] She had 5 years' postgraduate experience. On the night of August 5, Hirano was off duty, but when the air-raid siren sounded, all off-duty nurses had to report to the hospital to assist those in the wards. She stayed throughout the night of August 5, preparing refuge shelters and then, without having slept, began her day shift at 8 a.m. Like the other nurses interviewed in this oral history, Hirano was totally unprepared for the intensity of the explosion: "A strong light flashed through the window onto my right shoulder and then, a strong blast hit us."[82] People were knocked down by its force. Glass, metal, and equipment exploded, shattering fragments everywhere. Hirano was determined to remain calm and prevent panic, just as the JRCS was trained to do. After the shock wave had passed, she simply asked the night nurses to continue the handover to the day staff. Hirano was "of course, anxious about what was happening, but I was the head nurse and the handover was not yet finished."[83]

188

The staff subsequently learned that a powerful bomb had been dropped on the city. All nurses were ordered to stay in what remained of the hospital building with the patients. Exercising her authority as a senior JRCS head nurse, Hirano visited the wards to assess the patients and instructed them not to move.[84] The wards at the Mitaki Army Hospital had large windows, which had shattered in the explosion. Being summer and the temperature quite high, patients who were in bed at the time were not covered by blankets, which otherwise might have protected them from debris. Those lying supine suffered penetrating abdominal wounds from glass and metal fragments, while others were injured in the back. Glass fragments had penetrated head nurse Hirano's shoulder too. The wound was painful and bleeding, but as Hirano recalled: "I didn't know what injuries I had, and I didn't have time to take care of myself."[85] As did the other JRCS nurses interviewed in this oral history, above everything, Hirano saw her obligation as seeing to the needs of her soldier patients. Thus, the JRCS nurses fully took in the training that they had received under the military government: that soldiers' needs were the nurses' priority.

Many of the patients, as Hirano discovered, even those with minor injuries, were completely terrified by the blast. They hid under their bed blankets, convinced that they were unable to move without help. Hirano decided that the best thing to do was to measure their blood pressure as a way of showing the soldiers that they were not ill. The soldiers respected her assessment and agreed to move to a safer location. Hirano then went to inspect the three wards where more than 100 tuberculosis patients were accommodated. She "only could observe all of them as a group, and had no time to see each patient."[86] Miraculously, only one had died in the building's collapse,[87] and when an army surgeon came to the ward, Hirano was able to give him a general report on the patients. The nurses then moved the seriously wounded patients to a shelter.[88]

Outside of the Mitaki Hospital, Hirano saw hundreds of civilian survivors heading from the city toward Hiroshima's suburbs. She was shocked by their appearance. Some had skin hanging off their bodies, and they begged her for water. As the severity and scale of the damage from the bombing dawned on her, "Suddenly, my mother flashed into my mind," but there was no way to obtain information about how peo-ple in other parts of Hiroshima had fared.[89] Hirano and her colleagues spent all of August 6 at the inpatients' refuge, expecting patients to arrive. None presented, because of rumors that the entirety of this hos-pital was completely destroyed.[90]

Another branch army hospital was at Eba, 3.5 km from the atomic bomb's drop zone. Like the Mitaki Branch, the Eba Branch consisted of more than 10 wards in improvised wooden buildings, which at capacity housed 800 beds for patients suffering from internal diseases, tubercu-losis, and infections. Damage was not extensive, and neither patients nor personnel were killed or even seriously injured. On the day of the bombing, 50 patients and 59 hospital personnel were on site, as most of the inpatients had been evacuated from this location in April and May 1945.[91] Eight doctors, a pharmacist, eight nurses, 20 medical order-lies, and 22 other hospital officers staffed the Eba Branch on August 6.[92] Among them was Imamura, a JRCS nurse who had completed her train-ing in March 1945. She was assigned to the Eba Branch hospital because of nurse shortages.

On the morning of August 6, Imamura was outside the Eba Branch hospital, preparing to participate in the Monday morning assembly, a weekly parade at which army surgeons issued new orders or gave lec-tures to the staff. Imamura recognized the sound of B-29 fighter planes approaching and wondered what to do because no alarm had been issued. Before she could decide, the bomb blast blew her off her feet.[93]

When she regained consciousness, Imamura recalled being carried by some patients. As she looked skyward, there was a strange crim-son yellow color and she felt that something unusual was happening. Slowly coming to her senses, her first thought was for her patients. On that morning, Imamura was "in charge of the special report [criti-cally ill] patients, and I [felt I] had to go and rescue them." Imamura made her way inside the hospital where she found the entire corri-dor covered in crushed glass and rubble and the roof fallen in. She headed for the critically ill patients' room, crawling along the corridor through the debris. Her hands and knees were cut by shards of glass as she made her way. The patients' ward, likewise, was full of rubble, and the patients had injuries from glass fragments and falling masonry.

Imamura searched for dressings and found bandages and cotton cloths that she could use.[94]

There were many, many people to attend to. Desperate for someone to help her with this mammoth task, Imamura left the wards to look for other nurses. She saw civilians rushing to the hospital entrance, forming long queues. They asked, "When can I have treatment? When can I have treatment?" At the entrance, the staff put in place their emergency training. They formed relief teams and began to attend to survivors. The Eba Branch's director established a first-aid station at the hospital entrance and sent physicians, nurses, medical orderlies, and other hospital workers there to provide relief. Staff then mobilized the able-bodied patients to assist the relief teams to provide first aid and prepare food.[95]

Imamura joined this first-aid effort, conscious that what care they could give was inadequate. As she explained: "civilians were still waiting in long queues, so we continued caring for them, even though all we could do was just to clean them up with water." Those presenting had deep burns and were covered in ash and soot. Nurses and their helpers bathed wounds with water and applied zinc oil (the only ointment available), but even this was time consuming and provided little relief. The Eba Branch had been well stocked with medicines, bandages, and food, but supplies depleted rapidly because of the sheer numbers of people presenting. The scale of the disaster and a sense of helplessness were a lasting and painful memory for this young nurse. Imamura recalled that, at one point, she was preparing to attend to the next person waiting in line for care and said: " 'Next please' but the next person did not come, because he had died while waiting for his turn."[96]

The volume of work was immense. Between August 6 and September 30, 1945, approximately 10,500 survivors presented to the Eba Branch hospital for treatment.[97] Over those 8 weeks, the nurses continued to work in teams and attended seriously injured civilians in hospital beds that previously were dedicated to soldiers. But the challenges in delivering care did not abate. With limited electricity in Hiroshima, the hospitals were subject to spontaneous blackouts that at times left them in total darkness. It was impossible to see the extent of survivors' wounds, and appropriate treatment could not be provided under such conditions. Even the simple task of giving water to patients was difficult, because most of the crockery and glassware had been destroyed. Imamura served water to her patients from a large pitcher. But it was a token gesture for the very critically ill at times, as Imamura lamented, "Sometimes, when I said, 'Here is some water', the victim had already died."[98] Along with her fellow nurses, Imamura felt powerless as more and more seriously injured people begged for care. Without necessary resources in terms of medicine, equipment, and staff, little could be done. Just 24 hours after the bombing, the medical staff suspended all active treatment. In the days and weeks that followed, all the nurses could do was comfort survivors and provide them with whatever water and nourishment were available.[99]

CONCLUSION

The scale of destruction resulting from the atomic bomb at Hiroshima was unprecedented in human history, with tens of thousands of people dying in the initial blast and then others throughout the first 24 hours. Nurses Hayashi, Matsumoto, Kobayashi, Hirano, and Imamura convey a sobering picture of the disaster as it unfolded on the front line. As this glimpse of events on August 6, 1945, demonstrates, the extent of the disaster was beyond the control and responses of mere mortals. The eyewitness testimonies of the five nurses illustrate just how difficult it was to make any meaningful response to the evolving chaos. The nurses also were survivors of the atomic bomb, and they bore injuries and/or shock. Some of their friends and work colleagues had been killed by the explosion or subsequent fires. The three women on duty at the First Hiroshima Army JRCS Hospital, being young student nurses, were unprepared clinically for the extent of trauma and burns that presented.

The nurses' narratives point to the complexity of their status as JRCS nurses under military command. Even though the nurses were part of the emergency themselves, the Japanese people looked up to these individuals. It was important for the nurses to maintain a sense of themselves as professional nurses, to be perceived as "in control" of an uncontrollable situation so as to prevent panic, to invite trust, and to elicit cooperation from those who had survived the bombing. However, because JRCS military rule governed the nurses and their practice completely, soldier patients, not Japanese civilians, were the JRCS nurses' primary responsibility. Ironically, with that level of military responsibility and obligation, the nurses had a clear and compelling focus in the midst of the disaster. That same obligation presented the nurses with difficult choices in attending to soldiers first and civilians second. Thus, providing the simplest of treatments and nourishments, such as drinking water for civilians with severe burns, was an ethical dilemma for these young women. What is more, their feelings of failure and incapacity to provide care to everyone who needed it have remained with them throughout their lives.

On day 1 of the disaster, the nurses and other hospital staff had little assistance from outside services. Collaboration in this context was almost an impossible ideal because of the sheer magnitude of what had befallen the city of Hiroshima. The collaboration that did occur on that first day emerged from within the hospitals' resources and from survivors, even if they were injured. The crisis called for a pooling of labors irrespective of status. Less seriously injured hospital workers and patients rescued nursing students from the dormitory, fought fires, delivered first aid, cooked, and distributed food in relief teams. Nurses identified bodies and relocated them for families to claim. What seems most surprising is that in spite of the insurmountable clinical presentations and mass destruction, the five nurses felt compelled to "nurse," in any way that was possible, as individuals or through teamwork. These five young women present at the Hiroshima bombing displayed an overt consciousness as nurses; they were at work as nurses; they responded as nurses. They felt that they had to save, rescue, care, and cure.

NOTES

1. Interview with Chieko Matsumoto, July 7, 2002.
2. For a full record of published memories of Hiroshima's bombing, see Ryoko Ohara, "An Oral History of Nurses Who Cared for the Atomic Bomb

Victims in Hiroshima From August 1945 to the End of That Year" (PhD diss., University of Sydney, 2009).

3. Chieko Matsumoto, "Seisyunjidai no Omoide" ["Memories of Youth"], in *Ryoyu: Nisseki dai 9 Kaiseibunsyusotsugyou 40 Syuunenkinen [Dormitory Friends: JRC Hiroshima 9th Graduates 40 Years Commemorative Publication]*, Ed. Matsumoto, C., Iguchi, T., Kataoka, C., and Nakagawa, H. (Hiroshima: Nisseki dai 9 Kaiser, January 1986), 32–33; Terue Kobayashi, "Sekijyuujiki no Motodenogassyou" ["Joining the Palms Together Under the Red Cross Flag"], in *Ryoyu: Nisseki dai 9 Kaiseibunsyusotsugyou 40 Syuunenkinen [Dormitory Friends: JRC Hiroshima 9th Graduates 40 Years Commemorative Publication]*, Ed. Matsumoto, C., Iguchi, T., Kataoka, C., and Nakagawa, H. (January 1986), 34–35; Masae Yukinaga, *Kinokogumo, Jyugunkangofu no Syuki [Mushroom Clouds: Memoirs of the War Nurses]* (Tokyo: Oulu Syuppan, 1984); Shige Hirano, "Hiroshima Rikugunbyouinmitakibuningenbakutoukazengo no Omoide" ["Memories of the First Hiroshima Army Hospital, Mitaki Branch"], in *Chinkon no uta [Melody of Repose of Souls]* (Hiroshima: Nihon Sekijyujisha Kangofu Douhoukai Hiroshima-Kenshibu [Japan Red Cross Society Hiroshima Chapter Nurses' Association], 1981), 117–118.

4. The oral history of 16 nurses was conducted by Ohara, "An Oral History of Nurses." In Japan today, the JRCS is referred to as "JRC" and sometimes "RC." In this chapter, the full title "JRCS" is used for historical accuracy and consistency.

5. Some of the interviewees have since died.

6. The nurses' silence on their atomic bomb experience stemmed from four things: survivor guilt, guilt about not being able to give adequate nursing care when it was needed, censorship, and shame at having been subject to the atomic bomb. The last two are particularly complex. Following Japan's occupation by the Allies in August 1945, censorship applied to any information about the atomic bomb; therefore, the Japanese people were not free to speak about their experiences. Stigma, also, was attached to female *Hibakusha*, a Japanese term that translates literally as *those who were bombed*. Radiation from the bombing produced gross birth defects and other effects on female reproductive capacity. This meant that female *Hibakusha* were limited in marriage prospects and many preferred to keep their radiation exposure a secret. For all of these reasons, the nurses believed that talking about their experiences was "a very sensitive and taboo topic." See Ohara, "An Oral History of Nurses." J. W. Dower addresses censorship in *Embracing Defeat, Japan in the Wake of World War II* (New York: WW Norton & Company, 1999). For more on marriage discrimination, see NHK Hiroshima

Kyuku, Genbaku Project Team, *Hiroshima Bakushinchi-sei to shi no 40 nen* [*Hiroshima Ground Zero—Forty Years of Survival and Death*] (Tokyo: Nippon Housousyuppankyoukai, 1984).

7. Ohara, "An Oral History of Nurses," 12.

8. Ibid., 28.

9. Michiko Kameyama, *Kindai Nihon Kangoshi 1: Nihon Sekijyuujisha to Kango* [*The History of Modern Japanese Nursing Volume I: Japan Red Cross Society and Nursing*] (Tokyo: Domesu Shuppan, 1997), 31–35.

10. Ibid. In Japan, since the bombing, all people who experienced the atomic bomb are referred to as "atomic bomb victims" (ABVs), including those who survived it. In this chapter, instead of ABV, the term "survivor" is used to differentiate those who survived the bombing from those who were killed.

11. Michiko Kameyama, *Kindai Nihon Kangoshi 2: Sensou to Kangofu* [*The History of Modern Japanese Nursing Volume 2: War and Nursing*] (Tokyo: DomesuSyuppan, 1997), 33–39.

12. Kameyama, "Japan Red Cross Society and Nursing," 11–80.

13. Ohara, "An Oral History of Nurses," 25.

14. Ibid., 145. The examination for entry into JRCS training was difficult and training was rigid and militaristic in style.

15. Midori Wakaguwa, *Sensougatsukurujyosezou* [*The Female Image Made by War*] (Tokyo: Chikuma Syoten, 1997), 164–216.

16. Michiko Kameyama, "Nihon no Kinndai no Yoake" ["Dawn of Modern Nursing of Japan"], in *Kangoshi* [*History of Nursing*], Ed. M. Kameyama (Tokyo: Medical Friend Sha, 2001), 78–79. Some of the 16 women who participated in this research did not live in Hiroshima but were sent there by the junta.

17. Hiroshima Soumubu Ken Rekishi Hensanshitsu [History Compilation Group at the Administrative Division of Hiroshima Prefecture], *Hiroshima Kenshi* [*History of Hiroshima Prefecture*] (Hiroshima: Hiroshima Prefecture Syuppan, 1969), 246–254.

18. Ibid., 329.

19. Yukinaga, *Mushroom Clouds*, i.

20. During WWII, this facility was in the Army's first military district. After the war, all the military names of hospitals were changed. For instance, the First Hiroshima Army Japanese Red Cross Society Hospital during the war became the Hiroshima Red Cross Society Hospital after the war. This situation has created some confusion about the "correct" names of Japan's

various hospitals during and after WWII. In the text of this chapter, the hospitals' military names are used because these applied during the war. Images in the chapter, however, carry descriptors that are in use currently at the Hiroshima Peace Memorial Museum. For more on the organization of Army hospitals during WWII, see *Hiroshima Kenshi* [*History of Hiroshima Prefecture*], 341.

21. Hiroshima City, *Hiroshima Genbaku Sensaishi, Dai1kan Sousestu* [*History of Hiroshima Atomic Bomb Disaster, Vol. 1 General Remarks*] (Hiroshima: Hiroshima Sougou Insatu Kabushiki Gaisha, 1971), 347. First-year students had not done any practical work, having begun their training courses in April 1945.

22. Ibid.

23. *Hiroshima Kenshi*, 246.

24. Ibid.

25. Yukinaga, *Mushroom Clouds*, 79.

26. Hiroshima City, *Genbaku Sensaishi*, 309. An air defense law was put in place in 1937 for the sounding and silencing of civil defense sirens and alarms. According to this regulation, local Army commanders were responsible for sounding alarms. It is not known whether this was still the procedure at Hiroshima in 1945. Histories of the bombing do not record the identity of the person responsible for the alarms and sirens on that day.

27. Hiroshima Prefecture, Ed., *Genbaku Hibakusha no Ayumi* [*History of Atomic Bomb Victims*] (Hiroshima: Hiroshima Prefecture Syuppan, 1986), 1. There is some disagreement about the height at which the bomb was deployed.

28. Nagata Shinobu, Sawada Syoji, and Anzai1kurou, "Kakukaihatukara Genbakutouka Made" ["From the Development of Nuclear Power to the Dropping of the A-Bomb"], in *Kyodo Kenkyu Hiroshima Nagasaki Genbaku Higai no Jissou* [*Joint Research of the Reality of the Atomic Bomb Damage in Hiroshima and Nagasaki*], Ed. Sawada Shojo (Tokyo: Shin Nippon SyuppanSha, 1999), 13–41.

29. Hiroshima Prefecture, *Genbaku Hibakusha no Ayumi*, 1. There is disagreement about precise numbers of deaths from the atomic bombing. Some estimates include people who survived the initial blast but died subsequently from radiation. Others included deaths up to a year after the bombing. See Hiroshima Peace Memorial Museum website at http://www.pcf.city.hiroshima.jp/index_e2.html.

30. Interview with Chieko Matsumoto.

31. Interview with Nobuko Hayashi, August 28, 2001, by R. Ohara [audiotape recording]; Nihon Sekijyujisha Hiroshima-Kenshibu [Hiroshima Red

Cross Society], *Nihon Sekijyujisha Hiroshima Kenshibu Hyakunenshi* [*100 Years' History of the Hiroshima Red Cross Society*] (Hiroshima: Gyousei, 1991), 80–87.

32. Interview with Chieko Matsumoto.

33. Hiroshima Genbaku Iryoushi Hensyuiinnkai [Hiroshima A-Bomb Medical History Editorial Committee], *Hiroshima Genbaku Iryoushi* [*A-Bomb Medical History of Hiroshima*] (Hiroshima: Gousei, 1961), 312.

34. Interview with Chieko Matsumoto.

35. Hiroshima City, *Hiroshima Genbaku Sensaishi*, 434. Like the official civilian death estimates, staff deaths are imprecise. These numbers are the minimum numbers of staff known to have perished.

36. Interview with Nobuko Hayashi.

37. *In Mushroom Clouds* (p.78), Yukinaga described the difficulty of this transfer. Some patients refused to go to the refuge, remaining in their beds. The nurses were obliged to stay with them in the ward.

38. This nurse explained that the military at this time in Japan was a privileged class, far from being deprived, whereas civilians were suffering from malnutrition because of food shortages.

39. Interview with Nobuko Hayashi.

40. Ibid.

41. Matsumoto, "Memories of Youth," 32–34.

42. Interview with Chieko Matsumoto.

43. The air defense hood was commonly used by women and children because metal was expensive and civilians could not afford such a helmet.

44. Interview with Terue Kobayashi, November 11, 2001, R. Ohara [audio-tape recording]. Mercurochrome was a red-colored antiseptic agent that contained mercury.

45. After the explosion, the mushroom cloud turned the sky dark.

46. Interview with Terue Kobayashi.

47. Hiroshima City, *Hiroshima Genbaku Sensaishi*, 447.

48. Interview with Terue Kobayashi.

49. Ibid.

50. This was radioactive soot and dust, which fell in areas to the northwest of the city, within half an hour of the initial explosion. It contaminated areas far from the drop zone. See Hiroshima Prefecture, *Genbaku Hibakusha no Ayumi*, 4–5.

51. Interview with Chieko Matsumoto.

52. Ibid.

53. Hiroshima City, *Hiroshima Genbaku Sensaishi*, 434.

54. Interview with Chieko Matsumoto.

55. Hiroshima City, *Hiroshima Genbaku Sensaishi*, 349.

56. Ibid., 448.

57. Interview with Chieko Matsumoto.

58. Ibid.

59. Ibid.

60. Hiroshima City, *Hiroshima Genbaku Sensaishi*, 437.

61. Hiroshima Genbaku Iryoushi Hensyuiinnkai [Hiroshima A-Bomb Medical History Editorial Committee], *Hiroshima Genbaku Iryoushi* [*A-Bomb Medical History of Hiroshima*] , 312.

62. Oshie Kinutani climbed into the building under the rubble, putting herself in considerable danger. Her bravery in the disaster was recognized in 1954 by the award of the Nightingale Medal; see Hiroshima City, *Hiroshima Genbaku Gensaishi*, 437.

63. Interview with Nobuko Hayashi.

64. Ibid.

65. Interview with Chieko Matsumoto. Chieko learned about her rescue by the university student years after the event. Hiroshima University was located nearby.

66. Nihon Sekijyujisha Hiroshima Kenshibu, 89.

67. Interview with Nobuko Hayashi.

68. Hiroshima City, *Hiroshima Genbaku Sensaishi*, 446.

69. Ibid., 435.

70. Kobayashi, "Sekijyuujiki no Motodeno Gassyou" ["Joining the Palms Together Under the Red Cross Flag"], 34.

71. Hiroshima City, *Hiroshima Genbaku Sensaishi*, 448.

72. Interview with Terue Kobayashi.

73. Interview with Nobuko Hayashi.

74. Ibid.

75. Interview with Toshiko Nagata, September 13, 2002, by R. Ohara [audiotape recording].

76. Hiroshima City, *Hiroshima Genbaku Sensaishi*, 451.

77. Interview with EmiIrimoto, August 28, 2001, by R. Ohara [audio-tape recording].

78. Ibid.

79. Yukinaga, *Mushroom Clouds,* i.

80. Hiroshima City, *Hiroshima Genbaku Sensaishi,* 409.

81. Hirano, "Memories of the First Hiroshima Army Hospital, Mitaki Branch," 117.

82. Interview with Shige Hirano, January 23, 2002, by R. Ohara [audio-tape recording].

83. Ibid.

84. Ibid.

85. Ibid.

86. Ibid.

87. Hiroshima City, *Hiroshima Genbaku Sensaishi,* 408.

88. Hirano [Memories of the First Hiroshima Army Hospital, Mitaki Branch], 117. The shelters were caves, which were being dug by patients as a place of refuge. The nurses took cooked rice balls to the cave during the digging.

89. Interview with Shige Hirano. Her only family, Hirano's mother, lived in a suburb of Hiroshima.

90. Hiroshima City, *Hiroshima Genbaku Sensaishi,* 408.

91. Ibid., 374.

92. There are conflicting reports about the exact number of nurses at each hospital. Hiroshima City, *Hiroshima Genbaku Sensaishi,* for example, reports (374) that there were only eight nurses. This assessment includes the military nurses but not the civilian JRCS nurses seconded to serve at those locations. Interviewee Imamura was a seconded JRCS nurse. In her JRCS unit (number 303), there were 20 nurses.

93. Interview with Mieko Imamura, December 22, 2001, by R. Ohara [audio-tape recording].

94. Ibid.

95. Hiroshima City, *Hiroshima Genbaku Sensaishi,* 375–376.

96. Interview with Mieko Imamura.

97. Hiroshima City, *Hiroshima Genbaku Sensaishi,* 375.

98. Interview with Mieko Imamura.

99. Ibid.

CHAPTER 8

The Bar Harbor Fire of 1947, Bar Harbor, Maine (USA)

Barbara Maling

> *Nurses never got the credit that they deserved. They just did what had to be done.*[1]

In July 2014, Dorothy "Dottie" Worchester, RN, stated these words in an interview concerning her role in the Bar Harbor, Maine, fire of 1947. She was right. As happens in most disasters, nurses, often working just behind the front line of care, continued to do what they always did—triaging patients from staging areas, delivering babies in obstetrical units, and providing care for those with chronic conditions along with attending to those affected by the disaster.[2]

On the morning of October 23, 1947, Dorothy and her husband, Warren, of Bar Harbor, Maine, awoke to the smell of burning wood in the air. While going through their normal morning routine, neither of them even considered they would not go to work and continue their day as usual. Dorothy was an operating-room nurse at the local Mount Desert Island (MDI) Hospital; Warren was a postal clerk in the nearby town of Southwest Harbor.

Dorothy Worchester, RN, 1946.
Photo provided by Dorothy Worchester.

The Worchesters were not concerned about the smell of smoke because they were aware that a forest fire had been burning on MDI for 5 days. Recent reports had informed them that the fire was just 6 miles from their apartment, but they, along with most Bar Harbor residents, believed the blaze was contained. The smell of burning wood and the haze in the air had been apparent to them since the fire had begun. The forest firefighters, unable to extinguish the flames, had called in help from local fire departments as well as national resources.

Dorothy and Warren ate breakfast and prepared for a normal day at work. Warren left home first, making the 10-mile drive to the Southwest Harbor post office on the other side of MDI. He knew nothing of what was to come—that he would not see Dorothy for 34 hours, not know of her status, or even if his home was still standing or had burned down. Dorothy left home a few minutes later and walked to the MDI Hospital, which was located in the center of Bar Harbor just a few blocks from the apartment on Elm Street. As Dorothy walked along, she noted that the fall air, normally crisp and clean in Maine during October, seemed

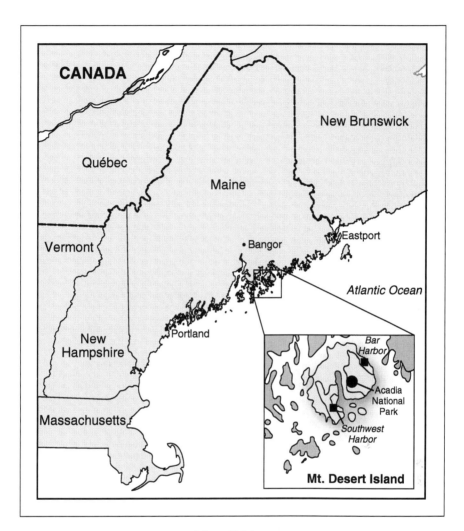

Map of Maine.

heavier with smoke than it had on the previous day. She could not shake a strange feeling that all was not well. Nurse Worchester was only 22 years old, but had already experienced the stress of separation from her husband during a crisis when he served in World War II (WWII). On arrival at the hospital, immediately prior to starting her shift, Dorothy called Warren and requested that he return home a bit early if possible.

Dorothy's feelings of apprehension were well warranted, but at the time, neither she nor Warren could have imagined that in a few hours much of Bar Harbor would burn and result in the town's worst recorded natural disaster. In fact, by evening, fire would forever change the economy and face of their small Maine town.[3] Unbeknownst to Dorothy, she would shortly become one of the numerous nurses who were actively involved in providing much-needed care to residents and firefighters. Working in collaboration with local, state, and national personnel from all walks of life, she would respond to the crisis without a formal disaster plan.[4]

NURSING IN BAR HARBOR

In 1947, Bar Harbor was one of the United States' most famous summer retreats for many of America's wealthiest residents. Nestled between parts of Acadia National Park on MDI, the town was and still is connected to central Maine's picturesque and rocky coast via a man-made bridge. In addition to numerous lavish estates, more than 30 high-end hotels dot the area. Tourists arrived by train and ferry to the gilded resort that at the time rivaled Newport, Rhode Island.[5]

WWII had ended only 26 months earlier on August 15, 1945, and was fresh in the minds of residents. The *Bar Harbor Times* often published articles of town events relating to the war. One such article on the front page of an early October edition announced that Victory Medals would be issued to naval veterans at the local American Legion Post.[6] Newspapers throughout New England contained updates of the Nuremburg trials, the aftermath of Hiroshima, and stories of the hardships and continued displacement of people throughout Europe.[7]

The nurses at the MDI Hospital had the respect of the community as well as the nation. Despite the fact that nurses were paid little (most earned approximately one dollar per hour),[8] the MDI Hospital had a full staff of dedicated nurses who felt the nation's post-WWII gratitude and the positive value of the profession.[9] Largely because Bar Harbor was well known as an elite summer resort with ample resources, finances, and natural beauty, the MDI Hospital, a 100-plus-bed hospital, was not suffering from the post-WWII nursing shortage that many communities throughout the United States were experiencing.[10]

Dorothy Worchester shared a professional pride of nursing with her peers.[11] Although she had only graduated 2 years prior to 1947, she had electively completed an additional surgical course postgraduation. She had considered enlisting in WWII, but the war ended just as she graduated from nursing school. Even with her limited experience, Dorothy's extra education afforded her an appointment as a charge nurse in MDI's operating room. Working closely with surgeons, Dorothy was tasked with the daily administration of the operating room's organization and equipment.

It is not known if the MDI Hospital had an evacuation or disaster plan in 1947. According to hospital officials, hospital records were lost sometime in the 1970s because of water damage.[12] Nevertheless, Bar Harbor and the hospital had the good fortune to attract a number of veteran WWII military physicians and nurses, some of whom had developed extensive wartime medical skills. Their familiarity and expertise with the care and treatment of fatigue, burns, smoke inhalation, and a wide variety of injuries were fresh in their memories and would serve them well when the disaster struck.[13]

In Maine at the time, firefighters sustaining acute injuries (mostly blisters on hands and feet, and smoke inhalation) were routinely taken to temporary first-aid stations behind established fire lines. These stations were staffed by both physicians and nurses whenever possible. If firefighters required more extensive care, they were transported by volunteers to local doctors' offices. Physicians and their office nurses treated patients, giving further instructions for follow-up care to family members. Those needing more intensive care than what a family could provide were admitted to area hospitals. This system worked fairly well as the MDI Hospital did not have an emergency room in 1947.[14]

NEW ENGLAND'S RED OCTOBER 1947

The same newspapers that reported postwar events also recalled that the autumn in Bar Harbor, as well as in the rest of New England, was a time of severe drought.[15] Ominous signs for possible forest fires began to appear as early as March. In the spring, an abnormally warm period caused snow to melt earlier than usual in the woods. For those engaged in forest fire control, this was a menacing sign of possible dry conditions during the upcoming months. Although the months from April through June were unusually cool and wet, by mid-July, a complete reversal of weather conditions occurred and continued well into October. During that time period, 108 days passed without any appreciable rain.[16]

Bar Harbor was just one of the numerous New England towns that were ripe for burning. During the fall of 1947, firefighters battled scattered fires from Maine to Massachusetts.[17] In Maine alone, from October 13 to 27, more than 200 forest fires ravaged the landscape. Officials estimated that Maine fires consumed nearly a quarter million acres of prime forest in addition to devastating or consuming entire towns.

The Maine counties of York, Oxford, and Hancock (in which Bar Harbor is located) were especially hard hit. Several other counties throughout Maine were also threatened. In many cases, these fires moved so rapidly that hundreds of homeowners escaped massive flame fronts with only the clothes on their backs. Businesses, livestock, family pets, and homes containing generations of heirlooms were lost in the blink of an eye. The *Bangor Daily News* headlines on October 22, 1947 and during the initial start of the MDI fire read, "Millions in Damage as Fires Rage Through Maine Forests." The paper further reported:

> Thousands of acres of Maine timber wood lands were laid waste and scores of homes and buildings destroyed with a loss that may reach millions as 35 forest fires, fanned by high winds and unchecked through various sections of the state rage today. The three worst fires appeared to be one in the Biddeford section which destroyed over 20 cottages, a hotel and several year-round homes at Goose Rocks Beach,

206

Cape Porpoise and vicinity and threatened Kennebunkport; another on Mt. Desert Island consumed several sets of buildings and was still raging out of control at a late hour in the Eagle Lake section after burning over more than 12 square miles including much valuable National Park territory; and one in Washington county which was reported eating its way into the town of Jonesboro last night.

The number of fires and the devastation they caused placed an enormous and sudden demand for aid on local, state, and national officials. The destruction that some communities endured and the resources that they needed were extensive. The same day that Bar Harbor burned, 200 homes and businesses were destroyed in Brownfield, a community of 750 residents located in the foothills of the White Mountains, 198 miles southwest of Bar Harbor. Brownfield was reduced to a wasteland of blackened chimneys and debris. On the morning of October 24, a local newspaper, the *Biddeford Daily Journal*, reported the town was so desolate that the only activity was an elderly man "walking with his dog down streets littered with fallen wires, peering into the yellow heat of cellar holes." The only other signs of life were two unattended horses and a few cows roaming in a pasture that miraculously had not burned.[18] The *Portland Sunday Telegram* headlined the same event as, "Scorched Ruins All That Remain of Brownfield," and wrote, "Virtually nothing was spared."[19]

The sheer number of towns, counties, and states devastated by fire made the prompt response of state and national officials especially difficult. Additionally, the immense manpower required to battle hundreds of burns throughout New England along with the need for prompt aid after fires was overwhelming. Available resources were stretched to their limits. For example, the American Red Cross budget report for New England's forest fire disasters of 1947 was $2,474,195. This was an exorbitant amount for the times. The same report included:

The most serious problem of this entire operation concerned case work personnel. During the emergency period and for the first month of the rehabilitation period there were no experienced and competent personnel. They were confused as to policy and what procedures to follow and felt swamped by the entire situation. Since they did not understand policies themselves, they were in no position to interpret to the community and the result was more confusion. The turnover in personnel was a serious handicap, for after intensive indoctrination had been given and a worker was just beginning to produce, he or she was withdrawn, or had to be released to regular jobs.[20]

PRELUDE TO A FIRE STORM, OCTOBER 17 TO 22

Bar Harbor would be very fortunate and receive more help than most Maine communities because of its local infrastructure, economic stability, and its proximity to Acadia National Park. Most of Bar Harbor's summer residents had left the island by October. However, the year-around residents continued their typical routines and many of the local residents, who cared for opulent summer estates, were busy winterizing them before the snow and cold began.

Year-around residents Claire Lambert and her husband were well aware of the drought conditions throughout the state, but never thought that they would be directly affected. Claire recalled that she and her husband had just bought their first home on Atlantic Avenue in Bar Harbor. The couple joyfully moved into their new home with their infant son. Both the Lamberts felt confident in their town's ability to prevent or contain any fires that might occur. In October 1947, however, Claire and her son would face emergency evacuation.[21]

Unlike many Maine towns, Bar Harbor had a well-trained and forward-thinking fire department led by a permanent fire chief, David Sleeper, who had a proven record of competence, skill, and devotion. Sleeper's men routinely trained with national park firefighters. Just a few months earlier, in the spring of 1947, the Bar Harbor Fire Department had tuned its skills by participating in a firefighting school sponsored by the National Park Service. Experienced instructors from Yellowstone National Park had worked with the Bar Harbor Fire Department along with local firefighters and those from Acadia National Park to update their firefighting techniques. Just a day prior to the MDI fire, the local fire department had used its new skills to easily squelch a forest fire accidently started by some hunters. As a result, the burn did not even engulf an acre of land.[22] Little did local firefighters know that over the next several days, their time would be consumed by an all-out battle to save their own station and the entire town.

During the early evening on October 17, the Bar Harbor Fire Department received a report of a fire in a cranberry bog approximately 7 miles southwest of Bar Harbor. Aware that the vegetation on the MDI was so dry that even a small fire could get out of control, Fire Chief Sleeper ordered a general forest fire alarm and sent a 150-gallon tank truck with every man he had to the area. Sleeper also called officials at Acadia National Park. Although the fire was not burning on official park lands, the park service, in cooperation with local authorities, sent equipment and a crew to help extinguish the flames.[23]

Dry conditions worked against firefighting efforts. Throughout the next 5 days, local and national park firefighters continuously monitored and pumped water on the burn. As the sun rose on October 21, a brisk wind sprang up from the northwest, whipping up clouds of smoke from the center of the bog. The fire then traveled 200 feet underground outside the established fire lines. The wind pushed flames through the dry Acadia woods at an alarming speed, causing Chief Sleeper to call for help from surrounding fire departments. Even though neighboring towns were at risk for outbreaks of fire themselves, their fire departments readily responded. Recognizing the grave crisis he faced, Chief Sleeper also asked for help from the headquarters of the 14th Fighter Wing of the U.S. Army Air Force at Dow Field, 40 miles west of Bar Harbor. The 14th Fighter Wing immediately sent more than 100 men.[24]

EMERGENT BEHAVIOR

In addition to firefighters and military personnel, volunteers from all walks of life came to the aid of MDI. For example, forestry students at the University of Maine immediately joined firefighting crews.[25] Among them was a young student, William "Bill" Maling, who traveled to MDI in the back of an open pickup truck with several other undergraduates. Leaving school with only what he could carry, Bill had a change of clothes, a box lunch, and a shovel that a friend gave to him. Although he was young and enthusiastic, he only spent 1 day on the fire lines before he sustained smoke inhalation injuries and was taken to a temporary aid station. There a volunteer nurse cared for his injury, gave him food and water, and arranged transportation for him to return home, so that his family could help him with his recovery. Bill never learned the nurse's name; he only recalled that she introduced herself as a nurse and that she was tall and had dark hair.

Following his injury on the fire line, Bill developed a debilitating cough that lasted for several months and forced him to withdraw from college. He never finished his degree. Years later, at 82 years of age, he was asked why he responded to the MDI fire of 1947 and if he would do so again. He stated, "I couldn't just let Acadia burn without doing something. Of course, I would do it again."[26]

It is not known how many of Bar Harbor's firefighters sustained life-altering injuries and how many were actively cared for by family members, unknown nurses, and other health care workers. On October 22, *The Bar Harbor Times* reported:

> It is impossible for one to name all the units and individuals who came forward unselfishly and unsolicited to take part in the battle. Canteen units from Northeast Harbor and Bar Harbor kept sandwiches and coffee on hand at all times, the latter being supplied by a large group of volunteers who worked day and night in relays. School teachers, nurses, business men, students, even printers pitched in to do their part. Apparatus from Brewer, Bangor and Old Town was sent here and used as stand-ins for the local department. The Bar Harbor Police Department, assisted by Military Police from Dow Field, maintained road blocks at several points to control the traffic. No words can express our praise for the cooperation and coordination of the many departments, agencies, officials and volunteers during the crisis.[27]

In the first few days while the MDI fire was being fought and while Bill Maling was battling flames with others, Dorothy Worchester continued her nursing work. Later, she recalled that the business of nursing at the MDI Hospital and in local physicians' offices was very professional and "mostly as usual." The only exception was the fact that several local nurses (in addition to their regularly scheduled shifts) donned pants and boots in place of their starched white uniforms and volunteered their nursing services to the injured and fatigued firefighters directly behind the fire lines.[28] It is not known what treatments these nurses provided or even the number of firefighters and personnel they cared for. No one kept records of their work; and no one paid them for their services.

AN INFERNO ROLLS INTO BAR HARBOR
"LIKE WAVES ON THE BEACH"

By Thursday morning, October 23, Bar Harbor residents knew of the MDI fire. However, they were still unaware that the conditions on the expanding fire lines were fast becoming more tenuous for their town. They had received word that several homes and farms had already burned along with acres of land within Acadia National Park. In addition, they were aware that 250 inhabitants of Hull's Cove, 3 miles north of Bar Harbor, had evacuated their small town. Nevertheless, *The Bar Harbor Times* newspaper went to press as usual in the morning and published an article on the "Condition of Health in Area" reporting:

> Good supplies have been coming from various towns and the public canteen is maintained with good nourishing food day and night at the fire station. A casualty station was immediately set up at the Fire House and manned constantly with two nurses and all returning fire fighters or anybody was treated. The majority of cases were irritation of the eyes from smoke and dry parched lips. There were a few sprained ankles. In fact, a remarkably few major instances occurred. An ambulance was constantly maintained in the parking ground for response to calls. While 300 of the Dow Field men were here, their medical corps with doctors was stationed with them. Also the hospital ambulance was utilized on one or two

cases....The hospital medical and surgical staff, nurses and personnel were constantly on the alert. The Bangor Chapter of the Red Cross sent two nurses to assist at the Casualty Station and the Ellsworth Chapter also sent nurses for one day. Other than that the Public Health Nurse of Bar Harbor and volunteer nurses remained on duty for untold hours at a time.[29]

Initially, during the morning hours, moderate winds eased the situation and gave the Bar Harbor residents a false sense of safety. Officials warned townspeople to be ready to leave if the fire changed direction, but the fire appeared under control. Midmorning conditions, however, suddenly changed. The velocity of the winds significantly increased and veered in the direction of the coastal resort town. Gusts between 63 and 70 miles per hour (112.6 kph) quickly stirred the blaze into a full inferno. Bar Harbor Fire Chief Sleeper remarked in an interview several years later that the fire was "like waves on the beach" as it rolled over houses and trees engulfing large areas in its path.[30]

In less than 3 hours, the wildfire was lapping the outskirts of Bar Harbor. It had traveled 6 miles, leaving behind a 3-mile-wide path of destruction including 67 palatial seasonal estates. As evening approached at 4:10 p.m., the Bar Harbor fire department sounded the seven whistles—the broadcast announcement for all residents to immediately evacuate.[31]

High winds had driven the fire so quickly that the sound of the whistle alert caught many residents off guard. Claire Lambert recalled that when she heard the alarm, she and her sister-in-law were walking Claire's infant son in a stroller several blocks from her home. She had done little to prepare for evacuation, even though her husband had been a volunteer on the fire lines for several days. He had stated, during intermittent breaks at home, that although the burn had not been extinguished, it was contained. He was busy fighting the blaze when it turned toward Bar Harbor. As a result, he was unable to warn or assist his family.

Like so many citizens, in their confusion, Claire Lambert and her sister-in-law had trouble organizing a plan of evacuation or even deciding what limited items they would take with them. National Guardsmen, the military from Dow Air Force Base, local policemen, and volunteers traveled from house to house up and down Bar Harbor streets giving evacuation instructions and helping those who needed transportation. One of Claire's neighbors who had a dump truck offered to transport whatever possessions Claire could pack into the back of his truck. She chose a cedar chest. It was a beautiful piece of furniture but it did not have any particular sentimental value and was not a traditional brides "hope chest." In fact, Claire used it to store yarn. To this day, she cannot explain why that one item seemed important at the time. Without question, her sister-in-law helped her load the heavy chest into the neighbor's truck. Then they packed the car with a few essentials before leaving to pick up Claire's mother-in-law and her two pets: a dog and a parrot.[32]

The Lambert group joined a slow-moving caravan of approximately 700 vehicles departing town on a designated evacuation route while alarms sounded.[33] Confusion and thick smoke filled the air while the evacuees took cues from police and followed word-of-mouth instructions from those around them. A cool autumn night as well as the fire were fast approaching; the only light available was that of the headlights from the bumper-to-bumper line of cars. Most people closed their car windows to prevent sparks and flaming bits of material that were flying through the air from entering their cars. Some were understandably anxious for fear the fire would overtake them and burn them to death as they slowly left town. Claire recalled that most people remained remarkably calm as they assisted their families, their neighbors, and even strangers to leave town in a somewhat organized fashion.

Part of the caravan ahead of the Lamberts was fortunate enough to escape the island before the fire completely blocked all land evacuation routes. Quick-thinking firefighters and officials rerouted the remaining cars, trucks, and buses back to Bar Harbor. The car containing the three Lambert women, the infant, dog, and parrot joined the group returning to town. On arriving in town, the evacuees received directions to park their loaded vehicles in a large athletic field on the outskirts of the community. National Guardsmen and police hastily steered residents toward the harbor with the intent to transport as many as possible across the sea to safety. Guardsmen planned to patrol the field and protect the villagers' belongings until the townspeople returned for them or until fire engulfed the field—whatever came first.[34]

By this time, the field was choked with automobiles containing prized personnel positions as well as domesticated animals. The three women sadly said good-bye to the dog and parrot when they were instructed to leave them in the car. Only later did they realize that many others had refused to leave their pets behind. Luckily, the fire never reached the field. The officials of the Society for Prevention of Cruelty to Animals and townspeople cared for the animals until they were reunited with their families. Later, reflecting on the incident, Claire Lambert laughed as she recalled that as they walked away from their car, the parrot continued a constant conversation with himself. She wondered how often National Guardsmen, who were given orders to direct all people toward the town pier, tried to locate the source of the banter.

Evacuation by sea, however, was not a simple process. On Bar Harbor's waterfront, driving winds tossed small fishing boats and private rescue vessels against the heavy municipal dock as the Lamberts and other townspeople arrived. One man fell into the cold waters as he hastily tried navigating from the dock into a boat. Luckily, he was quickly rescued by fellow evacuees.[35] Fifty-one-year-old Raymond Karrst suffered an apparent heart attack and died on the Bar Harbor pier[36] in a crowd that by evening had surged to more than 4,000 people.[37]

Some individuals were too afraid to leave by boat. Claire's mother-in-law told her that she would "go into the sea" if the fire came rather than getting on a boat in the dark while gale force winds swept all around them. The three women choose to remain together with Claire's young son at the seaside while closely monitoring the approaching fire as it lapped the edges of town.[38]

THE DUTY TO CARE

The darkness, storm, and fire did not change the fact that MDI Hospital still contained patients requiring care for chronic and acute illnesses. MDI nurses remained on duty despite the fact that their family members and friends were being evacuated or were unable to contact them. Moreover, some had homes in the path of the approaching inferno. Dorothy Worchester stated, "I cannot remember one nurse who suggested leaving her duties" to salvage personal belongings or to "save herself." Dorothy's husband, Warren, at 91 years of age, still could recall his feelings of helplessness when he was unable to contact his wife during the crisis. He stated, "I tried to reach her by car, but was turned back by soldiers. Other roads were blocked by the fire. I couldn't even catch a boat to Bar Harbor so I sat in Southwest Harbor not knowing what to do or if she needed help. I kept trying until the next morning when I finally got through on a back road."[39]

Earlier in the evening, MDI Hospital nurses had sought ways to safely move patients who were able to tolerate transport. Some patients were safely evacuated to Ellsworth Hospital, the closest mainland facility, before Bar Harbor became landlocked by fire.[40] While caring for patients, the nurses had also begun systematically triaging appropriate patients into the care of their families, friends, or volunteers. Nevertheless, after the town became isolated, the nurses quickly realized that safe patient transportation was becoming problematic. The exit by bridge was cut off and darkness and gale force winds made sea evacuation difficult even for those in the best of health.

COORDINATION AND COOPERATION

Complicating matters, Bar Harbor's contact with the outside world was precarious. Telephone lines were destroyed as fire swept over them. Only one line was still functional during the evening of October 23. Earlier, Bar Harbor police had sent a call for help to a Coast Guard station on the other side of the island in the town of Southwest Harbor. In turn, the Coast Guard dispatched ships from southern Maine and Boston, Massachusetts, to aid residents. Even at full speed, the cutters were still unable to cover the required distance in time to reach the town when they were needed. Quick-thinking police instructed Charlotte Stuart, a telephone operator who was by then working the only functioning communication line left in town, "to call every boat" in the area. Fishermen and private boats from nearby Winter Harbor, Gouldsboro, Southwest Harbor, Northeast Harbor, and Lamoine responded. Taking turns picking up residents stranded on the dock, the men managed to evacuate at least 400 people by sea.[41]

Another source of help came from the Maine Sea Coast Mission. They immediately volunteered and coordinated the sea evacuation of patients with the MDI Hospital nurses and authorities, even though gale force winds and smoke were at their worst. The Mission's main office of operation was in Bar Harbor and it maintained a ship, *Sunbeam II*, to travel to island communities throughout mid to Downeast Maine. This vessel was ready at all times to accomplish the Mission's goals of providing nondenominational services along with health and youth development. Springing into action, the *Sunbeam II* and its crew made two evacuation trips of stable MDI patients and others in need to nearby islands.[42]

Image of a patient being transferred from an unknown boat to the Sunbeam II
*under optimal weather conditions during the 1940s. Captain Bill Berry is in
the far right side of the picture.*
Photo from Maine Sea Coast Mission Archives, Bar Harbor, Maine.

People involved in evacuation and firefighting worked with those around them on many different levels, doing whatever was needed. For example, after coordinating the evacuation of patients with nurses and authorities from the hospital, the captain of the *Sunbeam II*, Bill Berry, and another crew member, Ray Colburn, went ashore and fought the fire directly. While the blaze continued, the Maine Sea Coast Mission officials offered the use of the *Sunbeam II* as a safe offshore floating billet for firefighters when they needed a break.[43]

Despite the fact that many patients were discharged from the hospital, the patient census increased during the evening. The largest surge in patient numbers was related to a sudden influx of elderly local residents rather than in a surge of patients with burns or other injuries.[44] Frail local residents, normally cared for by family members at home, were unable to tolerate the stress and physical strength needed for evacuation during an autumn Maine night in a smoke-filled town. In one case, an elderly resident, Mrs. Arthur Pray, died from "heart seizure" early in the mandated evacuation.[45] An acceptable option left to the towns-people was leaving their fragile loved ones in the care of nurses at the MDI Hospital. These invalid people were not officially admitted as patients. Nevertheless, nurses readily accepted them, and fed and cared for them along with the "official" patients. Moreover, by nightfall, the hospital lobby was filled with soldiers and National Guardsmen. They were using the hospital to take much-needed breaks from hosing water on the hospital's roof and squelching fires on the surrounding grounds. Their job was to protect the hospital from falling burning debris that was being swept around by high winds.[46]

As the night progressed, conditions in the town worsened, adding to the difficulty in delivering nursing care. The fire engulfed and destroyed the Bangor Hydro Company's only transformer to the island, abruptly terminating power to the hospital as well as to the entire town. The darkness in the hospital wards made the intermittent bright sparks hitting the windows clearly visible to nurses and patients alike. Nurses continued their care by simply moving patients to central locations within the hospital's interior and "making do" with what portable lighting they had. Isabelle Forbis was in her ninth month of pregnancy and went into labor during the crisis. Nurses coached her through a successful delivery of her infant daughter with the aid of lighting equipment that was supplied to the hospital from the Ellsworth fire department. The young mother was discharged soon after delivery, but her infant daughter remained with nurses for further monitoring until she could be evacuated by her father later in the evening.[47]

While carrying out their duties, nurses prepared for the worst and took charge of the situation in the best way they could. One nurse collected several anesthetic agents and then pushed an anesthesia machine to the main hospital building for safe keeping if an emergent operation needed to be performed. She transferred the equipment not only because of the loss of lighting but also because the operating rooms were located in a wooden wing off the main brick building. She worried that the operating room and all its equipment could easily become compromised and lost by fire. Other nurses filled their pockets with morphine and standard medications so that they would have them readily available for patients if they were required to quickly evacuate everyone. All nurses were given responsibility for specific patients so that none of the patients or their newly added elderly charges would be lost in the confusion.[48]

Local community and Red Cross nurses outside of the hospital were also busy. The Red Cross quickly mobilized nurses to MDI at the onset of the fire and they remained on duty throughout the crisis and in the aftermath of recovery. The "Emergency Medical and Nursing Service and Arrangements for the Continued Care of Ill and Injured" Report recorded utilization of 169 volunteer Red Cross nurses in Maine during October.[49] Bar Harbor historian Debra Dyer recalled that her mother, an office secretary for a local physician, was asked to report for work along with all the office nurses. The physician told all his employees that they had "lots of work to do." He correctly anticipated that their services would be needed when inevitable injuries or illnesses developed during the evacuation or on the fire lines. Mrs. Dyer's mother arrived at work without hesitation, along with the entire nursing staff. They labored throughout the night and never joined residents who were being evacuated. Mrs. Dyer's mother never relayed if she or the office nurses had a plan of escape, only that they worked through the disaster.[50]

A quick evacuation plan was, however, developed by the MDI Hospital nurses in collaboration with local police and National

Guardsmen. They decided that if the fire became perilously close to the hospital or if any part of the hospital caught fire, the staff would assist and/or carry patients to a back exit, nearest the ocean, and follow a path to the town dock and the sea if necessary.[51] A medical detachment from Dow Field stood by with litters if the need for the hospital evacuation developed. Local physician Dr. Larrabee also remained in the hospital to help with the escape and to care for patients while they remained in the facility.[52]

Firefighters continued to wage war throughout the evening against the fire to protect the hospital and many local physicians' offices in what Fire Chief Sleeper labeled "the battle for the vital heart of Bar Harbor."[53] The fire came rolling out of the hills burning outlying homes in its path on the west side of Bar Harbor along with a large and lavish hotel, the DeGregoire. The DeGregoire was only a few short blocks from the harbor; so most of the people on the town pier looked on with fear as it became engulfed in flames.[54]

SHIFTING WINDS

Just when many thought the situation was at its worst, winds suddenly shifted to the north.[55] Firefighters were able to finally make a successful stand where the DeGregoire had once majestically stood. Protected by wet blankets, heroic crews on the other end of town moved forward with hoses to spread streams of water on advancing flames. They too were able to divert the inferno. The fire was not stopped, but it was diverted east of town. It continued to burn and raced down the coast before it eventually blew itself out over the ocean in a massive fireball. As the fire skirted Bar Harbor, a bulldozer came into town and pushed the burning rubble from the DeGregoire out of the road to clear it. Finally, an evacuation route was reopened by land for the residents who had been trapped.

At 9:10 p.m., the police instructed the townspeople on the pier to form a second caravan of evacuees. This time, the group was able to cross the scorched rubble and reach the Trenton Bridge connecting MDI to the mainland. From there, the vehicles proceeded to the town of Ellsworth where Red Cross organizers had arranged for short-term shelter for the evacuees. The volunteers registered, fed, and sent the people to families or churches in Ellsworth and surrounding towns, where they had temporary lodging until they could return home.

Overall, the daring evacuation of Bar Harbor was a success, but it was marred by a traffic accident that resulted in injury and death. The accident occurred when a military truck loaded with soldiers collided with a station wagon. One of the soldiers, Warrant Officer William Coates, died instantly. Several other soldiers were injured and taken by ambulance to a nearby medical center. Sixteen-year-old Helen Cormier of Bar Harbor, a passenger in the station wagon, suffered a skull fracture, resulting in her death 3 days later at the Ellsworth Hospital.[56]

By late morning on October 24, all the patients in the MDI Hospital had been evacuated. Local nurses and doctors transferred patients to mainland hospitals and the transient elderly population who had sought shelter in the facility were reunited with family or transported to Red Cross centers in Ellsworth for continued care. The hospital was closed and did not reopen until several days later when power was restored and water was tested for safety. However, Bar Harbor physicians and nurses remained on duty or call. Several resident physicians never closed their offices. Along with their nurses, these physicians cared for any remaining residents, firefighters, and support crews.[57]

The Red Cross had given aid throughout the MDI fire, but increased its efforts substantially during and after October 23. A Red Cross Summary Report about MDI from October 24 documented:

> Radio reports indicate one-half of Bar Harbor destroyed with property damage estimated at fifteen to twenty million dollars. 3,500 residents evacuated to communities on mainland. 400 to 500 persons in Red Cross shelters and private homes. Eight mobile canteen units operating on Island....Arrangements have been made with Coast Guard for portable mobile radio transmitters and receiving equipment to reestablish communications where it has failed. At 8:00 a.m. this morning Coast Guard informed us that highways had been reopened and Army trucks were evacuating residents of this section over

land. Although Coast Guard and Navy assembled 40 vessels for evacuation, it is possible that no further sea evacuation will be necessary. Three deaths were reported as result of automobile accident with several persons injured.[58]

Another Red Cross Report included the following:

During the emergency period shelters were staffed with volunteer nurses and doctors.... Emergency first aid was given to fire fighters, as well as displaced persons. All serious injuries or medical cases were transferred to a hospital.... The doctors and nurses assigned to the shelters and the emergency medical stations were responsible for examining the people coming into the shelters, to screen out any with communicable diseases. And those burned or suffering from exhaustion and smoke inhalation were treated.[59]

The need for increasing resources placed even greater demands on an organization that was simultaneously helping other communities throughout Maine.

Local nurses were given the option of temporarily evacuating Bar Harbor after October 23, but many chose to stay. Officials welcomed their contributions. They continued their usual employment in physicians' offices and many volunteered time to help care for firefighters or assist in other ways during the crisis.

CONCLUSION

Almost 2,000 more acres of land and forest burned before the MDI fire was declared under control on October 27. Sargent Collier, in "Mount Desert: The Most Beautiful Island in the World," wrote:

Those who beat out the flames remember it as three weeks in which they seldom removed rubber boots from drawn and blistered feet. Benzedrine pills by the pocket full kept them going without sleep for as long as five consecutive nights.[60]

Even after rain and snow had fallen, the vegetation on the forest floor, along with deeply embedded tree roots, fostered the continuation of underground fires. As firefighters continued to battle the fire, nurses and physicians provided them with care and aid for weeks after the initial crisis was over. The MDI fire was not declared completely extinguished until 4 p.m. on November 14, 1947.[61]

The collaborative efforts of locals, including the nurses, with state and federal agencies help explain the remarkably small number of recorded injuries and deaths in the 1947 Bar Harbor Fire. Residents were fortunate to have such an accomplished fire department in their town and the help of the surrounding local communities. Additionally, because of Bar Harbor's elite summer resort status, its ample natural resources, and its financial stability, the town attracted a wide array of individuals whose skills could easily be put to use in a disaster. In Bar Harbor, these individuals ranged from physicians and nurses with wartime knowledge to fishermen who were able to easily adapt their seamanship skills to evacuate residents during a storm. Local MDI residents also worked with each other and with the Red Cross, the National Park Services, the National Guard, the military, and numerous other state and government organizations. The essential role that local people played in averting many potential catastrophes during the Bar Harbor Fire illustrates the importance of strong local infrastructures for disaster preparedness.

With every passing year, there are fewer Bar Harbor residents who are able to recall details of the 1947 fire, much less the activities of nurses during that time. Most stories center around the remarkable and heroic activities of the firefighters. Nurses, like many in support services, are rarely mentioned. Dorothy Worchester, at 90 years of age, stated when interviewed in 2014 at her Southwest Harbor home, "Nurses never got the credit that they deserved. They just did what had to be done." Even professional nurses in Bar Harbor have trouble verbalizing exactly what nurses did during the fire. In the confusion, little was documented. A history of the MDI Hospital, written in 1997 by Mrs. Clarice Hall Hamlin, devoted one paragraph to the nurses who gave care in October 1947:

> The personal concern of hospital employees was never more clearly demonstrated than at the time of the Bar Harbor fire,

in 1947. Although this was the first disaster in the memory of the hospital, or the town, there was no panic. Mr. George Berry, who was a patient at the time, said that although they realized what was happening outside, inside the hospital all was calm. The patients were taken from the wooden structure to the brick wing; otherwise the regular routine was followed. On the following day, bed patients were moved to the Eastern Maine General Hospital in Bangor. Through it all, Mr. Berry emphasized the work of the nurses. Although several of them knew that their homes were in danger, and even destroyed, they remained on the job all day and all night until their patients were evacuated.[62]

Nurses throughout Bar Harbor, nevertheless, played a vital role in the care of residents during the town's greatest natural disaster. Whether traveling to fire lines, working in private physicians' offices, assisting the Red Cross, or on duty in the MDI Hospital, nurses provided necessary skills to their community when they were needed. Through their devotion and in collaboration with officials and local physicians, nurses provided a sanctuary during the storm.

On the morning of October 24, 1947, Dorothy Worchester, RN, finished a harrowing 18-hour shift of duty. Her white uniform had long lost its highly starched creases prior to her leaving the hospital. During her walk home, she noted that the usually quiet morning activities in her quaint coastal village had been replaced with the sounds of active military personnel, firefighters, and emergency vehicles that were still fighting flames to the southwest of town. Most of Bar Harbor's residents had been evacuated and businesses were closed. Bar Harbor seemed more like a military outpost than the resort retreat it had been just a few days ago. She knew it would take months for Bar Harbor to recover. Utter exhaustion had replaced her earlier feelings of apprehension, but she also had a sense of accomplishment. While making do with the equipment and supplies that were available, Dorothy cared for the elderly, the vulnerable, patients with acute and chronic illnesses, as well as those affected by the disaster. Like all the nurses in Bar Harbor, she did "what had to be done."[63]

NOTES

1. Dorothy Worchester (Charge Nurse, MDI Hospital, 1947), personal communication with the author, June 20–21 and July 10, 2014.

2. Ibid.

3. Joyce Butler, "Down Millionaires' Row," in *Wildfire Loose: The Week Maine Burned* (Camden, ME: Down East Books, second edition, 1987), 49–74.

4. Worchester, personal communication, June 20–21, 2014.

5. The Bar Harbor Historical Society, accessed June 2014, http://www.bar-harborhistorical.org/gildedage.html.

6. "Veterans Medals to Be Issued at Legion Meetings," *The Bar Harbor Times* XXXIV, October 2, 1947, 1, Column 2.

7. Butler, *Wildfire Loose*.

8. Worchester, personal communication, June 20–21, 2014.

9. Phillip Kalisch and Beatrice Kalisch, "When Nurses Were National Heroines: Images of Nursing in American Film, 1942–1943," *Nursing Forum* 20, no. 1 (1981): 14061.

10. Karen Egenes, "History of Nursing," in *Issues and Trends in Nursing: Essential Knowledge for Today and Tomorrow*, Ed. Gayle Roux and Judith A. Halstead (Sudbury, MA: Jones and Bartlett Publishers, 9th edition, 2009), 18. Following World War II, the United States experienced one of its most drastic shortages of nurses. Many nurses who returned from the war sought the idealized role of wife and mother. Until the 1960s, nurses who worked in hospitals were expected to resign from their positions when they married. In addition, returning military nurses who had experienced such profoundly autonomous roles during the war were now reluctant to return to the subservient role of staff nurse in a hospital. During the years that immediately followed the end of the war, despite the acute nursing shortage, nurses were paid far less than elementary school teachers, the professional group to whom nurses were most often compared. In fact, a study conducted in 1946 by the California Nurses Association found that the majority of staff nurses were paid only slightly more than hotel maids and seamstresses. Additionally, nursing leaders of the time were well known and dynamic. They included Lavinia Dock (1858–1965), Mary Adelaide Nutting (1858–1948), Isabel Maitland Stewart (1878–1947), and Mary Breckinridge (1888–1965). Lavinia Dock was a lecturer, author, and activist. Her campaign for women's suffrage and participation in antiwar protests sometime led to her arrest. She authored many nursing textbooks and, because of her leadership in the International Council of Nurses, served as

an editor for the *American Journal of Nursing*'s Foreign Department. Mary Adelaide Nutting was appointed head of the Department of Nursing and Health at Teachers College of Columbia University. She became the world's first professor of nursing. Isabel Maitland Stewart was a professor of nursing at Teachers College of Columbia University. She worked tirelessly for the establishment of a standardized nursing curriculum. She insisted on the need for nursing research to give the profession a solid scientific base. Mary Breckenridge, a nurse midwife, founded the Frontier Nursing Service to provide maternity services to women in the Appalachian mountains of eastern Kentucky. The organization is still in existence today. Since this development, it has significantly lowered the maternal mortality rate of the region served.

11. Worchester, personal communication with author, June 20–21, 2014.
12. Brenda Sprague (MDI Hospital Public Affairs), e-mail message to author, May 28, 2014.
13. Worchester, personal communication with author, June 20–21, 2014.
14. Ibid.
15. Butler, *Wildfire Loose.*
16. *The Fire of 1947: The Year Maine Burned,* directed and produced by the Maine Forest Service (Bucksport, ME: Northeast Historic Film), 1984.
17. Ibid.
18. Robert Crocker, "Limerick Countryside Lies Desolate in Ruins," *Biddeford Daily Journal*, October 24, 1947.
19. Frankline Wright, "Scorched Ruins All That Remain of Brownfield," *Portland Sunday Telegram*, October 26, 1947.
20. American Red Cross Records, DR-1959.08, "Final Report Vol. II Areas, New England Forest Fires, October 20–29, 1947"; The Rehabilitation Semi-Monthly Report, Period Ending January 31, 1948, "Final Report, Helen Corken, Case Work Supervisor," National Archives and Records Administration, College Park, MD.
21. Claire Lambert (Bar Harbor resident and retired town librarian), personal communication with author, June 28, 2014.
22. Butler, *Wildfire Loose*, 50.
23. Acadia National Park Archives, Mount Desert Island, Fire Management Program, 1930–1979 (ACAD-341), Annual Fire Summaries 1940–1949.
24. "Thousands of Acres of Timberlands Burned: Hulls Cove Threatened; Fire Still Burning," *The Bar Harbor Times* XXXIV, no. 1721, October 23, 1947.
25. *The Bangor Daily News*, October 23, 1947.

26. William Maling (University of Maine undergraduate in 1947), discussion with author, November 2007. William Maling is the author's father. After being diagnosed with terminal cancer, he spent time relaying events in his life to his family. His part in fighting the 1947 Mount Desert Island (MDI) fire was one account that he relayed. His story was directly responsible for the author's decision to research the participation of nurses in the 1947 MDI fire.

27. "Thousands of Acres of Timberlands Burned," *The Bar Harbor Times*, October 23, 1947.

28. Worchester, personal communication with author, June 20–21, 2014.

29. "Condition of Health in Area," *The Bar Harbor Times*, October 23, 1947.

30. *The Fire of 1947*. This film contains an interview with Chief Sleeper.

31. Butler, *Wildfire Loose*, 62.

32. Lambert, personal communication with author, June 28, 2014.

33. Butler, *Wildfire Loose*, 64.

34. Lambert, personal communication with author; Maling, personal communication with author. Lambert's account of evacuation is echoed in Butler's *Wildfire Loose*, 64–74.

35. Ibid.

36. Richard Hale, Jr., *The Story of Bar Harbor* (New York, NY: Ives Washburn, Inc., 1949), 32.

37. Butler, *Wildfire Loose*, 69. Per Butler, "Around eight o'clock at the office of the *Press Herald* in Portland, an Associated Press wire dispatch came in saying 4000 people were trapped on the wharf at Bar Harbor."

38. Lambert, personal communication with author, June 28, 2014.

39. Worchester, personal communication with author, June 20–21, 2014.

40. Butler, *Wildfire Loose*, 63.

41. Ibid., 71.

42. Maine Sea Coast Mission Archives, Bar Harbor Maine.

43. Ibid.

44. Worchester, personal communication with author, June 20–21, 2014.

45. Butler, *Wildfire Loose*, 71.

46. Worchester, personal communication with author, June 20–21, 2014.

47. "Baby Born During Burn," *The Bar Harbor Times*, October 20, 2014. This article was printed in *The Bar Harbor Times* on the 67th birthday of Monica Forbis. Ms. Forbis was born in the MDI Hospital to Isabelle and Welch Forbis of Southwest Harbor during the 1947 fire.

48. Worchester, personal communication with author, June 20–21, 2014. Worchester's account of nurses' actions in the MDI Hospital during the 1947 fire is echoed by Joyce Butler in *Wildfire Loose* as well as in October issues of *The Bar Harbor Times*.

49. The "Emergency Medical and Nursing Service and Arrangements for the Continued Care of Ill and Injured." Report recorded utilization of 169 volunteer Red Cross nurses in Maine during October.

50. Debra Dyer (Bar Harbor Historical Society Curator), personal communication with author, August 10, 2014.

51. Worchester, personal communication with author, June 20–21, 2014.

52. Butler, *Wildfire Loose*, 63.

53. *The Fire of 1947.*

54. Butler, *Wildfire Loose*, 71–72.

55. American Red Cross report, DR-1959.08, "Final Report, Vol. II Areas, New England Forest Fires, October 20–29, 1947." Description of area in which disaster occurred.

56. "Road Tragedy: Dow Field Officer Dies at Hull's Cove," *Bangor Daily Commercial*, October 24, 1947.

57. Worchester, personal communication with author, June 20–21, 2014.

58. American Red Cross Records, DR-1959.08, "Final Report Vol. II Areas, New England Forest Fires, October 20–29, 1947," National Archives and Records Administration, College Park, MD.

59. Ibid.

60. Sargent Collier, *Mount Desert: The Most Beautiful Island in the World* (Boston, MA: Houghton Mifflin, 1952), 52.

61. Acadia National Park Archives, Mount Desert Island, Fire Management Program, 1930–1979 (ACAD-341), Annual Fire Summaries 1940–1949; Acadia National Park Service, U.S. Department of the Interior, "Acadia: the Year Maine Burned" (Washington DC: U.S. Government Printing Office, 1994), 500–769.

62. Clarice Hall Hamlin, *A History of the MDI Hospital* (Bar Harbor, Maine: Bar Harbor Historical Society and in cooperation with the MDI Hospital, 1997).

63. Worchester, personal communication with author, June 20–21, 2014.

CHAPTER 9

The SARS Pandemic in Toronto, Canada, 2003

Sioban Nelson and Adrienne Byng

> *[SARS] brought nurses closer together. Nurses who I worked with on the different units were more compassionate with each other. Sometimes in nursing you get so busy that you don't care that much about your colleagues, you're focused so much on your work. But in SARS we had more time to reflect, and the caring attitude came out in a lot of us.*[1]

THE CRISIS

Severe acute respiratory syndrome (SARS) found its way to Toronto in February 2003 through a series of events that started with a 64-year-old physician with flu-like symptoms who checked into the ninth floor of Hong Kong's Metropole Hotel. Unbeknownst to this individual—who had been working to contain an outbreak of a mysterious respiratory ailment that had first emerged in Foshan, China, in November 2002—he would act as a locus of infection that would extend around the globe and trigger a world health emergency.[2]

Map of Toronto, Ontario, Canada.

Although the mechanism of SARS transmission at the Metropole is yet to be ascertained, the physician's brief residency was sufficient to transmit the disease to 17 other patrons, of whom two were Canadians. Of those infected, Mrs. K—a 78-year-old matriarch of a large Toronto family in the Scarborough district, east of the city—would become the index case for the Toronto outbreak.[3] Although initially asymptomatic, 2 days after the conclusion of her 10-day trip to China, Mrs. K developed the high fever, muscle aches, and dry cough that would later become the hallmarks of SARS. Unaware of the epidemic of atypical respiratory illness festering in China, doctors classified Mrs. K's illness as a case of community-acquired pneumonia. As a result of this categorization, her death on March 5, 2003, was not looked upon with suspicion.[4]

As March unfolded, the family members with whom Mrs. K shared her apartment became ill. Of the five infected, Mr. T—Mrs. K's 45-year-old son—was the most severely afflicted. On Friday March 7, 2003, he was transported via ambulance to the Scarborough Grace Hospital. Presenting with acute pneumonia, Mr. Y remained unmasked and in close proximity to other patients for 16 hours while waiting for an acute care bed.[5] Precautions were similarly not used following his transfer to 4D—a medical floor—and, subsequently, the intensive care unit (ICU).

By March 13, 2003, Mr. T was dead and the remaining four members of the T family—his sister, his brother, his wife, and his infant child—were sick. In the days that followed, public health officials, infectious disease experts from across the Greater Toronto area (GTA), and physicians–infection control staff at the Scarborough Grace Hospital attempted to gather as much information as they could about this new, unknown disease.

Two things were becoming clear about this mystery disease. First, it posed considerable risks to health workers, and second, it was extremely challenging to contain. For instance, despite wearing protective equipment and following precautions, a physician and three nurses were infected after intubating one patient. Worse still, this particular patient's family members also contracted the disease. When they eventually were admitted through the emergency department (ED), their presence infected seven ED visitors, two patients, one staff member, three ED nurses, two clerks, and one housekeeper. Two of those infected individuals were subsequently admitted to a different hospital where they were neither isolated nor treated with precautions, resulting in further spread of the disease.[6]

By Sunday March 23, 2003, officials on a municipal and provincial level realized that the efforts to contain SARS had failed. In addition to the legal obligation that hospitals now had to report SARS cases, public health units were also given the power to make orders with respect to SARS cases; the most notable of which was a mandatory 10-day quarantine for any individual who had come into, or had potentially come into, contact with a suspected or known SARS case. It was the first imposition of quarantine in Toronto in 50 years.

MITIGATING RISK

By March 26, 2003, the extent of SARS transmission across Toronto forced the premier to issue a state of provincial emergency. Under this order, hospitals were now required to establish isolation units, to implement the use of respirators such as the N95, and to restrict patient transfers between institutions. Staffs were instructed to use precautions in all areas of the hospital and were limited to work at one institution. These measures were intended to break the chain of infection that had been forged between institutions as well as to reduce the incidence–likelihood of community transmission.

Despite these measures, by the end of March, it was apparent that SARS was continuing to run rampant throughout the GTA hospital system. Suspected and probable cases were increasing in numbers at approximately 8 to 10 cases per day and a number of emergency departments across the city were being flooded with patients displaying symptoms of SARS.[7]

As the presentation of new cases began to abate in April, authorities optimistically and controversially relaxed the infection control precautions throughout the GTA hospital by later that month. The province formally lifted the state of emergency on May 17, 2003. The consequences of this premature move, however, were disastrous as SARS once again quickly spread throughout Toronto's hospital system. By May 22, the government was forced to concede that a second SARS outbreak (what became known as SARS 2) had arrived.

As this second wave of disease began to subside with the onset of summer, the funerals of health care workers began. On July 4, 2003, the first funeral service was held for a Canadian health care worker who had contracted SARS while at work. This service was followed by a second on July 20, 2003, and a third on August 13, 2003, when a nurse and physician who contracted SARS during the first wave of the outbreak succumbed to their illnesses.

In the final stage of the epidemic between February and September 2003, Toronto officials recorded 438 suspected cases and 43 deaths. Across the world, the death rate was 775, with the pandemic largely centered in acute care hospitals with patients and health care workers at the greatest risk of infection and death. Two nurses and one doctor were among the Toronto deaths. Although nursing has a long history of providing patient care during epidemics, what became clear through the Toronto experience was the tension between the health workers' altruistic and service-oriented responses to the risks of providing care, on the one hand, and the nurses' rights to a safe working environment, on the other. The need to manage issues such as mandatory quarantine, the public's stigmatization of health workers, and the demands for full access to information challenged epidemic response groups and the organization of nursing during a crisis.

Based on a secondary analysis of nurse interviews that are available on the public record and the funds received from a recent scholarship to study SARS in Toronto, this chapter highlights the challenging labor issues and emotional debates about the rights and responsibilities of nurses to protect themselves and their families as nurses and other health care workers experience the dangers and uncertainties of pandemic care in a modern 21st-century health care system.[8]

COLLEGIALITY, PROFESSIONAL OBLIGATION, AND ETHICAL DILEMMAS

At the beginning of the outbreak, I thought I didn't want to be a nurse anymore. Then I thought "what the hell am I thinking?" Never once in nursing have I turned away from danger. (Saverina Sanchez, Emergency and Intensive Care Nurse[9])

For hundreds of nurses like Saverina Sanchez, the 2003 Toronto SARS crisis constituted a time of intense professional and personal turmoil. Especially during the first wave of the pandemic, nurses had to decide whether they would continue to report for work, given the very real potential for exposing themselves and their loved ones to what might prove to be a fatal illness. In spite of their intense commitment to the profession, many nurses struggled with the ethical dilemma of reporting for work during the SARS crisis as they weighed their personal duties to their families against their professional obligations to their hospitals, colleagues, and patients. Although some nurses were reluctant to report for work due to the unacceptable risk that their participation in the crisis posed to the health of their families, hundreds of men and women continued to go to work out of a strong sense of duty to their colleagues and to their patients. Indeed, as a Scarborough Grace Hospital nurse said, "[As a nurse, my duty] is to look after *people*! ... Your job, as a nurse, is to *be at work.*"[10]

Various reasons have been identified in determining why nurses continued to report for work during the crisis in spite of the inherent risks posed by SARS nursing. The major reasons cited, however, were the nurses' recognition of their personal obligation to nursing colleagues, and their professional obligation to the patients. An examination of the nurses' reflections in the SARS and post-SARS period produces evidence that despite the dangers posed to their health and the health of their families, many nurses chose to continue to work in order to support and sustain their colleagues who were working extended shifts with increased workloads amid constantly changing infection control directives, as well as rumored reports of staff falling ill. As one Scarborough Grace Hospital nurse recalled,

> Why did [I] come to work? There is a sense of dedication. There is a sense of duty. ... It's not to the hospital. ... It is to the profession, for me. So, although ... I'm very happy working here, it is an organization. [My duty is] to the profession, I think. And ... to my co-workers, I think. It's to the people I work closely with.[11]

Although quotations such as the preceding one are repeated ad nauseam in SARS nursing narratives, the question to ask is: Why did these nurses feel this sense of duty and obligation both to their profession and their colleagues? In examining nurses' decisions to report for work during the SARS crisis, Williams suggests that the decisions to report for work were highly contextual and predicated on personal assessments of each individual's financial–familial situation as well as assessments of personal risk. In cases where familial risks were judged to be negligible, Williams suggests that nurses were more likely to continue to accept hospital duties. But how could the actions of those nurses who chose to continue to undertake hospital duties despite having preexisting medical conditions that predisposed them to contract the disease be explained? As one SARS veteran nurse remarked:

> I did receive notification from the Ministry through Occupational Health of the Hospital that...SARS should not be a problem for people with [medical conditions such as mine]. However, I questioned that and I did go to my doctor, and he was very concerned....And he did offer to put me off on sick leave. At which time I said "No," I would go to work. Because I firmly believe that *I'm supposed to* go to work![12]

Why did nurses such as these eschew medical advice to fulfill an unstated obligation to their colleagues? For some nurses, the obligation they felt to their colleagues was rooted in their perception of the profession itself. As one Scarborough Grace nurse stated:

> The truth of it is, it is my job and I *do have* a responsibility. And yes, I have to go....It's your obligation. You have to do it! It's your obligation...to the patients...I think everybody struggled with this, but the bottom line is, you did go into this profession, and you have an obligation. If we all said, "Oh well, we can't go!" who would care for the patients? So you just *have to go*.[13]

For these nurses, continuing to report for work was congruent with fulfilling the mandate set out by the nursing profession itself. Failure to report to work was constructed as akin to failure to fulfill the profession's duty to care. Conceptualized in this context, reporting for work was nonnegotiable. Although many nurses surveyed in the post-SARS period indicated that when they first entered the profession they had not realized they were agreeing to place their lives in danger, these nurses felt that risk—particularly the risk associated with outbreaks and pandemics—was an inherent part of the profession itself. Entry into the profession thus meant acceptance of that risk.

Although the theme of professional obligation and the subsequent duty to care underwrites the majority of SARS nursing narratives, it is but one of the variables that motivated nurses to continue to report for duty. Indeed, in reading nurses' accounts of SARS, it appears that the need for understanding, intimacy, and psychosocial support motivated many nurses to continue to operate in their positions. As a result of being ostracized by their families, friends, and communities, many nurses, unable to draw on those usual sources of intimacy, turned to their colleagues to help them weather the storm. According to a Scarborough Grace nurse:

> During SARS...the people we worked with became our confidantes and we spent more time with them, but also [we] were probably more, I'll say, intimate with them just because you couldn't be intimate with your family at home because one of you was always wearing a mask! [And] you're ten feet away talking, and you see them for only 2 hours (not the usual length of time) because people had been working longer [during the outbreak].[14]

Infection control protocols reshaped both the space and nature of interactions nurses were able to have with one another. They donned personal protective equipment (PPE) and sat in the hospital cafeterias at a regulated distance between one another. In spite of these regulations, their perception that they were united in the hardships they faced on the hospital floor, at home, and in the community fostered a renewed sense of collegiality among them.

This strengthened sense of collegiality between and among nurses not only was a source for emotional, physical, and psychosocial support, but it also became a source of information at a time in which an intense distrust was fostered in the hospital administration. Although many nurses have acknowledged in the post-SARS period that unit and hospital administrators did their best to keep staff abreast of changes in infection-control directives and of any updates regarding the health statuses of ill colleagues, many felt at the time of the crisis that they were not properly supported by senior staff. Although some nurses did report that they felt adequately supported by hospital management, many felt a sense of abandonment. This feeling arose from the perception that senior administrative staff failed to be physically present during the crisis, to communicate changes in infection control policy to hospital units (thus, making the nurses and other staff more vulnerable), and to check in with staff to see how they were faring during the crisis. This sense of abandonment was particularly acute for nurses during the second round of SARS (SARS 2). They felt their concerns regarding the reappearance of the disease were not taken seriously by the administration. Even worse, before SARS 2 was officially declared, nurses were prevented from taking precautions that would have protected themselves and others from infection. As one Scarborough Hospital nurse so eloquently stated:

> It seems to me that those who have been most traumatized by it all, some of whom never had SARS, were the ones for whom it raised or resurrected, I think, issues of abandonment.... They felt, in my psychological jargon... abandoned by Mother Institution. "I *told* you that I wanted to wear a mask and you said, 'That's silly, you're gonna scare people!' I *needed* to wear a mask, and you wouldn't let me! I got sick with SARS *because* you told me not to wear a mask. And then when I was home sick, or in another hospital, not *one word* from my manager!"...And those are the...people coming back to work now who are still *pissed off!* And some of them aren't going to come back! Some of them are not going to ever walk in the doors of this place again.[15]

For those nurses who felt abandoned by their institutions, fostering stronger relationships with other nurses became essential not only for their emotional survival but also for their physical survival. Indeed, many nurses have quoted at length that they relied on their colleagues to keep them abreast of changes in hospital policy, proper infection control measures, and changes in the health statuses of nurses afflicted with the disease. Nursing relationships at the time of the crisis became essential repositories of information that made nurses feel more comfortable and capable in performing their duties. As one nurse remarked:

> If there was a SARS 3, my first reaction would be to get the next plane out of here! [No,] if there was SARS 3, I think I would probably be in...[but] not necessarily on the SARS unit. But I've learnt a lot from this, and I know what not to do and what to do and I think I would be more *adamant* about how I want things to be run. I would be in there and try and give as much support from what I learned from it, and from the mistakes that people have made in my case, and try to guide my colleagues and patients about SARS.[16]

Strengthened nursing relationships also became a conduit through which nurses were able to vent their frustrations about the organization and the quality of patient care. For many of those surveyed, the implementation and use of PPE created distances between themselves and their patients in a manner that prevented them from providing care at the bedside in their usual manner. Due to the 15-minute time restriction placed on nurses when remaining in SARS patients' rooms, many felt that the quality of care they were able to provide to these patients was diluted and subpar. This was especially true when nurses found themselves caring for SARS-afflicted colleagues. As one emergency nurse recalled in caring for felled colleagues:

> To watch this unfold, I don't have the vocabulary to express it. Just thinking about it has been difficult. I think you can't comprehend, especially SARS I, how scary it was at that time because we had no idea. As we were shipping these people out to West Park and we are gloved, gowned and masked and you are reaching to touch these people not knowing if you will ever see them again, helping them get onto the bus, all we knew in the media was that people were dying. They probably had no idea what they were facing either. Looking back, I think at the time because we were tired and we were working, because it was so surreal you didn't have the opportunity to absorb it.

> That's when the nightmares came. The going in circles, the questioning, did we do it right, could we have done it better?[17]

This nurse expressed the enormous pain and concern felt by nurses charged with caring for their colleagues who had contracted the disease. Tempered with feelings of compassion, guilt, and fear—particularly fear of contracting the disease itself and transmitting it to their loved ones—nurses' recollections of caring for colleagues demonstrate just how closely the crisis bound these men and women together.

SARS AS A LABOR ISSUE

During the first SARS outbreak (February to May 2003), nursing SARS-afflicted patients was voluntary and did not include any form of additional financial compensation. Early SARS units appeared on an ad hoc basis as the disease spread throughout the GTA hospital system. Courageous men and women worked in the highly contagious units without clear direction at a time when the precautionary principles of SARS treatment were yet to be fully developed.

However, nurse staffing both within and outside of the SARS units soon became complex. Prior to the pandemic, significant government-funding cuts had created a severe nursing shortage across the province. In its report on the nursing experience with the 2003 SARS pandemic, the Registered Nurses Association of Ontario (RNAO) identified staffing shortages facilitated by Ontario Premier Mike Harris's *commonsense revolution* as a major impediment to local efforts to contain the disease. The RNAO argued that the government's push under Harris to reduce costs created system-wide deficiencies that placed the health of nurses and patients in jeopardy.[18] Most notable, the RNAO emphasized the need to retrench full-time nursing positions rather than the part-time, casual, and agency nursing used during this period. They laid the blame for the uncontrolled spread of SARS and the high rate of infection of nurses and other health care personnel squarely on the government. The RNAO argued that the creation of a large, transient nursing workforce resulted in reduced surge capacity with tragic results, and, ironically, in higher costs that threatened the viability of the entire health care system.[19]

Prior to the dramatic cuts to health care in the 1990s, a high proportion of nurses had been employed full time. As Baumann and others have observed, "part-time nurses [were intended to provide] routine coverage of absenteeism and a pool of casual workers were [to be] accessed during periods of heavy demand [only]."[20] This arrangement created a stable nursing workforce because it emphasized the use of full-time employment as the principal means to meet growing population needs. In the years leading up to the SARS pandemic, the population of Toronto grew exponentially beyond the number of nurses employed in the city itself.[21] In the 1990s, however, an unpredictable funding climate induced hospital managers to reduce operating costs. Chief among the solutions devised was to eliminate supposed "overstaffing" by systematically replacing full-time and regular part-time staff with staff employed on an ad hoc basis.[22] Referred to as the "just-in-time" staff policy, this measure promoted the en masse casualization of the nursing workforce and fostered an overreliance on part-time, casual, and agency-based nursing services. This created and promoted an accordion-like image of the nursing workforce that expanded by adding part-time, casual, and agency labor only when crises exhausted the capacity of the health care system to meet population needs. Following the resolution of the "threat," any additional staff who had been brought in to supplement a threadbare nursing workforce would be laid off or fired in order to allow the system to contract back to noncrisis levels. Although this concept appeared sufficient on paper, it would not work because the number of nursing positions prior to the SARS crisis was already insufficient to provide adequate health care services.

This trend toward part-time, casual, and agency employment led to a dramatic deterioration in the number of nurses available. With part-time and casual positions offering nurses neither stability nor benefits, many nurses found themselves coping with employment insecurity by seeking additional nursing positions.[23] As nurses took on two positions to make up for one full-time job, they created a trend toward multiple employment, which in turn negated the flexible nursing workforce the progenitors of the "just-in-time" policy had envisioned.[24] Indeed, as Barbara Wahl—then president of the union, the Ontario Nurses Association (ONA)—noted, government cuts to health care budgets and health care restructuring that fostered the trend toward multiple employment actually reduced the number of nurses available.[25] This was particularly evident during the SARS crisis when infection-control directives prohibited hospital staff from working in multiple institutions. Any nurse working two jobs in two places was no longer available to help with the crisis. Suddenly, the realities of the nursing shortage were blatantly obvious. What took place was the result of the accordionesque nursing system that had been implemented during Mike Harris's Common Sense Revolution during the early to mid-1990s to facilitate an expandable and contractable nursing workforce based on part-time labor. Although this accordionesque staffing model was able to compensate for staff attrition that resulted from on-the-job injuries, illnesses, and absenteeism in noncrisis situations, it was unable to accommodate staff losses that occurred as a result of illness and quarantine at the height of the SARS crisis. Indeed, as many nurses have noted in the post-SARS period, the dangerously low staffing levels that resulted from the hospital systems' overreliance on part-time, casual, and agency nursing resulted in workloads that were untenable and, in many instances, unsafe. These conditions are perhaps best captured by one nurse, who, in her recollections of the working conditions experienced during SARS, remarked:

> So I only spent at home maybe 8 hours, 9 hours, tops. And on my days off I still worked because [of the lack of staff]. It was really hard. We would work two weeks straight. And it's 12-hour shifts.... There was a lot of staff who didn't want to come in [because] they were scared. There was a few people that got sick, on our staff too.... So we had to cover their shifts. And they didn't have the manpower to do it. Eventually they got extra people,... For three weeks we worked full 7 days– 21 days straight—it was pretty hard.[26]

The concept of agency-based nursing was not just popular with hospital administration, many nurses themselves found it very attractive even though agency-based nurses were viewed with a particular vehemence due to their cost, lack of competence, and the destabilizing effects that they had on the team.[27] Due to the premium rate pay, many nurses chose to pursue agency-based employment in the wake of the massive layoffs and job displacements that occurred in the late 1990s. Rather than work for a permanent employer, qualified nurses with specialty skills could make more money by loaning themselves to institutions in the grips of a staffing shortage. Regular staff nurses were being paid between $21.00 and $31.00 an hour, whereas private agency nurses were being offered up to $100 to perform the same duties.[28] Although this arrangement was tenable during times of noncrisis, the strain of the SARS epidemic revealed the problems that arose when utilizing this labor source. In its examination of the SARS work environment, the RNAO found that the use of agency-based nurses created significant problems at the operational level. In examining post-SARS nursing testimonies, the RNAO established that many nurses resented the deployment of agency-based staff not only because they were more highly remunerated for their services but because their lack of accountability to and unfamiliarity with the unit decreased the quality of care provided and added greatly to the already untenable workload of "regular" staff.[29] In addition to this, many nurses reported that agency-based staff members were often deployed to units without the requisite skill set to operate safely on the unit, which in turn also added to staff frustration and increased workloads.

Another rupture to the collegial bonds that unified nurses during the pandemic was the implementation of "danger pay" offered to staff at the SARS Alliance Hospitals. As noted by the Naylor Report, the selective payment of extra monies proved to be a contentious and divisive issue and created inequities between staff both within and between institutions.[30] Although intended by then Health Minister Tony Clement as a compensatory measure for nurses working under stressful conditions in SARS-designated hospitals, the provincial push for double pay challenged the profession's long-standing image as a vocation and, in the process, fractured long-standing nursing relationships.

In response to rising anger from nurses, the provincial government cobbled together a deal for danger pay that had regular staff working in designated SARS hospitals, ICUs, emergency departments, and SARS units. However, because receiving danger pay could potentially violate the nurses' collective agreements with the hospitals, they made efforts to negotiate shorter shifts and longer breaks while maintaining the same pay.[31] At the same time, Premier Ernie Eves announced that a $190 million compensation package would be organized for nurses and health care workers alike who suffered a loss in wages as a result of the SARS crisis.[32] Although the nursing unions were skeptical about these overtures, many nurses were pleased with this proposed direction. Indeed, as one nurse recollected:

> I can remember one day we were told by my manager that from now on we were getting time and a half because we were working in that unit. We thought that was wonderful! It was kind of like danger pay. We thought, that's super! We didn't have to have as many shifts that way. That was the first initial thought—you'd work fewer shifts and still get your full time hours in because those shifts you'd work for at time and a half.... So that sounded really good.[33]

The enthusiasm with which regularly employed nurses embraced the province's initiative to shorten working hours and lengthen breaks without a reduction in pay was short-lived, however. During the SARS 2 outbreak (May to July 2003), the province allocated funds to double the wages of hospital staff nurses employed on SARS units in an effort to attract and retain staff. Framed as an incentive to work and as compensation for the inconveniences nurses faced when providing care to SARS patients, these funds were an effort to quell widespread anger over the standard rate offered to agency nurses. Although payment of these monies was well received by "eligible" staff who had worked and continued to remain on SARS units during the second wave of the crisis, others were angry. Health care workers who were overlooked or deemed ineligible for the payments of extra monies were furious over this new pay scale. Although there was a push from hospital staff to ensure that all those who reported for duty during the crisis received remuneration for the danger and hardships they encountered while providing care, enhanced wages were made available only to those who worked on SARS units or who provided direct care to SARS patients. This infuriated staff who felt that the inability of the hospitals to guarantee that they would not be exposed to SARS if serving on "regular" units meant that they too should be entitled to some form of compensation. The same was true for nurses who did not provide direct care to SARS patients, but who did have SARS patients housed on their units. Indeed, as one nurse remarked:

> Oh, I agree [people should have gotten the extra pay], but I think everybody should get paid that. Not just the people that are—I mean, we're *all* potentially at risk. I think everybody that was working with or had been with—We have respiratory patients on our floor....And you don't know if *that* guy has it, or is carrying it. You don't know.[34]

These sentiments were similarly expressed by another nurse who stated:

> So, now they're coming to work and getting regular pay. And somebody else is coming to work and she's getting more than they are, she's getting *double pay*, because she's going into *that* room. So, there was—How can you say, Today *she's* sitting there—(she may not go into that room, she's just running as a gopher for the staff)—she's getting the *premium* pay, but other nurses [on the floor] are not. So *that* caused problems. *Definite* problems.[35]

This payment of extra monies during the second wave of the crisis also caused considerable frustration among nurses who volunteered or were conscripted for duty during the first wave. At the time of the initial outbreak, little was known about the disease's transmission, clinical course, and long-term health-related outcomes postinfection. Unlike nurses who reported for SARS duty during the second wave, the initial group of SARS staff did not have clear direction with respect to the use of PPE nor was their care of suspected or probable SARS cases guided by the precautionary principle. First-wave nurses were paid a regular wage, worked full 12-hour shifts, and had to do so while operating with insufficient types or amounts of PPE. Because of the inherent danger they faced in providing care to SARS patients, these nurses were considerably angry when—after the promise of double wages in the second wave—nurses previously unwilling to volunteer for SARS duty began to clamor for postings on these units. As one nurse stated:

> Then the double time came. And then you *really* saw people's true colours come about.... People that had no *interest* and who would not volunteer from Day One, now wanted to work on that unit. People were *fighting* to get work on this unit. And they were only coming, blatantly, for the money. They weren't coming because they wanted to do it, or they felt they needed to do it, or that people were lacking care. They were coming strictly for *cash,* and cash *only.* I think that had a lot of impact on the staff that were there from Day One.... [And nurses] were *very* upset that they didn't get this money the first time around. And rightfully so.[36]

There was also anger among first-wave nurses who felt that the offering of extra monies during the second wave of the crisis compromised and diluted the quality of patient care. As one nurse poignantly stated:

> Yeah, I think [duty of care] *was* compromised quite a bit because, for one, nobody wants to go in [to the SARS unit] unless they're going to get paid *a lot* of money. Honestly, I feel that—I know that for a fact because we've had this conversation since I've been back with my colleagues [about] who went where and how much money they got paid and who got double time for how many weeks, that sort of thing. And the reason [they worked with SARS patients] was for the *money.* And it *wasn't* because they cared about people, and it *wasn't* because they wanted to make a difference.[37]

Although first-wave nurses have been documented at length as being able to forgive those who did not volunteer in the first wave due to medical conditions, familial obligations, or fear, statements such as these demonstrate that some nurses felt that the acceptance of

SARS postings on the basis of "danger" pay cheapened patient care. Indeed, statements such as the aforementioned one appear to indicate that many nurses were upset that professional obligation did not factor into the acceptance of SARS duties. Although many believed that nurses could not truly be reimbursed for the danger or burdens they encountered during the first wave of the outbreak, many felt that the use of financial incentives to attract nurses to SARS units was inconsistent with the profession's duty to care. Indeed, as one nurse remarked:

> For me and for…those of us who initially volunteered, I don't think [money] was ever an issue.…And I find this concern about the pay and not the patient inconsistent with the sense of a duty to care.…And I think that's what we witnessed. That's what we definitely did witness.…There was, among some people, a [lack of duty to care], certainly there was, yeah, definitely so. And is that someone you really want looking after your loved one? I don't think so.[38]

Clearly, the SARS epidemic brought to light the considerable and very real divide between nurses who saw their profession in terms of their strong commitment to their duty to care (vocation) and others who viewed nursing as an occupation that did not and should not entail a threat to their lives or livelihoods. An important lesson from the SARS crisis is that for those nurses who did volunteer, it did affect their view of their colleagues and indeed of their profession in less than positive ways. As one nurse recalled:

> It was hard for me to see staff not come into work. And…some staff are just coming back now. I mean, a year later!…That's hard for me because the next time we have something happen like this, are [they] going to walk away again?…And these are staff that weren't off sick, but just refused to come in—fear!
>
> And being on code orange…you'd work 12 hours, and you'd work way above and beyond your schedule. That's

what code orange is about. You're supposed to come back and help in disasters—and people weren't coming back.[39]

Thus, the nursing response to SARS was both collaborative and divisive. The new remuneration schemes for risk associated with SARS 2 created deep rifts between nurses that the hospitals struggled to manage. The government's clumsy attempts to compensate nurses for their service and for the risks associated with nursing during the pandemic merely served to deepen the divides among colleagues. Meanwhile, outside of the hospital, SARS created divides between nurses and the public, their friends, and even their families.

SARS AND THE FAMILY: THE QUARANTINE EXPERIENCE

For nurses who chose to report for work during the crisis, a significant psychosocial toll was exacted on themselves and their families. In spite of hospital assurances that infection control policies would protect them from contracting the disease, many nurses limited their contact with their spouses and children to lower the risk of exposure and transmission.[40] Although some nurses chose to send their children away to live with relatives residing outside of the Toronto area, others were more limited in their options to safeguard the health of their loved ones. This was especially true for nurses who were forced to remain in their family home during their quarantine—a mandatory 10-day in-home isolation period imposed on them following any possible exposure to SARS or their development of flu-like symptoms. For these nurses, the home quarantine dramatically altered the nature and scope of their relationships with their children, spouses, other family members, and friends. Confined to their homes (large or small) and forced to don an N95 respirator at all times, these nurses ate separately from their family using a dedicated set of dishes and utensils, slept in different rooms and even on different floors if possible to create distance from their loved ones, and avoided most, if not all, physical contact with live-in family members.[41] These altered conditions not only caused considerable stress and frustration but also created significant distance between nurses and their loved ones at a time in which they needed considerable emotional and physical support.

The imposition of mandatory home quarantine, in particular, created significant challenges for nurses with young children; they found themselves torn between needing to create physical distance from them to ensure their safety and maintaining a close physical relationship to support the children emotionally during the crisis. Although nurses for the most part chose to adopt the precautionary principle in their interactions with their loved ones, they faced difficulty when sensational media reports and hearsay created fear in their children and made it necessary for these nurses to be present with their children in as "normal" a way as possible. Indeed, as one Scarborough nurse observed:

> Hearing on the news about Scarborough General and Scarborough Grace...made it a little difficult at home for me because my kids wouldn't come very close to me. I had to educate them about the conditions. [One time] {laughs} they brought my breakfast to me in bed, but they left it at the door, they wouldn't come into the room. And I had to sit them down and say, "You know, this is not what you're thinking. Your mom [follows all] the precautions and hopefully, she's safe so don't be scared."[42]

Assuaging the doubts of their children—especially young children—was difficult for the nurses, however, when they had to communicate from behind a mask. Indeed, as many nurses recalled in the post-SARS period, it was difficult to convince their children that everything was fine while they continued to don PPE at home. As one nurse recalled:

> She thought I was going to die, because, of course, at school, they were educating them, but not enough for them to know that...[only] if it's something you have, you *could* die from it. But of course children are going to take that as, "Okay, if your mother's wearing a mask, she's contagious, she's going to die." And they had said to any students in the school whose parents are nurses or work in the hospital, they need to be

even more careful. So *that* didn't help. So when my daughter saw me [wearing a mask,] she broke down screaming and crying. And I'm trying to talk to her *through* this mask and I couldn't and finally I just took it off. And then when she saw me take it off, my [toddler], he just freaked! He was like "Oh my gosh, Mummy, you're going to die, you're going to die," and I'm like "No, I'm not going to die! This is something I have to do, [it's precautionary]."[43]

Worse still, the ability of the nurses to reassure their children was affected by their own fear that they inadvertently were bringing home the disease. The inability of hospitals to contain the outbreak—particularly in the first wave of the crisis—sensitized nurses to the very real possibility that they too may unknowingly contract the disease. This fear daily influenced their interactions with their children. As one nurse recalled:

[M]y children wanted so much to hug and kiss me, but I wouldn't let them. And for my [toddler] that was *really* hard. At one point he said, "Don't you like me anymore?" And I was like, "Ahh! No! I love you! But I love you enough that I'm not even going to risk hugging you." I didn't even bathe my children. Their dad did it. So that was really, *really* hard because I couldn't reach out. And if he fell or hurt himself or if he wasn't feeling well, I couldn't do anything.[44]

These sentiments were echoed by another nurse in describing the actions of her colleague:

One woman had her only grandchild visiting...and she said she was so paranoid about seeing her grandchild that she would kneel down about three feet away in front of her grandchild and say, "how are you doing?" And the kid would run up and say "Grandma! Pull down the mask!" And she would freak right out! Because she was *scared to death* she was going to give SARS to this little kid.[45]

The nurses' fear of potentially transmitting the disease to their children was powerful and continued to occur even after the epidemic subsided. Indeed, as one nurse remarked several years later: "To this day, I still don't kiss my children on the mouth."[46]

The frustration and helplessness that nurses experienced in caring for their children extended to their relations with other family members. Although the majority of nurses reported considerable support and understanding from their spouses—particularly after outlining their duty to care—few reported similar interactions with extended family members. As one nurse remarked:

> Our family didn't really want us, and they didn't want to come into the house, even....We weren't infected; we knew we were safe. And we would've been happy to have them. But we knew that they were anxious about how [being with us] might impact their employment....Yeah, there was a lot of that kind of stuff and there was just so much irrational fear about it.[47]

Indeed, familial concerns about how interactions with health care workers may facilitate the transmission of the disease prompted many extended family members to keep their distance from their loved ones who were health care workers. This distancing was often due to employment concerns, with many worried that confirmed contact with health care workers may prompt their dismissal from work, thus sending them into financial straits. Given the preponderance of media coverage detailing the dismissal and/or involuntary quarantine of those who had confirmed or suspected contact with potentially exposed health care workers, this was a rational fear.

There was also the fear that confirmation of contact with a health care worker may inadvertently facilitate the stigmatization and ostracism of family members from the community. Indeed, as one nurse recalled:

> We stayed away from church, for instance, because we knew that people didn't really want us there. And we were invited to a bar mitzvah. Friends of ours that we've known...many

250

years....The father phoned me just before it was about to happen and he told us...that some of his relatives from New York weren't going to come if we were there. So I said I think we'd better stay away...I felt sad [about this]...more sad than anything. I think [we also felt] a sense of relief that we weren't going to have to go there and face the fears and anxieties of other people, that we weren't going to be a source of that for them....I was sad to miss that one-time event in her life, but it would have been harder to go.[48]

This avoidance of friends and loved ones was a common experience for nurses who weathered the crisis. Although many worked hard to dispel the stigmatization that arose as a result of public misinformation, others felt exhausted and defeated in their attempts to transcend negative images of the nursing profession. This was particularly true during SARS 2, when nurses began to be viewed as vectors of the disease rather than soldiers combating it. One nurse described how she found herself unwelcome in her shared household:

I [shared] a house [at the time]...[and] somebody came up to my room and asked me, do I mind going to another room [in the basement] where I would be in quarantine....But then it began to escalate, and people were getting more upset....So not only was I told to move from my room [to the basement], I was also being given food on a tray, with disposable everything, and the tray was just left outside my door. And the person who was bringing me the tray was also. People were questioning *her* about why she was doing this, [saying] that *she* was going to contaminate the rest of the place.[49]

Sadly, this particular nurse's experience with public fear and ostracism is remarkably similar to post-SARS accounts from others in the profession. A wide range of material—including governmental, organizational, and mainstream media—details at length the pariah status bestowed on nurses at the time of the crisis. Chief among these reports are accounts of spouses or children being temporarily dismissed from work, appointments being cancelled, neighbors avoiding contact, and taxi cabs refusing to transport anyone connected to a health care institution. In dealing with this ostracism, many nurses recalled experiencing a profound sense of loneliness. Cut off from their peers, these individuals had limited or nonexistent systems of moral support to help them weather the crisis. It is no wonder that so many reported feeling isolated, anxious, and depressed.

CONCLUSION

Toronto's "spring of fear" was a modern-day pandemic crisis that highlighted the incapacity of a pressured, understaffed health care system to respond to an emergency. How was it that a modern, sophisticated, and wealthy country could have such a seemingly inept and uncoordinated response to a pandemic? Citizens expressed a loss of faith that the system would protect them. Nurses and other health workers experienced a serious crisis of confidence in the system, in their employers, in their relationship with the public, and, most critically, with each other.

Although the human tragedy brought out the bravery and devotion to duty of some nurses, others were reluctant to put themselves or their families at risk by continuing to care for SARS patients. The tensions between colleagues created by these entirely predictable responses in the nursing workforce were further exacerbated by the political maneuverings of the union, in its fight for danger pay, and the professional association, in its efforts to secure gains for nurses from the government. Meanwhile, the widespread public and private shunning of nurses as the crisis continued deeply wounded individuals who had placed themselves and their families at risk for the public good.

NOTES

1. Robert Sinclair Williams, "The Lived Experiences of Hospital Staff During the SARS Outbreak of 2003: A Phenomenological Study" (PhD diss., Institute of Medical Sciences, Joint Center for Bioethics, the University of Toronto, 2007), 258.

2. The government of Ontario, *Spring of Fear, Vol. 2*, by the Independent Commission to Investigate the Introduction and Spread of Severe Acute Respiratory Syndrome (SARS), 1–4249-2822–2 (Toronto, Ontario: Publications Ontario, 2006), 39.

3. Ibid., 44.

4. Ibid.

5. Ibid., 67.

6. Ibid., 142.

7. Ibid., 235.

8. One important source for this chapter is the dissertation of Robert Williams, who interviewed nurses from the Scarborough General and Scarborough Grace Hospitals, the latter of which was closed to admissions during the pandemic and the nurses quarantined there. These in-depth interviews undertaken around 2005, only 2 years after SARS, and quoted at length in the phenomenological dissertation that explored the lived experience of health workers during SARS, provide a rare and relatively immediate first-person reflective account of the events. A second key source is the Campbell Commission; in its report entitled *"The SARS Commission: The Spring of Fear,"* the commission made recommendations for renewing the Ontarian public health system through a chronological investigation of the introduction and spread of SARS in the Greater Toronto area (GTA) hospital system. Based on the information culled from public hearings, hospital and government documents, and confidential interviews of more than 600 individuals connected with the SARS outbreak, this document addressed the deep problems of Ontario public health infrastructure and glaring deficiencies evidenced in Ontario health protection and emergency response laws (SARS Commission, 2006).

9. Sonia Verma, "I've Never, Ever Turned Away From Danger," *Toronto Star*, April 26, 2003, A27, accessed July 10, 2013, http://search.proquest.com/docview/438594280?accountid=14771.

10. Williams, "The Lived Experiences of Hospital Staff," 311.

11. Ibid., 305.

12. Ibid., 198.

13. Ibid., 182.

14. Ibid., 307–308.

15. Ibid., 195.

16. Ibid., 221.

17. The government of Ontario, *Spring of Fear*, 229–230.

18. A. O. Baumann, J. M. Blythe, and J. M. Underwood, "Surge Capacity and Casualization: Human Resource Issues in the Post-SARS Health System," *Canadian Journal of Public Health* 97, no. 3 (2006): 230.

19. Registered Nurses Association of Ontario (RNAO), *SARS Unmasked: Celebrating Resilience, Exposing Vulnerability* (Toronto, Ontario: Registered Nurses Association of Ontario, 2004), 13, accessed July 22, 2013, http://search.proquest.com/docview/438599544/accountid=14771.

20. Baumann, Blythe, and Underwood, "Surge Capacity and Casualization," 230.

21. RNAO, *SARS Unmasked*, 13.

22. Baumann, Blythe, and Underwood, "Surge Capacity and Casualization," 230.

23. RNAO, *SARS Unmasked*, 13.

24. Baumann, Blythe, and Underwood, "Surge Capacity and Casualization," 231.

25. Barbara Wahl, "Ontario Nurses Association (ONA): Presentation to the Commission to Investigate the Introduction and Spread of Severe Acute Respiratory Syndrome (SARS)" (Presentation at the SARS Public Hearings, Toronto, ON, September 29, 2003), 16–17.

26. Williams, "The Lived Experiences of Hospital Staff," 306.

27. Baumann, Blythe, and Underwood, "Surge Capacity and Casualization," 230.

28. Theresa Boyle, "SARS-Weary Nurses Demand Danger Pay; Private Hires Blamed for Morale Drop: Agency Nurses Get $100/hr., Others $21," *Toronto Star*, May 29, 2003, A01, accessed July 9, 2013, http://search.proquest.com/docview/438593464?accountid=14771.

29. RNAO, *SARS Unmasked*, 25.

30. Health Canada, *Learning From SARS: Renewal of Public Health in Canada*, by The National Advisory Committee on SARS and Public Health, 0-662-34984-0 (Ottawa, Ontario: Health Canada Publications, 2003), 154.

31. Tanya Talaga and Theresa Boyle, "Deal Will Lighten Load for Nurses; Same Pay for Shorter Shifts at Affected Units: Higher Pay for Agency Nurses Still a Sore Point," *Toronto Star*, May 30, 2003, C06, accessed July 12, 2013, http://search.proquest.com/docview/438590137?accountid=14771.

32. Ibid., C06.

33. Williams, "The Lived Experiences of Hospital Staff," 298–299.

34. Ibid., 289.

35. Ibid., 388.

36. Ibid., 298–299.

37. Ibid., 289.

38. Ibid., 266.

39. Ibid., 231.

40. Sonia Verma, "Tales From the Front Lines; SARS Workers Are Stressed at Work, Stressed at Home; For Weeks, Many Have Limited Contact With Children, Spouses," *Toronto Star*, April 27, 2003, A07, accessed July 10, 2013, http://search.proquest.com/docview/438590684?accountid=14771.

41. Gloria Galloway, "For Healthcare Workers, It Is Not Life as Usual; One Nurse at Scarborough Grace Is Quarantined While She Is at Home," *The Globe and Mail*, March 1, 2003, A08, accessed July 10, 2003, http://search.proquest.com/docview/347458465?accountid=14771.

42. Williams, *The Lived Experiences of Hospital Staff During the SARS Outbreak of 2003*, 259.

43. Ibid., 329.

44. Ibid., 328.

45. Ibid., 185.

46. Ibid., 220.

47. Ibid., 193.

48. Ibid., 194.

49. Ibid., 331.

CHAPTER 10

Hurricane Sandy, October 2012, New York City (USA)

Barbra Mann Wall, Victoria LaMaina, and Emma MacAllister

In my estimation, [nurses] are the highest.[1]

The aforementioned statement from Jo-An Tremblay-Shepherd revealed her awe of the nurses who helped save her son Jackson. He had to be evacuated from the neonatal intensive care unit at New York University's (NYU) Langone Medical Center after Hurricane Sandy hit the northeastern coast of the United States in 2012. Langone was one of the two major hospitals in flooded lower Manhattan that had to be evacuated. The other was Bellevue Hospital, New York City's leading public facility. Nurses, physicians, medical students, orderlies, and other staff workers moved hundreds of patients down several flights of stairs and did not lose a single patient from either hospital.

On October 29, 2012, a disastrous hurricane struck in an unfathomable way. According to Red Cross records, 117 people encompassing a four-state region died, the majority being older than 65 years.[2] Although the storm's winds and water were deadly, downed trees and the resultant power loss and massive flooding caused thousands of people to lose their homes and property. Hurricane Sandy reached winds peaking at 115 mph.[3] It was the most severe storm to hit this region and the second most powerful storm to hit the country, second only to Hurricane Katrina in 2005. Although the storm affected all of the states along the eastern coast of the United States, it wrecked the Jersey Shore, shut down New York City for 3 days, and caused an estimated $108 billion in damage.

Sociologists argue that "some groups of people are known for their ability to remain cool and stay clear-headed under pressure, including veteran military officers, fire, and police commanders."[4] Although they do not mention nurses, it is clear that nurses are part of this response. As the storm struck, NYU Langone Medical Center evacuated 300 patients, and the next day, staff at Bellevue Hospital evacuated 700 patients.[5] No evacuation activities had been rehearsed in any disaster plan, yet evacuation did occur successfully. This illustrates the important collaborative roles that nursing and medical personnel, other hospital staff, and police and fire department workers play in emergency evacuations during disasters.

At the same time, although each hospital had disaster plans in place, none had accounted for failed backup generators and flooding in elevators. This chapter examines how the disaster affected hospital staff and the problems that occurred that existing disaster plans could not prevent. It also enhances the reader's understanding of the role of group behavior after disasters.

Research on group behavior at the height of a disaster has been a significant feature of disaster studies. Sociologist E. L. Quarantelli has examined how groups react during a disaster and debunks the myth that people panic afterward. The assumption is that individuals are "stunned" and "emotionally traumatized or psychologically incapacitated, and generally react selfishly and in self-centered ways during and immediately after a disaster."[6] Yet, research shows that panic does not occur. Survivors do not run away or "run around aimlessly," they do not go into hysterics, and, in fact, "they do what they can for themselves and others in the situation."[7] Most problems that occur during

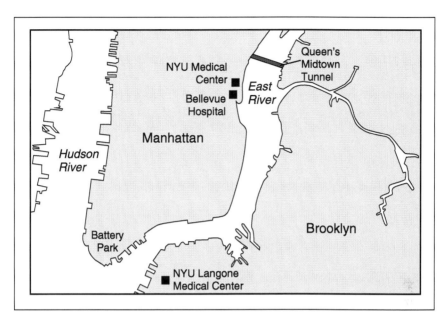

Map of New York City, New York.

the emergency phase of a disaster are found in the organizations that are attempting to help.[8] An examination of nursing responses after Hurricane Sandy validates these findings.

Hospitals depend on electricity for the majority of their care. Intravenous pumps for fluids or pain, all heart rate and blood pressure continuous-monitoring equipment, portable suction machines, and many other devices necessary for treatment require electricity to function. According to The Joint Commission, which accredits and certifies hospitals, electricity must be maintained in "all intensive care units, post anesthesia units, obstetrical delivery units, nurseries, and urgent care units."[9] Yet, although the Joint Commission mandates that all hospitals have generators, what happens if they do not work? This occurred in the case of NYU Langone Medical Center and Bellevue Hospital.

LESSONS LEARNED FROM HURRICANE KATRINA

Much of what happened in response to Hurricane Sandy was a reaction to the debacle that occurred after Hurricane Katrina hit the southeast coast of the United States in 2005. Patients in more than two dozen hospitals had to be evacuated after flooding and massive electrical power losses. Helicopters could be used by some hospitals that had the resources; for others, boats had to transport patients to locations where they could get ground transportation or helicopters. All the transports—boats, helicopters, or ambulances—could take no more than one or two patients per trip, and the duration of transport was agonizingly long. Although some hospitals in New Orleans were able to remove all patients successfully, others did not.[10] Tulane Medical Center ran on generators for 36 hours before they ran out of fuel. It was not able to evacuate all of the patients during this time to the Superdome and other hospitals.[11] Patients, nurses, medical school faculty, and others were waiting to be rescued, whereas help was slow to come because of the surrounding flood waters. For days, health care providers provided hand ventilation to patients in shifts until the parking garage was transformed into a makeshift helipad a few days following the storm. After flooding damaged Charity Hospital's generators, which were in the basement, it became clear that patients had to be removed, especially those in the intensive care unit. Eventually, more than 350 patients were evacuated, a process that took nearly a week.[12] Even more catastrophic events occurred at the Memorial Hospital in New Orleans when help for evacuations arrived extremely late. Health care personnel were accused of intentionally hastening the deaths of some patients. Eventually, authorities found 45 bodies.[13]

Studies about nursing care after other hurricanes were also informative for responses to Hurricane Sandy. Danna et al. conducted a study of the experiences of nurse leaders who survived Hurricane Katrina. They found that nurses experienced a breakdown of communication because phones did not work, so there were many problems throughout the hospital while organizing the transfers of patients. Tulane staff members were locked out of their medicine dispensers, causing patients not to have access to certain pain medications. Furthermore, at Tulane, there were many issues with patient belongings being lost during the evacuation. Nurses reflected that the evacuation was "extremely chaotic" because the city's "emergency preparedness command center was overwhelmed with thousands of evacuation requests," and ambulances were not able to travel on the streets because of flooding.[14] Danna et al. recommended having a chain of command in place to make decisions for hospitals. They also noted that it is important to have leadership involving physicians, nurses, the administration, and all support personnel involved so that in a time of emergency there are people in each role to take charge and make decisions. Establishing an emergency phone line or having a charged cell phone for emergency use was also important so that there would be a better way to communicate than by walkie-talkies. The researchers found that if individualized plans for the patients were made prior to the storm, the evacuation and disaster preparedness went much more smoothly. The prior planning increased the sense of order needed in an evacuation. Grouping patients according to risk and evacuating those in the higher risk category first provided order to the evacuation plans, rather than just sending every patient downstairs to be evacuated all at once.[15]

Following the Katrina fiasco, hospitals across the country redesigned their emergency evacuation plans. The Joint Commission set standards to prevent this type of hospital-care disaster by requiring hospitals to review their organizational charts, prepare for equipment failure, and practice evacuation. Other writers noted the problem with generators in hospitals: "generators' failure, for reasons that seemed to vary from institution to institution, is one of the most striking and disappointing parts of the post-Katrina experience."[16] Thus, a major standard mandated that hospitals have backup generators with the capacity to power the entire hospital as well as one elevator. Another step was taken in 2006 when President George W. Bush signed into law the official Pandemic and All-Hazards Preparedness Act (PAHPA). This act addressed the need to have a deliberate, coordinated plan for responding to various types of emergencies (natural, accidental, or deliberate) and to "utilize informational technology to improve situational awareness during these events."[17] As a result, state and local governments as well as businesses and health care institutions have all developed plans for potential crises.

NYU LANGONE MEDICAL CENTER
AND BELLEVUE HOSPITAL EVACUATIONS

As Hurricane Sandy approached New York City, administrators of hospitals faced similar problems that had occurred in New Orleans: whether or not to evacuate. They were well aware that the storm was powerful. A year earlier, when Hurricane Irene hit the city, officials did issue an evacuation order for hospitals in low-lying areas because of fears of flooding and loss of power. This resulted in approximately 10,000 patients being transferred from seven acute care hospitals and 39 non-acute care facilities. In 2012, as Hurricane Sandy neared, two other hospitals evacuated, and others discharged their more stable patients. Officials at NYU Langone Medical Center and at Bellevue did the same, but they were concerned that patients, especially the critically ill, might die during pre-storm transfers, and they did not expect flooding. Thus, they made the decision to stay but not to accept any new cases.[18]

In the late afternoon of October 29, 2012, as winds and rain increased in intensity, nurses and other staff at NYU Langone Medical Center began moving patients from higher floors to a lower one where there was an extra generator. This transition went very smoothly and was organized. By evening, however, as lights began to flicker and monitors shut off, it became apparent that the backup generator at the hospital was not functioning. One generator was in the basement; although others were on higher floors, their fuel tanks were in the basement.[19] The Joint Commission standards emphasized that backup generators should allow hospitals to function alone for 96 hours, but that did not happen. As nurses realized what was going on, they prioritized care, calmed their patients, and, anticipating evacuation, grabbed pain and sedation medications from drug dispenser carts that they knew they would need.

By early morning of October 30, it became obvious that the hospital could not function, and administrators ordered an evacuation. For the next 15 hours, day-shift nurses stayed on duty to assist with the emergency protocol; throughout the night and early morning, nurses ran up and down the stairs to remove the patients. NYU medical students came to help escort patients out of the hospital and light the hallways with their cell-phone flashlights. The New York Police Department (NYPD) and Fire Department of New York (FDNY) also helped with the evacuation, physically carrying patients and all the battery-powered equipment down the stairs.[20] Although sources mention only that city responders, doctors, nurses, and medical students helped out, no doubt respiratory therapists, orderlies, nurses' aides, maintenance workers, housekeeping and laundry personnel, x-ray technicians, and others were all part of the mix of responders.

The workers evacuated patients in intensive care units first because they were in immediate danger. Many of the patients could not breathe on their own, and were on ventilators requiring electricity. Unfortunately, the generators were losing power quickly. Without electricity, teams of nurses alternated hand ventilating the patients to keep them alive. The evacuation process included nurses and others placing patients on a red toboggan-like sled and physically sliding them down all of the flights of stairs.[21] Not only did hospital personnel cooperate but so did the patients. They did not complain while being evacuated, and some were even concerned about the well-being of the caretakers, asking how the emergency personnel were doing, if they had time to eat dinner, or if they could help them in any way. Ambulances were waiting to carry patients to other hospitals in the region.[22] Evacuating the babies from the neonatal intensive care unit was especially a challenge. Many people were needed to attend to the infants who required critical care. Each infant had to be moved down nine flights of stairs in its isolette while remaining connected to oxygen tanks, monitors, and all other necessary medical equipment. Moving the infants while keeping them stable was an exacting process. But all of the babies were carried down the stairs safely and evacuated.[23]

The same problems occurred at the Bellevue Hospital. Because Bellevue was a public hospital, city officials were in charge. Before the storm, the city's health commissioner made the decision not to evacuate the hospital in consultation with the state health commissioner. They too feared that the loss of life during an evacuation was a real possibility. By 9 p.m. on October 29, however, the hospital's basement was quickly flooding. Unlike at Langone, the backup generators that had been placed on higher floors were working. Even though nurses, medical residents, and other hospital personnel carried supplies of fuel up 13 flights of stairs to keep the main backup generators running for days, the staff faced other problems due to the flooding. The unprecedented depth of water entering the basement destroyed the water pumps that were located there. Consequently, Bellevue lost its entire water supply.[24] Nurses also calmed their patients, rationed their water supply, and double checked the machines to make sure they were fully charged in the event of the generators failing. The next morning, all 32 elevators were out of commission, limited compressed air was available for oxygen therapy and ventilators, phone communication was lost, and water faucets had run dry. City officials and administrators called for evacuation and asked the National Guard to help. One source reported that a patient with a recent heart bypass had to walk down 20 flights of stairs. Other patients were evacuated on sleds down 13 to 15 flights of stairs, in the dark, with one person dragging oxygen tanks and another hand ventilating patients.[25] As at Langone, dozens of ambulances were waiting.[26]

LESSONS LEARNED FROM NEW YORK CITY HOSPITALS

Obviously, many of the systems put in place after Hurricane Katrina worked, because there was no loss of life during the evacuations. New York hospitals had evacuation equipment available. Because of a federal ambulance contract made after Hurricane Katrina, New York had 350 more ambulances for use in the city, and many were available and waiting to transport the evacuees. In addition, the Department of Health and Human Services sent 1,000 health care personnel to assist in the response, and the Federal Emergency Management Agency (FEMA) had search-and-rescue teams on site as the storm hit the coast.[27]

Yet, problems did occur. Because this event happened so recently, there is little empirical evidence available, and accounts published after the storm focus on "lessons learned." One theme that emerges in the literature is that lessons about organizational behavior during the hurricane still need deconstruction. In 2012, Tia Powell, Dan Hanfling, and Lawrence O. Gostin published an article in the *Journal of the American Medical Association* with the subtitle "The Lessons of Hurricane Sandy." Although the authors praised the successes, they noted that hospitals had not planned for 14-foot flood waters. The hospitals were prepared for flooding of up to an unprecedented 12 feet of water; however, the flooding caused by Hurricane Sandy rose as high as 14 feet. The hospitals also had no clear guidelines for evacuation in place, and personnel were not prepared to evacuate obese patients. Indeed, Bellevue left two overweight patients in place when elevators were not available to help move them. A major recommendation was that preemptive moves to lower floors might have prevented this from happening.[28] The authors also called on public health officials and emergency managers to develop guidelines for decision making as to when to evacuate.

The damage sustained at NYU Langone Medical Center shut the hospital down for 3 months. Bellevue was closed for 4 months, and the electrical damage took a full year to repair.[29] The nurses from these hospitals temporarily relocated to other area hospitals. This involved learning new electronic health systems and working with unfamiliar staff and materials.[30]

In 2012, Irwin Redlener and Michael Reilly published an article in *The New England Journal of Medicine* with a title, "Lessons From Sandy." They addressed problems that occurred with access to health care, mental health problems as a consequence of disasters, and infrastructure needs in hospital buildings with generators and pumps in basements. They also found a need for improvements in the standards for all hospitals when designing them in the future. These include special considerations for flooding, where the generators are located in the buildings, how patients can be evacuated in the event the elevators do not work, and how many stairwells are available in the building.[31]

LESSONS LEARNED FROM OTHER HOSPITALS

With so many people left homeless or in need of care after the storm, nurses stepped into leadership positions in various settings throughout New Jersey. At Jersey Shore University Medical Center (JSMC), Vice President and Chief Nurse Executive Mary Anne Donohue was at work when the hurricane hit. A week before, in response to warnings, she immediately began working with state disaster personnel to coordinate their activities to ensure that they had enough supplies, medications, and food for a full week.[32] The hospital became a site where outsiders flocked in the days following Hurricane Sandy, and nurses played a major role in JSMC's ability to manage the 60% increase in visits to the emergency department (ED).[33] In response to this major influx of patients, the JSMC ED created two additional areas within the department, and nurses helped to manage them. One unit monitored patients being admitted who were waiting for beds, and another helped patients being discharged while they waited for transportation to a safe area. Nurses were crucial to the implementation of these changes and the creation of a safe, smooth, and efficient system. As Donohue stated, "Being a nurse does help you be a leader, because you see what needs to be done and do it."[34] Nurses not only seamlessly stepped up as leaders in their areas, but they also were resilient in their response to the disaster. Donahue wrote about her nursing staff voluntarily staying on for a double shift after the hurricane hit.[35] Although many nurses did not know if they still had homes to go to at the end of the day, they agreed to stay at JSMC because of the anticipated surge of patients.[36] Patricia Barnett, New Jersey State Nurses Association (NJSNA) chief executive officer, noted that nurses throughout the rest of the state exhibited this same selflessness. Despite widespread destruction from the storm, so many nurses responded to the NJSNA's request for help online that the organization had to take the message down.[37]

Many nurses who responded to the hurricane spoke of the immense need for mental health services after the storm. Anxiety, depression, and posttraumatic stress disorder (PTSD) were all common symptoms noted by nurses caring for the community.[38] This likely occurred in other responders, as well. Terrianne Christopher, an advanced

266

practice nurse specializing in psychiatric care who volunteered at the Monmouth University temporary shelter, discussed her experience in the *New Jersey Nurse & Institute for Nursing Newsletter*.[39] Christopher and two other nurses were in charge of health care for the 300- to 400-person refuge site. As the overnight managers, the three nurses were not only responsible for providing care, such as monitoring blood sugars and providing oxygen, but they also had to decide whether or not patients needed to be transported to an ED. Due to severe flooding and limited access throughout New Jersey and New York, a supply shortage immediately after the storm was apparent. Christopher described her experience with limited supplies at the shelter as reminiscent of the TV show *M*A*S*H**, which depicted medical staff during the Korean War. Still, Christopher and her two nurse colleagues were able to safely care for and support their patients. They described their feelings of a great sense of accomplishment when the night was over.[40]

Although Christopher felt prepared to care for the vast psychiatric needs of the shelter residents, providers in other areas did not always have access to her expertise. The health care workers in the North Shore Long Island Jewish (LIJ) Health System's Mobile Health Unit (MHU) did not anticipate the number of people who would approach the clinic with mental health issues related to the hurricane.[41] The typical MHU team included one to two physicians from various specialties, a registered nurse, a driver who also served as a security officer, and one administrator. With this group, the MHU did not initially have the appropriate staff on hand to respond adequately to mental health issues. Teams eventually adapted to meet the needs of their populations, however, by incorporating a social work consult service to their daily efforts. The MHU staff acknowledged that it would have been more ideal to have mental health services in place from the beginning and expressed the hope that this change could be implemented from the start in any future crisis.

Although it is important to have the appropriately trained staff during a disaster, it is also vital to have access to information. The health care professionals from the MHU described the difficulty they faced in providing care with no access to medical history and an inability to follow up with their patients. They were especially concerned for the patients with chronic health conditions involving complicated treatment and requiring equipment that had become scarce in the immediate aftermath of Sandy.[42]

David Abramson and Irwin Redlener, in an article with the title "Hurricane Sandy: Lessons Learn, Again," reported problems with communication. As communication at all levels is extremely important during a disaster, the lessons learned in this arena have particularly large implications for disaster management in the future. During the storm, civilians were urged to look at social media sites, such as Twitter; government websites; or wait for instruction via text message. When the power went out as a result of the heavy winds and rain, these methods of communication were no longer effective because people could not get an Internet connection or charge their phones and computers.[43]

Another problem identified by Abramson and Redlener was the lack of effective preparation and communication between disciplines. Sandy had some of its most debilitating effects on the nation's energy distribution network. There is no denying the heroic actions of nurses, physicians, medical students, and other responders all over the city; however, the authors point out that when a generator fails, these medically focused individuals do not have the skills or knowledge base to respond. Severe gas shortages and electrical outages not only limited medical response teams and the region's supply chains, but they also led to widespread desperation for families in the community who tried to meet basic needs. There were at least eight carbon monoxide–related deaths tied to Hurricane Sandy in New York alone that resulted from families using stoves or generators to heat their homes. The authors suggest that these widespread failures represent "preparedness gaps" within the disaster plan.[44] Although fixing problems with emergency generators are not the purview of medicine or public health, provisions of coordinated relief were lacking, despite "considerable public investment" in standardizing command and communication systems. These authors assert that, although coordination did occur, it was unorganized, and "[e]fforts should be made to broaden those coordination channels to include more diverse and emergent groups."[45]

CONCLUSION

It is clear that, in hospitals and other health care facilities after Hurricane Sandy, city officials, medical and nursing personnel, hospital staff, technicians, ambulance drivers, police and fire personnel, and the National Guard from all over the region put aside their own fears and inconvenience in order to provide the best care to those affected by the storm. Consistent with findings by sociologists,[46] they coped with the demands of the emergency and rose to the challenges they faced when equipment and systems were far from ideal. For the purposes of this chapter on disaster nursing, nurses showed great resilience, and many arose as leaders during the disaster relief efforts. Nurses were crucial in making decisions about patient discharges before the hurricane made landfall, and they acted as liaisons between evacuating hospitals and receiving hospitals once the storm hit.[47] Other nurses recognized that in a crisis such as hurricanes, hospitals attract many people seeking refuge, and some prepared for the event in advance. And nurses were critical to ensure safe and efficient patient transfers. Indeed, large numbers of nurses and other health care personnel doing extraordinary things under extremely difficult conditions have become evident. They improvised with great creativity when equipment failed and supplies were limited.

The reauthorization of PAHPA in 2013 testifies to the prevailing importance of up-to-date disaster protocols in any future emergency response.[48] At the same time, examination of the existing literature reveals that disaster drills should include practice in evacuating patients. Nurses and students can do this in new state-of-the-art simulation laboratories that are being built across the country in hospitals and schools of nursing. Furthermore, it is not new that better advanced planning, better communications, and better coordination are needed after disasters. These are the same problems that occurred after Hurricane Katrina[49] and need further examination. The use of social media, such as blogs, Facebook, Twitter, and LinkedIn, can allow for quick messages to be posted,[50] albeit without jeopardizing patient confidentiality. Through development of their own body of disaster knowledge, nurses can further increase public understanding of what it is they contribute to the field.

NOTES

1. Robert Kolker, "A Hospital Flatlined: Inside the NYU Langone Medical Center Evacuation," *Daily Intelligencer* (posted 11/3/2012), accessed May 29, 2014, http://nymag.com/daily/intelligencer/2012/11/hospital-flatlined-inside-the-nyu-evacuation.html.

2. Centers for Disease Control and Prevention, "Deaths Associated With Hurricane Sandy—October–November 2012," *Weekly* 62, no. 20 (May 24, 2013): 393–397; Keller, 2012.

3. Blake, E., et al., "Tropical Cyclone Report: Hurricane Sandy," *National Hurricane Center*, February 12, 2013. Retrieved from http://www.nhc.noaa.gov/data/tcr/AL182012_Sandy.pdf.

4. R. Havidan Rodriquez, Enrico L. Quarantelli, and Russell R. Dynes, Eds., *Handbook of Disaster Research* (New York, NY: Springer, 2007). Quotation is on p. 49.

5. Tia Powell, Dan Hanfling, and Lawrence O. Gostin, "Emergency Preparedness and Public Health: The Lessons of Hurricane Sandy," *Journal of the American Medical Association* 308, no. 24 (December 26, 2012): 2569–2570.

6. E. L. Quarantelli, "Human and Group Behavior in the Emergency Period of Disasters: Now and in the Future" (Preliminary Paper #196) (Newark, DE: Disaster Research Center, University of Delaware, 1993), 1.

7. Ibid., 2. For an earlier source, see N. Smelser, *Theory of Collective Behavior* (New York, NY: Free Press, 1963).

8. Russell Dynes, *Community Emergency Planning: False Assumptions and Inappropriate Analogies* (Newark, DE: Disaster Research Center, University of Delaware, 1990).

9. The Joint Commission. Joint Commission Requirements for Emergency Management, 2013, accessed May 30, 2014, http://www.jcrinc.com/Joint-Commission-Requirements/Hospitals/#EM/.

10. Bradford H. Gray and Kathy Hebert, "Hospitals in Hurricane Katrina: Challenges Facing Custodial Institutions in a Disaster," *Journal of Healthcare for the Poor and Underserved*, 18 no. 2 (2007): 283–298.

11. C. Burdeau, "Ex-La. Governor Halted Hospital Reopening," *The Associated Press*, July 14, 2009. Retrieved from http://savecharityhospital.com/content/ap-honore-ex-la-governor-halted-hospital-reopening.

12. Gray and Hebert, *After Katrina*.

13. Sherri Fink, "The Deadly Choice at Memorial," *Pro Publica*, August 27, 2009, accessed May 28, 2014, http://www.propublica.org/article/the-deadly-choices-at-memorial-826.

14. D. Danna et al., "Experiences of Nurse Leaders Surviving Hurricane Katrina, New Orleans, Louisiana, USA," *Nursing Health Science* 12, no. 1 (March 2010): 9–13. Quotation is on p. 11.

15. Ibid.

16. Gray and Hebert, *After Katrina*, 16.

17. 109th U.S. Congress, "Pandemic and All-Hazards Preparedness," December 14, 2006, accessed May 4, 2014, https://www.govtrack.us/congress/bills/109/s3678/text.

18. The Daily Briefing, "Why NYC Hospitals Did Not Evacuate Before Sandy," November 2, 2012, accessed May 28, 2014, http://www.advisory.com/daily-briefing/2012/11/02/why-nyc-hospitals-did-not-evacuate-before-sandy.

19. Kolker, "A Hospital Flatlined: Inside the NYU Langone Medical Center Evacuation," *Daily Intelligencer* (posted 11/3/2012), accessed May 29, 2014, http://nymag.com/daily/intelligencer/2012/11/hospital-flatlined-inside-the-nyu-evacuation.html.

20. Powell et al., "Emergency Preparedness"; David M. Abramson and Irwin Redlener, "Hurricane Sandy: Lessons Learned Again," *Disaster Medicine and Public Health Preparedness* 6, no. 4 (2012): 328–329; G. Deutsch, M. Dorian, and A. Sechrist, "Nurses Who Saved NICU Babies Remember Harrowing, Triumphant Hurricane Night," *ABC News*, November 3, 2012, accessed May 30, 2014, http://abcnews.go.com/Health/nicu-nurses-saved-babies-remember-harrowing-triumphant-hurricane/story?id=17632993.

21. D. Ofri, "The Storm and the Aftermath," *The New England Journal of Medicine* 367, no. 24 (2012): 2265–2267.

22. Ibid.

23. Kolker, "A Hospital Flatlined"; Deutsch et al., "Nurses Who Saved NICU Babies"; Abramson and Redlener, "Hurricane Sandy."

24. Powell et al., "Emergency Preparedness."

25. Ibid.

26. Anemona Hartocollis and Nina Bernstein, "At Bellevue, A Desperate Fight to Ensure the Patients' Safety," *The New York Times*, November 1, 2012.

27. Powell et al., "Emergency Preparedness."

28. Ibid.

29. Ibid.

30. A. A. Adalja et al., "Absorbing Citywide Patient Surge During Hurricane Sandy: A Case Study in Accommodating Multiple Hospital Evacuation," *Annals of Emergency Medicine* 64, no. 1 (2014): 66–73e1. Published online January 13, 2014, accessed May 30, 2014, http://dx.doi.org/10.1016/j.annemergmed.2013.12.010.

31. Irwin Redlener and Michael J. Reilly, "Lessons From Sandy—Preparing Health Systems for Future Disasters," *The New England Journal of Medicine* 367 (2012): 2269–2271.

32. Susan Trossman, "Flooding and Fury: Nurses Respond to Needs During Hurricane, Suffer Losses," *The American Nurse* (November/December 2012): 1, 8–9. Quotation on p. 8, accessed May 28, 2014, http://www .TheAmericanNurse.org.

33. M. A. Donahue, "Hurricane Sandy Devastated New Jersey: Jersey Shore Medical Center Meets the Challenge," *New Jersey Nurse & Institute for Nursing Newsletter* 43, no. 1 (2013): 6.

34. Trossman, "Flooding and Fury"; Donahue, "Hurricane Sandy Devastated New Jersey."

35. Donahue, "Hurricane Sandy."

36. Ibid.

37. Trossman, "Flooding and Fury."

38. C. Lien et al., "Community Healthcare Delivery Post-Hurricane Sandy: Lessons From a Mobile Health Unit," *Journal of Community Health* 39, no. 3 (2013): 599–605.

39. Terrianne Christopher, "Volunteering After Sandy," *New Jersey Nurse & Institute for Nursing Newsletter* 43, no. 1 (2013): 7.

40. Ibid.

41. Lien et al., "Community Healthcare Delivery Post-Hurricane Sandy."

42. Ibid.

43. D. Abramson and I. Redlener, " Hurricane Sandy: Lessons Learned, Again," *Disaster Medicine and Public Health Preparedness* 6 no. 4 (2013): 328–329.

44. Abramson and Redlener, "Hurricane Sandy."

45. Ibid. First quotations are on p. 328. Last quotation is on p. 329.

46. See Quarantelli, "Human and Group Behavior," for example.

47. Adalja et al., "Absorbing Citywide Patient Surge."

48. H. R. 307, "Pandemic and All-Hazards Preparedness Reauthorization," January 18, 2013, accessed May 30, 2014, https://www.govtrack.us/ congress/bills/113/hr307.

49. Abramson and Redlener, "Hurricane Sandy."

50. R. M. Merchant, S. Elmer, and N. L. Lurie, "Integrating Social Media Into Emergency-Preparedness Efforts," *The New England Journal of Medicine* 365, no. 4 (2011): 289–291.

Conclusion

Arlene W. Keeling, Emma MacAllister,
and Barbra Mann Wall

Each of the disasters highlighted in this book is unique, yet common themes emerge. First of all, it is clear that nurses play an important role in every disaster in all parts of the world, and that often that role is overlooked or taken for granted. Time after time, during bombings, floods, fires, hurricanes, or epidemics, nurses simply did what they were trained to do to meet the needs of the public—no matter which country they served, or in which setting they worked. Second, the book underscores the importance of cooperation and collaboration in disaster responses, while revealing conflicts that resulted during those responses when multiple teams converged on a disaster scene—as in the Italian earthquake—or when communications failed—as they did in Alaska during the influenza epidemic. Third, the book provides examples of instances in which quarantine measures worked—as in Shishmaref during the flu—and others in which they did not, as was evidenced in Nome, Alaska, during the same epidemic. Emergent behavior among individuals and organizations at the local, regional, and state levels is a fourth theme that appears as people, realizing the extent of an emergency, work together to help their fellow human beings. During disasters, nurses sometimes worked in traditional roles and followed traditional routines and behaviors; at other times, they blurred racial, social, and professional boundaries in order to do what they had to do.

Sometimes, the nurses' response came with great risk to the nurses themselves. For example, in the 19th-century hospitals in Tasmania, an infectious disease crisis resulted in four nurses dying from typhoid fever, and 30 others required substantial convalescence after becoming ill. Likewise, in 2003, nurses risked their own lives when they mobilized to respond to the severe acute respiratory syndrome (SARS) pandemic. Some nurses were later ostracized by their friends and communities for the services they provided to others. More recently, fear of Ebola has resulted in the same ostracism in the United States when health workers returned from western Africa.

In wartime disasters, nurses suffered injuries themselves and their priorities were tested. For example, in 1941, nurses risked their own lives to care for the injured as bombs fell over Pearl Harbor; in 1945, nurses and nursing students in Hiroshima struggled with their own injuries from the horrific blast while they continued to provide care for others. When confronted with the problem of helping their injured colleagues or caring for soldiers, they ultimately followed their training and chose first to attend to the needs of the soldiers.

The theme of nurses putting themselves in danger of sacrificing their own health for the sake of their patients is one that transcends all eras, countries, and events. It is as if when one dons the role of the nurse, he or she accepts personal risks as an unavoidable consequence. In fact, at 13.1 per 100 full-time workers, nurses in the United States face the highest incidence of nonfatal occupational injury or illness of any profession and industry in the country. This number is more than double the incidence of nonfatal injury for construction workers, which is often considered a high-risk job. Thus, as disasters continue to occur, the expectations for how nurses will respond and the risks they will take are more relevant than ever.[1]

So why did nurses put themselves at risk? For some, as noted by a British nurse after the London and Manchester bombings in World War II, nursing was a means to participate in a drama that allowed one to perform meaningful and rewarding work. Other nurses during wartime were driven by nationalistic motivations to protect citizens and keep up a "fighting spirit." Nurses also felt a responsibility to care for patients because of the profession they chose. When they have found themselves in conflicting situations that pit their professional ethics against their own or their family members' personal safety, they routinely made decisions guided by their "duty to care."

Choosing the profession of nursing entails accepting risks that come with the work. Nurses often are emboldened to accept risks when they believe their education and training make them the best-qualified professionals to perform dangerous work. This occurred in their response to disasters throughout the 19th and 20th centuries. In each case, it was important for nurses to maintain their professionalism and win their patients' trust. It is important to note, however, that nurses' bravery does not come without personal fears. Indeed, when nurses witnessed members of their own profession dying with SARS, for example, many worried about their own health and feared bringing the virus back to their families.

The Ebola crisis today has some of the same elements as other disasters highlighted in this book. Health care workers, including nurses, risked their own lives to respond; the WHO coordinated the construction and staffing of treatment centers in Liberia, Sierra Leone, and Guinea; Médicine Sans Frontières (Doctors Without Borders) sent in physicians and nurses; and the U.S. and British governments sent in troops to build new Ebola clinics. According to *The New York Times*, "Crates of food and medicine are flowing into the port, and planeloads of experts seem to arrive every day—Ugandan doctors, Chinese epidemiologists, Australian logisticians, even an ambulance specialist from London."[2] Clearly, there is a front-page documentation of international cooperation. What is also clear is that there is conflict—at national and international levels—about how and when to respond, how much help to send, and how to implement proper burials, airport screenings, and quarantines to protect the public's health, not only in Africa, but all over the world.

As an example, as mentioned in the Preface, African nurses have played a key role in the disaster response to Ebola. Josephine Finda Sellu, the deputy nurse matron of the government hospital in Kenema, Sierra Leone, defied the wishes of her family to quit her job and remained strong when a group of nurses from her hospital threatened her life if any more nurses fell ill from the deadly virus. She knew that younger nurses looked to her for guidance and, thus, she refused to abandon her duty. Other nurses on Ms. Sellu's staff spoke of abandonment by their spouses and shunning by their community because of their choice to continue working with Ebola patients; yet the call of their profession was so strong they did not hesitate in their loyalty to the job. Similar narratives can be heard in every hospital and health care center all across Sierra Leone, Guinea, and Liberia, the countries most affected by the Ebola epidemic.

Although different types of disasters often require different responses from nurses, several constants remain. One such constant is the importance of cleanliness, fresh air, nutrition, and proper waste disposal. Florence Nightingale espoused these principles after she nursed in the Crimean War in the 1850s, and they remain true today. Another disaster relief constant is the blurring and overlapping of professional roles as responders work quickly to deal with emergencies. Indeed, general observers at a disaster scene might have difficulty identifying who are nurses, doctors, emergency medical technicians, or student nurses. Finally, another constant of disaster response is the continuing need for education and refinement of skills. Alice Fisher wrote after the Italian earthquake in 1908 that nurses needed to be well trained and disciplined to meet any disaster with "skill and precision," and those requirements are still essential.

Because disaster nursing poses risks, nurses need to know that they can protect themselves and their families. They require proper resources, equipment, skills, and knowledge to do so. Nurses also need skilled and knowledgeable nursing leaders. As Connie Ulrich and Julie Fairman note, "No nurse should fear reprisal from administration for voicing concerns about inappropriate patient care delivery. Guidelines, however, are urgently needed."[3] To this end, faculty at the University of Kochi, the University of Hyogo, the Tokyo Medical and Dental University, the Chiba University, and the Japanese Red Cross College of Nursing have developed an interprofessional Disaster Nursing Global Leader Degree Program in Japan. Graduates are prepared to work in local, national, and international arenas to ensure security for all people, establish international partnerships, and build greater scholarship in disaster nursing.[4] The goal of this book has been to enhance this scholarship by highlighting the successes and failures of past disaster efforts so that readers can apply this knowledge to meet future needs and challenges.

NOTES

1. Bureau of Labor Statistics, "Economic News Release," http://www.bls.gov/news.release/osh.t05.htm.

2. Jeffrey Gettleman, "Despite Aid Push, Ebola Is Raging in Sierra Leone," *New York Times*, November 28, 2014, 1. (In November alone, WHO reported more than 1,800 new Ebola cases in Sierra Leone.)

3. Connie Ulrich and Julie Fairman, "Ebola, Epidemics, and Nursing Care," historian.nursing.upenn.edu/2014/10/21/ebola_and_nursing_care/#more-505.

4. Hiroko Minami, "Expected Contribution of the New Journal, *Health Emergency and Disaster Nursing*, to the Development of Nursing Science," *Health Emergency and Disaster Nursing* 1 (2014): 2–5.

Index

Note: Throughout the index, Alaskan influenza epidemic, Italian earthquake, Ohio flood, and typhoid fever epidemic pertain to the events that happened in the years 1918–1919, 1908, 1913, and 1885–1887, respectively.